Alvar Aalto

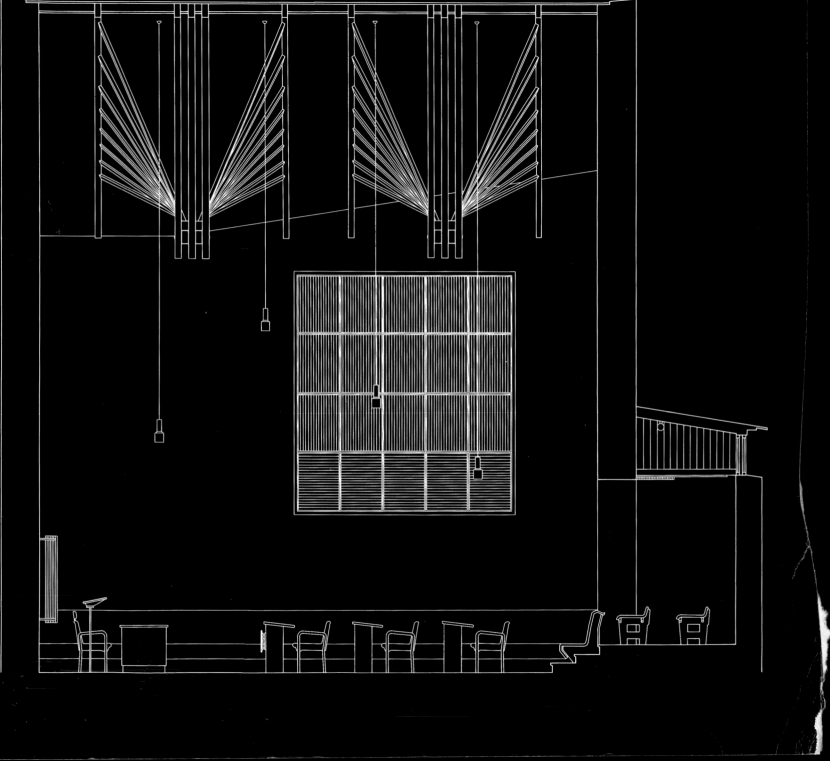

Alvar Aalto

Richard Weston

Phaidon Press Limited
Regent's Wharf
All Saints Street
London N1 9PA

First published 1995
Reprinted 1996
Reprinted in paperback 1997, 1999

© 1995 Phaidon Press Limited
ISBN 0 7148 3710 5

A CIP catalogue record for this book
is available from the British Library

Printed in Hong Kong

The cover photographs of Saynätsalo
Town Hall are © Simo Risto. The
drawn section of the council chamber
in Saynätsalo Town Hall, on p. 2,
is by Darren Stewart Capel.

Acknowledgements

Although I have been interested in
Nordic architecture since my student
days, my introduction to Finnish
culture and the direct experience of
Aalto's work came several years later
through the generous hospitality of the
architects Käpy and Simo Paavilainen.
Simo's pioneering studies of Nordic
Classicism are essential reading for
anyone interested in the long
neglected architecture of the 1920s,
and I have benefited enormously from
many conversations with him about
architecture in general, and Finnish
architecture in particular. Käpy and
Simo employed a former student,
Darren Stewart Capel, whose untiring
work in the Aalto archives and on the
drawings for earlier books on the Villa
Mairea and Säynätsalo Town Hall were
of enormous help; Darren has also
contributed many thoughts on Aalto's
work, commented helpfully on the text,
and assisted in various other ways in
the realization of this study.

I would also like to extend my thanks to
the many other Finnish architects and
friends who have made my regular
visits to their country such a joy. For a
British architect, spending time in a
country where modern architecture is
respected and valued is a special
pleasure, and I trust they will forgive
the tendency, shared with many others,
to idealize the experience of what is
still apt to seem – the recent economic
recession notwithstanding – an
architect's paradise. For five years I led
an architectural tour of Finland,
organized by Victoria Thornton, and
learnt much from repeated visits to key
buildings and conversations with other
Aalto enthusiasts.

The Museum of Finnish Architecture is
an invaluable resource, and I am
grateful to Marja-Riitta Norri and her
colleagues for their help, and in
particular to Elina Standertskjöld for
assistance with illustrations. Likewise,
Göran Schildt and Joakim Hansson
generously helped in facilitating
access to the Aalto Archive, still being
catalogued under the auspices of the
Alvar Aalto Foundation in the studio in
Munkkiniemi. Aalto's buildings are
difficult to photograph, and the
distinguished Finnish photographer
Simo Rista has provided a splendid set
of colour transparencies: his skill and
willingness to produce more material
than book budgets normally permit are
greatly appreciated. I am grateful also
to Reino Kurki and his colleagues at
Artek for help with illustrations of
Aalto's furniture and for their support
in my endeavours to promote Finnish
culture, and to Elizabeth Whitehead for
her careful re-drawing of many of the
plans and sections. I would like to
thank the staff at Phaidon. Finally,
special thanks go to my parents for
their unfailing support: this book is
dedicated to them.

Picture Acknowledgements

The publishers wish to thank all
individuals, photographers and
institutions who have kindly supplied
illustrations for this book.

The picture positions are abbreviated
as l= left, r= right, t= top, c= centre
and b= bottom.

The following are courtesy of the
Museum of Finnish Architecture,
Helsinki: 8 (r), 9 (tl, tcr), 11 (l, r), 19, 22
(r), 24 (tl, tr), 28 (t), 29 (b), 36 (t, b), 40,
45, 49 (c), 56 (c), 57 (tl, tc), 60, 61 (t), 62
(t, c, b), 63 (t, c, b), 64, 65, 66 (t, cr), 67
(t, b), 71, 72 (tl, tr, b), 73 (tl, tc, tr, b), 74
(tr), 75 (t, b), 76 (t, b), 78 (t, b), 79 (t, b,
cr), 80 (bl), 97, 98, 99, 100, 101 (tl, cl, r),
102 (b), 104 (r), 105 (t, b), 106, 107 (t, c,
b), 108, 109 (t, b), 110 (t, b), 111 (t, c, b),
112 (t, c, b), 113 (l, c, r), 114, 124, 139 (l),
147, 149 (r), 150 (r, l), 151 (tl, tr, cl, cr, bl,
br), 156, 157 (t, tc, bc, b), 164 (bl, t), 170
(t), 174 (t, cr), 175 (lc, lb, tr, cr), 194 (b),
198, 200 (r, c, l), 201, 212 (t, b), 213 (tl,
b), 214 (tr, c, b), 215 (bl, br), 216 (t), 217
(t, b); MFA/© Pietinen: 8 (r); MFA/ ©
Igor Herler: 24 (bl); MFA/ © N. E.
Wickberg: 24 (br); MFA/ © Simo Rista:
26 (c, b); MFA/© Aitta Mag: 30 (b);
MFA/© Gustaf Welin: 37 (t, c, b), 41 (tl),
42, 43 (tl, bl and br), 46, 47, 59 (tc, r), 61
(cl, cr, bl, br), 66 (b), 68 (t, b); MFA/©
Kari Hakli: 41 (tr, c), 43 (tr); MFA/ P.
Ingervo: 58, 170 (b), 217 (c); MFA/©
Heikki Hauas: 164 (tl); MFA/© Johnny
Korkman: 69; MFA/© Ilmari Kostiainen:
213 (tr); MFA/© Eva Ja Pertti Ingervo:
213 (c). The following are © Alvar Aalto
Foundation: 18, 21 (l), 23 (b), 28 (c, b),
29 (tl, tr), 31 (t, tc, c, bc, b), 32, 33 (cl,
bl, cr), 35 (t, b), 38, 41 (bc, b), 54 (bl), 56
(tc, tr), 70, 74 (tl), 80 (t, br), 81, 93 (r),
104 (l), 122, 126 (t, tc, bc, b), 127 (t), 128,
146, 172, 188, 216 (b).

Artek: 73 (c), 101 (bl), 102 (tl, tr).
The photograph on p. 80 (bc) is ©
Peter Cook. Those on the following
pages are © Simo Rista: 14 (c, b), 16
(tr), 17 (b), 39, 51, 52, 53 (t, c, b), 54 (tr),
55 (t, b), 59 (tl), 77, 82, 85, 87, 88, 89 (tl),
96, 103 (t, c, b), 115, 116, 118–9, 119, 120
(tl, tr, b), 121, 123, 125 (tr, tl, tc, bc, b),
127 (b), 129, 130, 133, 134–5, 135 (t, b),
136 (tl, tr, bl, br), 138, 139 (tr, tcr, tr, bcr,
br), 140, 141 (t, tc, bc, b), 142, 143, 144,
145, 152, 153 (t, b), 159, 160 (t, b), 161,
162–3, 165 (tr, bl), 166, 167 (t), 168, 169
(b), 173, 178–9, 180 (t, b), 182 (tr), 183,
185, 186, 187, 190 (b), 191, 192 (bl),
192–3, 196, 197 (t), 199, 202, 203 (b), 204
(t, c, b), 205, 206, 208–9, 210, 211 (t, c,
b), 215 (t), 219, 220, 221, 222 (tl, bl),
222–3, 224 (c, b), 225. The photograph
on p. 7 is © Göran Schildt. The
photograph on pp 92–3 is © Rauno
Träskelin. Richard Weston: 9 (cl, r), 10
(l, r), 12 (l, c, r), 13 (tl, cl, bl, r), 14 (t), 15
(l, c, r), 16 (cl, cr, b, tl), 17 (t), 20 (l, r),
21 (tr), 22 (l), 26 (tl, tr), 30 (tl, tr, c), 34
(tl, bl, r), 44 (t, c, b), 57 (bl, tr, cr, br),
84, 89 (tc, tr), 90 (tl, tc, tr), 91 (t, b), 94 (t,
b), 95, 148 (l, r), 149 (l, c), 154 (tl, tc), 171
(tl, tr), 176 (tr), 177, 179 (l, r), 181 (t), 182
(tl), 189 (t, tc, c, bc, b), 192 (tl, cl), 195
(t), 214 (tl).

The sketches on pages 23 (tl, tr) and 28
(t) are courtesy of the Swedish
Museum of Architecture. The plans on
page 25 (t, b) are courtesy of the
Archive of the City of Jyväskylä.

Elizabeth Whitehead executed the
drawings on pages: 48, 49 (tr, br), 50
(br, bl), 56 (tl), 117 (tl, br), 154 (br), 155
(t, b), 157 (cl), 158, 164 (br), 165 (cl), 167
(cr, br), 169 (tr), 176 (bl), 181 (b), 182 (c,
b), 190 (t), 195 (b), 197 (c, b), 203 (t), 207
(t, b), 218 (t, b), 224 (t); and Darren
Stewart Capel is responsible for the
drawings on pages: 83, 86 (l, r), 89 (c,
b), 131, 137, 194 (t).

Contents

Aalto
and
Finland

Alvar Aalto and Finland occupy a special place within the history and mythology of Modern architecture. The Paimio Sanatorium, designed in 1928 at the remarkably young age of thirty, was immediately hailed internationally as a major achievement; subsequent successes with the Finnish pavilions at the Paris and New York World's Fairs of 1937 and 1939 confirmed Aalto's reputation as one of the leading exponents of Modernism. Le Corbusier praised the Paris Pavilion's 'deep-rooted authenticity', reflecting the view that Aalto's work represented a unique, regional interpretation of Modernist orthodoxy.[2] This was a 'combination', as the architectural theorist Sigfried Giedion was later to put it, 'of standardization with irrationality'.[3] As he developed an increasingly personal style which seemed to defy systematic analysis, the myth of Aalto, the romantic humanizer of austere Modernism, steadily grew: the warmth and naturalness of his work seemingly a self-evident reflection of his ability to do 'what comes naturally'.[4]

Throughout the Fifties and Sixties, Aalto happily cultivated the romance of the designer whose work flowed intuitively from his 6B pencil. Reluctant to engage in theoretical debates, he was an architect who did 'not answer in writing . . . but buildings'. In 1958, in response to an invitation to contribute to the Finnish Architectural Review Arkkitehti, he offered a piece entitled 'Instead of an Article', which took the form of an imaginary Socratic dialogue with Giedion. He suggested that the, 'Creator created paper for drawing architecture on. Everything else is, at least for my part, to misuse paper.'[5] This was a remark doubtlessly directed at the lively circle of architect-theoreticians focused around Aulis Blomstedt and the magazine Le Carré Bleu, which formed the dominant 'rationalist' counterpoint to Aalto in Finnish architecture.

Since his death in 1976, Aalto's work and life have been subjected to increasing scrutiny and a much richer picture, both of the man and of the architecture, has emerged. His friend, Göran Schildt's three-volume biography has provided invaluable insights into his personality, access to hitherto unknown texts, and new ideas about his architecture. Extensive early designs in a classical style have been published and analysed; links with, and debts to, other pioneers of Modern architecture have been explored in depth; his ideas have been examined in the context of European thought and subjected to searching critical analysis; and attempts have been made to analyse his elusive formal language.[6] Yet, while Aalto is an altogether more complex figure than the intuitive

Finland is with Aalto wherever he goes. It provides him with that inner source of energy which always flows through his work. It is as Spain is to Picasso or Ireland to James Joyce. **SIGFRIED GIEDION** [1]

1 (Previous page) Alvar Aalto.
2 Acanthus logo, 1943: Aalto designed this logo for the Finnish Association of Architects (SAFA) during his first year in office as their chairman (1943–59). 3 View of Saimaa: the glaciated landscape of Finland is characterized by numerous undulating lakes weaving their way between seemingly endless coniferous forests. 4 Lars Sonck, summer villa, Hjortösund Sound, Finström: the design was a picturesque assemblage of rounded logs in the Swiss-chalet style, spiced with Karelian features. 5 Medieval stone church, Hollola. 6 Gesellius Lindgren Saarinen, Hvitträsk, Lake Vitträsk, 1901–3: designed by the three architects, Herman Gesellius, Armas Lindgren and Eliel Saarinen, as their home and studio. 7 Akseli Gallén-Kallela, Kalela, Ruovesi, 1895: this studio-house was largely self-built by its designer, a painter.

northern romantic of popular myth, the major themes of his work are inseparable from Finnish culture and any examination of them must begin with it.

Alvar Aalto was born in 1898 and brought up in Jyväskylä, the principal town of central Finland where a lively intellectual culture flourished; it is still occasionally referred to, half-jokingly, as 'the Athens of Finland' because of its strong educational traditions. His father was a surveyor, responsible for mapping the landscape of central Finland and setting out the routes for new railway lines and roads; Aalto later reminisced about the importance of the 'great white table' under which he played as a child and at which he was sometimes allowed to draw with his father. The possible impact of Aalto's natural affinity with the forest will be considered when we explore his attitude to landscape, but we should be wary of over-emphasizing this aspect of his upbringing: the Aalto family had many ties with forest-based industries, but this was hardly uncommon in Finland in the early years of the century and remains, as we shall see, integral to the national psyche.

Aalto matriculated from the Jyväskylä Lycée in 1916 and, after a summer working for a local architect – who encouraged him to consider a journalistic rather than architectural career! – left for Helsinki to study at the Finnish Polytechnical Institute. His studies were interrupted by the Civil War, which broke out in 1918 following Finland's declaration of independence from Russia, and he finally graduated in 1921. Little is known about his education, but the foundation of the course remained a rigorous *Beaux Arts*-influenced curriculum, with its emphasis on the holistic understanding of architectural form using the disciplines of orthogonal projection, enriched by the conventions of picturesque composition favoured by the National Romantic school. Armas Lindgren, who became the Professor during his time there, Aalto always looked back on with particular affection.[7]

Following a year of military service, Aalto set up his own office in Jyväskylä in the autumn of 1923. A year later he married his indispensable assistant, Aino Marsio, remarking that he owed her so much money, this was the only way out. Two years older than Aalto, Aino complemented him perfectly: she was highly practical, able to moderate some of her husband's more romantic flights of fantasy, and a gifted draughtsman. Aalto himself reputedly found draughting tedious compared to free-hand drawing, and, despite his mastery of detail in formal terms, the

inadequacy of his knowledge of building construction was the subject of much amusement in his office long after his death. Aino had a particular gift for interior design, and some of the glassware she designed was outstanding. Judging by the few examples of buildings known to be from her hand – and with the singular exception of the Villa Flora, which we examine in the following chapter – she was not outstandingly gifted as an architect; however, her importance to Aalto, both professionally and personally, can hardly be exaggerated, and he was utterly devastated by her early death in 1949. Three years later he married another of his assistants, the recently graduated architect Elsa Kaisa Mäkiniemi, to whom he always referred as Elissa; she outlived him by twenty-six years, continuing to run the office of Alvar Aalto and Company until her death in April 1994.

Although to the outside world – and especially in his later years – Aalto was happy to cultivate the image of the silent romantic for whom design was a matter of sheer intuition rather than rational thought, within Finland he was seen as a cosmopolitan, internationally minded artist whose architecture related more to the mainstream of progressive European culture than to any specifically national traits. To comprehend

his work it is none the less vital to understand something of the singular history, landscape and culture of his native land.

Situated on the northern fringe of Europe, a third of Finland's land mass lies within the Arctic Circle. It was first populated by tribes of Finns, Tavasters and Karelians from the south and east, but the twelfth century saw the beginnings of Swedish settlement and the arrival of organized Western Christianity. The Reformation introduced under Gustav Vasa (1523–60), gave Finns equal rights with inhabitants of Swedish origin, and the Lutheran Church remains to this day an important component both of Finnish identity and of its solidarity with the other Nordic countries. Under Vasa's successor, John III, Finland became a Grand Duchy of Sweden, and remained so until the early nineteenth century. In 1808, Tsar Alexander I of Russia invaded and Sweden was forced to cede its right to Finland and the Åland Islands.

Throughout the period of Swedish rule, Finland had little sense of national identity and its culture was dominated by the Swedish-speaking élite. With the arrival of Russian rule the situation changed unexpectedly and the 'Finns found in Russia', as Albert Christ-Janer observed, 'the foster-mother of their nationality'.[8] In 1812, the capital was moved from Turku on the west coast to Helsinki on the northern coast of the Gulf of Finland; originally founded in 1550 as a rival to Tallin in Estonia, it traded extensively with Russia and the Hanseatic League. The Tsar appointed the German-educated architect Johann Carl Ludwig Engel (1778–1840), who had mastered the Neo-classical 'Empire Style' while practising in St Petersburg, to create the major government buildings and cathedral for the new capital and to superintend the design of public buildings throughout the Grand Duchy. Following a disastrous fire in Turku in 1827, the university was also relocated to Helsinki where Engel designed its new accommodation around Senate Square, the finest Empire Style space outside St Petersburg.

The population of Finland was divided between the aristocratic, Swedish-speaking Svekomans and the Finnish-speaking Fennoman majority. The Russians were happy to encourage the nationalist sentiments stirring in the early nineteenth century, but the Finns were understandably fearful that Russian might be imposed, like Swedish before it, as the official language. One of the leaders of the Fennomans, Ivar Arvidson, famously summed up their cultural ambitions: 'We have ceased to be Swedes; we cannot be Russians; so let us be Finns.' A focus

for the emergent patriotism and national sentiment was found in promotion of the Finnish language and appreciation of the Finnish landscape.

In 1831, the Finnish Literature Society was founded to provide a focus for efforts to promote the Finnish language. Meanwhile, a country doctor, Elias Lönnrot, was busy collecting the orally transmitted runes of the Finnish bards, mostly in the remote eastern district of Karelia, far from Swedish influence and the supposed fount of authentic Finnish culture. Lönnrot compiled and published his material as the poetic narrative *Kalevala*; the first edition appeared in 1835 and a greatly enlarged version in 1849. Lönnrot's ambitions in assembling the material were, as its recent English translator Kevin Bosley writes, 'to present the Finnish nation and language as capable not only of poetry, but of epic', comparable to Homer's *Iliad* and *Odyssey*.[9] The *Kalevala* was adopted as the national epic poem and offered a multi-faceted account of the adventures and animistic beliefs and rites of the ancient, forest-dwelling Finns; its stress on their affinity with nature, emphasized through wonderful evocations of the landscape of 'whirling gravels . . . sands that jingle . . . marshy hollows . . . spruces that whisper . . . firs that sough and sigh', was to become a key aspect of the emerging Finnish identity.[10]

The cause of the Finnish language achieved a notable advance in 1858 with the founding of the first Finnish-speaking secondary school in Jyväskylä – a hundred years later, a distinguished graduate, Alvar Aalto, would return to address its jubilee gathering.[11] In 1863, Alexander II called a meeting of the four estates – nobles, clergy, burgesses and peasants – and the Finnish Diet, or parliament, was convened for the first time. A constitutional monarchy was established and the Diet met regularly, but, as the century drew on, Finland's growing self-sufficiency led to increasing tensions with Russia, itself under internal stress from the nationalist Slavophile movement opposing the cultural Westernization instigated by Peter the Great. In 1890, the postal and telegraph services were taken under Russian control and, following the accession of Nicholas II in 1894 and the appointment in 1898 of General Nicholas Bobrikov as Governor-General, a series of increasingly hostile measures was introduced: Russian was to be taught in schools and used as the official administrative language, and the tiny Finnish army was merged with the mighty Russian forces; Bobrikov finally provoked widespread dissent with the issue of the February Manifesto in 1899, in which he

decreed that all Imperial legislation, apart from purely local matters, was to be the sole responsibility of the Tsar.

A 'Pro Finlandia' petition of more than half a million signatures – including over a thousand intellectuals – was gathered in little more than a week. When the Tsar refused to receive their deputation, the Finns sought international support, but Nicholas II would not receive the French Senator Trarieux when he took the petition to Russia. After a short lull, the Tsar introduced further measures intended to reduce Finland's ability to manage her own affairs and in 1903 gave Bobrikov dictatorial powers: he was assassinated the following year against a background of growing unrest. With Russia beset by internal problems resulting from its war with Japan, the Finns regained some measure of autonomy and in 1908 a new Diet was elected under universal suffrage; Finland was the second country in the world, after New Zealand, to allow women to vote. Relations with Russia deteriorated again, and the Tsar re-assumed legislative powers in 1910. Matters inevitably came to a head with the Russian Revolution of 1917, when threatened by a Red Russian drive to promote the revolution on Finnish soil, the Finns, under the leadership of General Mannerheim, marshalled their resources and declared independence.

Against the turbulent political background of the 1890s, the arts assumed a greater importance as a means of promoting cultural identity, resulting in a stylistic phase now generally referred to as National Romanticism.[12] The term is far from satisfactory, for it was neither as 'national' nor as 'romantic' as the name suggests, and can be interpreted, especially in architecture, as the culmination of the general reaction against stylistic eclecticism and the search for a 'new style' suited to modern needs and means of construction.[13] During a period of economic depression after the prosperity of the previous decade, this manifested as a critique of the opulent Neo-Renaissance style which had flourished during the 1880s. The Swedish historian Björn Linn has suggested 'National Realism' as an alternative, due to the stress on technique and craftsmanship. Similar national sentiments were, of course, being expressed to a greater or lesser extent throughout Europe and emerged as regional interpretations of the Arts and Crafts movement, such as the English Free Style, *Art Nouveau* and *Jugendstil*. National Romanticism did flourish briefly in other Nordic and European countries, but only perhaps in the *modernismo* of Barcelona, fuelled by similarly intense

aspirations to cultural identity and independence on the part of Catalonia, was it matched by the same nationalist fervour as in Finland.

The first manifestations of National Romanticism were felt in literature, music and painting, and characters and events in the *Kalevala* became favourite subjects: Lemminkäinen and the Swan of Tuomela, for example, featured in a symbolist drama of the poet and dramatist Eino Leino; in a tone poem by the composer Jan Sibelius (1865–1958), whose work also included such overtly nationalist pieces as the 'Karelia Suite' and 'Finlandia'; and in the paintings of Akseli Gallén-Kallela (1865–1931) who was perhaps the most zealous of all in his pursuit of nationalist ideals and veneration of nature. 'He who lives and works much out in nature,' he declared, 'can almost catch himself talking to the trees of the wood . . . Our folklore witnesses to the fact that a deep experience of nature is a characteristic of the Finns. It can be said, perhaps, that we tend to personify nature, which expresses itself in our art and literature'.[14] Christened with the Swedish names Axel Waldemar Gallén, he adopted the Finnicized form Akseli Gallén-Kallela informally during the 1890s and officially from 1907, by when such a change of name had become relatively common practice.

In architecture, no one had yet managed to express the national spirit or achieve the cultural eminence of Finnish literature, art and music; the need was felt, as Ritva Tuomi has written, for an architect who, 'would elevate architecture, possibly all the way to world fame, and hopefully help architecture redeem its place as the great mother art'.[15] Norway, with its extravagant 'Dragon' style, and Sweden with the so-called 'Ancient Nordic', had already shown a way towards national expression through timber building; similar interests gradually appeared in Finland, with particular attention being paid to the traditions of the remote eastern province of Karelia. Two of the first examples came not from architects, but artists: during 1893–4 Emil Wikström built a studio at Visavuori – an eclectic mix of the Swiss chalet-style, the Ancient Nordic style, and East-Karelian folk buildings; and in 1895 Gallén-Kallela moved into his studio-home, Kalela.

Designed and largely self-built on a remote lakeside site at Ruovesi, Kalela was modelled on Karelian farmhouses, which were thought to be largely untainted by foreign influence. In the depths of the Continuation War with Russia in 1941, Aalto eulogized the authenticity of Karelian architecture, but later acknowledged that the farmhouses were actually derived from the two-storey timber houses of the Russian boyars.[16] This fact would no doubt have greatly disturbed Gallén-Kallela's equilibrium in his wilderness paradise – he spoke of a 'Russian stink' whenever he sensed a Russian or Byzantine influence.[17]

Kalela was organized around a large, double-height room focused on a massive plastered and sculpted fireplace, reflecting Gallén's belief that: 'a fire in the hearth has its place deep in the soul as a symbol of our common Finnish spirit'.[18] Despite his love of the primitive and of working in the Finnish wilderness, Gallén-Kallela was a cosmopolitan, widely travelled artist. He trained in Paris, spoke several languages, and ensured that a steady stream of international books and magazines reached Kalela to keep him in touch with wider developments.

Also, at this time, the twenty-four-year-old architect Lars Sonck was completing his own summer villa.[19] Magnificently sited on Hjortösund Sound in his native parish of Finström, the design was a picturesque assemblage of rounded logs in the Swiss chalet-style, spiced with Karelian features recorded by his friends on a trip to Karelia. Sonck built several such eclectic log villas, culminating in 'Ainola', the permanent home into which Sibelius moved with his family in 1904 to join the artistic community developing along the shores of Lake Tuusula in Järvenpää. This included the painters Pekka Halonen and Eero Järnefelt and the writer Juhani Aho, and the lakeside sites offered the opportunity for direct communion with nature; however, unlike Gallén-Kallela's remote retreat in Ruovesi, these were also conveniently located a few miles north of Helsinki.

In the heightened political atmosphere of the late 1890s, Finland's participation in the planned Paris World's Fair of 1900 was the source of great controversy, and the Finns' right to be represented by their own pavilion was only won in the face of concerted Russian opposition. A competition for the design of the pavilion was announced in 1898 and in a leading article the main daily Swedish-language newspaper, *Hufvudstadsbladet*, clearly identified the challenge facing the competitors. The paper noted the hope expressed by the organizers that each pavilion would be in the country's own style and materials: 'Unfortunately,' it observed, 'we have no style of our own'. The Finnish wood-built style was condemned as, 'an artificial product laboriously invented in the ivory towers of more or less idealistic architects' which, even worse, 'will almost certainly be viewed as a Russian style in the eyes of laymen – in

other words, by practically everybody'.[20]

The competition was won by the young practice of Herman Gesellius, Armas Lindgren and Eliel Saarinen, who had formed a partnership in December 1896, while still students at the Finnish Polytechnic Institute. The design was freely based on Medieval churches and the robust Neo-Romanesque style of H. H. Richardson, and capped by a bizarre tower, which, as Marika Hausen has aptly observed, 'defied all attempts at description'.[21] The interior displayed a wide range of Finnish arts and crafts, and was extensively decorated with frescos on *Kalevala* themes by Gallén-Kallela and paintings by other artists depicting the Finnish landscape and national life. Scenes such as Pekka Halonen's *By the Ice Hole*, which showed a lone woman washing a sheet, and Juho Rissanen's *Fishing Through the Ice*, must be read as both literal depictions of peasant life and emblems of the country's rugged individuality in the face of natural and political hardship.

The Finnish Pavilion was hailed by contemporary critics as the 'pearl of the exhibition' and, 'indisputably the most simple and the most beautiful pavilion'.[22] Its success was clearly a considerable boost for national self-confidence. Recent scholarship on National Romanticism stresses the architects' manifold borrowings from international sources. In retrospect it is easy to dissect into component sources and thereby, to some extent, undermine its claims to being a peculiarly 'national' style,

but its reception at the time would clearly have been rather different. As John Boulton Smith points out: 'The fact that the design for the Finnish Pavilion was a synthesis of national and international motifs was probably not appreciated by the public of the day. To the Finns its reminiscences of old Finnish churches and Karelia would have struck a chord, while to the foreigners in Paris it would have looked striking and different to other exhibits, and as they would have known little if anything about Finnish culture it would have been easy to accept the building for a genuine Finnish style.'[23]

In 1901, the office and apartment block for the Pohjola Fire Insurance Company, designed by Gesellius Lindgren Saarinen, was opened. The name Pohjola ('the Nordic home' or 'north country') was taken from the *Kalevala* and the architects took every opportunity to bring the epic to life in their detailing of a rich array of forest motifs – trees, bears, squirrels, foxes and birds intermingled with fanciful witches and mythical demons. The building caused a sensation. Bertel Jung reported that, 'hardly anyone passes it with indifference', and Sixten Ringbom notes that, 'crowds of people watching and discussing the details of the building were a common sight'.[24] Buildings still have the same power to become the focus of public debate today in Finland in a way almost unknown elsewhere.

At the official opening, the chairman of the board Sebastian Gripenberg (himself an architect) suggested that the new style could be called 'Finnish Naturalism' because, 'the salient feature in this building is that every material speaks its own natural language, and that the ornamentation is based solely on themes derived from the Finnish flora and fauna.'[25] Summing up this period of his work, Saarinen was later to remark that 'we went back to the nature of the material and tried to find a simple and honest way of using this material . . . Material was our only guide.'[26] The Pohjola building's debts to Spanish commercial buildings, the Richardsonian Romanesque and Continental *Jugendstil* can be readily discerned; to its contemporaries, however, this massive cliff of a building successfully maintained the fiction of representing an authentic national architecture, grounded in the nature of its native materials. Soapstone was primarily usd in this case, although granite was the more typical material having special significance as the literal geological foundation of the country, its toughness emblematic of national resolve and, as Vilhelm Helander puts it, 'the gravity of the Finnish mentality'.[27] Although Aalto

was later to distance himself from the 'absurd birch-bark culture . . . which believed that everything clumsy and bleak was especially Finnish', the terms of his own return to 'natural materials' during the 1930s were largely set by the architecture of the turn of the century.[28]

Gesellius Lindgren Saarinen built their own studio-home, Hvitträsk (1901–3), on a spectacular elevated site overlooking Lake Vitträsk a few miles west of Helsinki.[29] It was one of several domestic projects in which the architects were able to realize the *Art Nouveau* ideal of the building as a *gesamtkunstwerk* ('total work of art'). Critics, such as J. M. Richards, inclined to read this period for clues to the eventual breakthrough of Modernism in Finland, have understandably not been slow to see intimations of 'the open plan' in Hvitträsk's 'treatment of space and . . . subtle use of changes of level'.[30] However, the architects' efforts to give each space a particular character – from the castle-like painted vaults of the dining room, to the cool, Mackintosh-inspired refinement of the children's bedroom – are just as notable and might equally convincingly be conjectured as precedents for Aalto's treatment of what Demetri Porphyrios calls, 'the autonomous room'.[31]

A similar differentiation and particularization of its component parts is apparent in Gesellius Lindgren Saarinen's major public project, the Finnish National Museum (1902–12). The design of this culturally and symbolically important building was the subject of much debate, culminating in the publication by a group of leading architects – including GLS – of a pamphlet entitled *Vårt museum* (Our museum), which described, using mostly German and Swiss examples, the 'agglutinative principle' by which they believed the building should be organized. As as result of this pressure, a competition was organized the following year, which GLS duly won. Their design consisted of an agglomeration of buildings whose major components would have been readily recognizable to a contemporary audience: a 'Medieval tower'; a 'church' with a prominent gable decorated with the geometric ornament typical of Medieval practice; and a 'castle' with partly rendered walls and massive masonry – the latter more powerful in the cyclopic bonding proposed in an alternative unbuilt version. The differentiation of the parts responded to the Museum's contents – ecclesiastical objects in the 'church' and weapons in the 'castle's' circular turret. In 1904, Saarinen won the competition for the Helsinki Railway Station with a design featuring a similarly Medieval-looking tower, a picturesque array of

12 Akseli Gallén-Kallela, Kalela, Ruovesi, 1895, view of interior and exterior: the studio-home centred around a massive, sculpturally elaborate fireplace; the feature was echoed over forty years later by Aalto in his Villa Mairea.
13 Fireplace in the Villa Mairea, Noormarkku, 1938–41: as in Kalela, the fireplace is sculpturally enriched, though here it takes on the type of sensuous and feminine shapes found in the reliefs of Aalto's friend, the artist, Hans Arp.
14 Gesellius Lindgren Saarinen, Hvitträsk, Lake Vitträsk, 1901–3.
15 GLS, Bear, Finnish National Museum, Helsinki, 1902–12.
16, 17 GLS, Pohjola Building, Helsinki, 1901, gremlins and view of facade: real and mythical animals were frequently used as motifs to enrich National Romantic buildings. **18** GLS, Hvitträsk: a picturesque approach to composition creates a marked stratification from the ground to the sky.

smaller towers and turrets, and ponderous stone walls.[32]

Despite its modern programme, the picturesque effect of the station design was decidedly Medieval in character, reflecting both the recent archaeological and architectural interest in the Finnish churches and castles of the Middle Ages, and the young architect's enthusiasm for all things Medieval. William Morris's ideas were widely respected in Finland, and the general conception of the most compelling *gesamtkunstwerk* of National Romanticism, Lars Sonck's Tampere Cathedral (a building Aalto greatly admired), was essentially Neo-Gothic.[33] In 1901, *Ateneum* magazine published an article by Armas Lindgren entitled, 'Two Medieval Churches in Finland' whose opening sentences are: 'The Medieval night was awe-inspiring, full of dreams and radiant visions. Its life is like a fairy tale to modern man, its dreams the hymns of saints.'[34] These sentiments, as we shall see, were anathema to the advocates of another kind of modern architecture, and truth to other materials.

Enthusiasm for picturesque design was reflected in the widespread interest in the ideas of Camillo Sitte, as set out in his book *City Planning according to Artistic Principles.*[35] Bertel Jung, probably the first architect in Finland to acquire the text, later recalled that Sitte's ideas 'worked like a spark in a barrel of powder' when he introduced them to Lars Sonck in 1897.[36] Inspired by this example, Sonck wrote the influential article 'Modern Vandalism' in 1898 in which he applied Sitte's ideas to Helsinki.[37] Reflecting the nationalist fervour for the land, he stated that, 'nature is our best domicile and everything … in the towns [that] seeks to preserve its beauty and playful nuances enhances aesthetic emotions and strengthens love for one's native district and home town'.[38] Sonck returned to the same theme three years later in 'The Arrangement of our

19

20

21

19 Gesellius Lindgren Saarinen, Hvitträsk, Lake Vitträsk, Helsinki, 1901–3, the castle-like ante room to the dining room. **20** Villa Mairea, Noormarkku, 1938–41: view showing the rear of the house. **21** Lars Sonck, Tampere Cathedral, 1902: the outstanding achievement of National Romantic architecture, it was one of Aalto's favourite buildings.

Small Towns', written for a special issue of *Ateneum* devoted to architecture.[39] He mounted an almost hysterical attack on the prevalence of grid-planning in Finland, which took no account of 'the dictates of nature', and attributed the 'proverbial drunkenness' of the small town inhabitants to these dreary 'set-square villages', in which the 'natural carpet of lingonberry scrub and heather, through which wild flowers emerge', was rejected in favour of the 'clean-shaven lawn . . . laid out, cultivated and weeded of everything that could give the impression of nature and freedom'. This equation of nature and freedom is encountered repeatedly in Aalto's writings. Sonck's ideas had considerable influence, and he realized several town plans, most notably the 'villa districts' of Eira in Helsinki and the nearby island of Kulosaari, in which the combination of picturesque planning and *Jugendstil* design aspired to stylistic unity in the development of the city as an extensive and harmonious total work of art.[40]

The Medieval motifs of the National Museum may have been justifiable programmatically, but were altogether more problematic for a railway station, and Saarinen's success provoked the publication of one of the most celebrated documents in Finnish architecture, which effectively marked the end of National Romanticism as a creative movement. Entitled *Architecture: a challenge to our opponents*, it was written in a highly polemical style by Gustaf Strengell and Sigurd Frosterus who, although only three years younger than Saarinen, represented the emerging ideals of the younger generation.[41] Frosterus had submitted an unsuccessful entry to the railway station competition, greatly influenced by the Modern style of his former employer, Henri van de Velde, and Strengell was to establish a reputation as Finland's leading architectural critic, in which capacity he was one of Aalto's earliest public advocates at home.

Strengell berated the jury's dependence on 'taste' and lamented the fact that Finnish architecture had, 'turned into something like decorative painting'. In a memorable image, he described the National Museum as being, 'like a plesiosaur reawakened in the midst of present-day animals'; he lambasted the Pohjola building's 'grinning heads of beasts of prey . . . and wild men with rolling eyes'; and castigated the railway station's 'eclecticism in which the most heterogeneous components are melted down into a lustrous alloy'. 'This art,' he asserted, 'which started by proclaiming TRUTH as the only norm, ends in the most inordinate

self-indulgence,' and suggested that, 'the future architect has far more to learn from the Atlantic steamer and the electric tram, from the racer and the motor car . . . than he does from art forms belonging to the past.' Frosterus also praised 'bicycles, cars . . . battleships and railway bridges' as exemplars of rational design, emphasized the importance of coming to terms with new materials such as iron and concrete, and pointed out that: 'even in Finland we do not live on hunting and fishing any more, as in the old days, and decorative plants and bears – to say nothing of other animals – are hardly representative symbols of the age of steam and electricity.' 'WE WANT INTERNATIONALISM ON THE BASIS OF WHAT IS COMMON IN WESTERN CULTURE' he proclaimed (capitals in original), '. . . AN IRON AND BRAIN STYLE . . . a vital mobility, answering the violent pulsating life of the capital, buildings like bared nerve bundles.'

I have quoted Strengell and Frosterus at length because the vividness of their language admirably expresses the vigour – and romance – of the rationalist position which formed such a potent counterpoint to the nationalist fervour. Their appeals to the forms of the 'machine age' may

not have been original, but they are surprisingly direct for this date, and would reappear in twenty years' time in the similarly passionate language of Le Corbusier. They also quickly dispel any suspicion that Finland was remote from the larger debates of the time – indeed, given their anxieties about their peripheral position, geographically and culturally, many Finnish artists at the turn of the century made considerable efforts to keep in touch with developments abroad and one could argue that the range of ideas and images circulating in the culture was as wide as almost anywhere in Europe.

National Romanticism was not a provincial version of ideas evolved elsewhere, still less the spontaneous flowering of a rooted national culture, but a concerted and brilliantly successful attempt to construct a national cultural identity. Its eclecticism reflected the anxiety to belong to Europe, and the passionate attention to domestic Medieval architecture and to the epic world of the *Kalevala* and Karelia, was a response to the urgently felt need to define a Finnish culture distinct from its former and present political masters. The emergence of Finland as a nation, and the identity which National Romanticism constructed, are inextricably intertwined and ripple through the rest of the century. We will note in subsequent chapters aspects of the specifically architectural legacy upon which Aalto was to draw, but here I wish to suggest some of the broader implications for Finnish culture.

In his recent, wide-ranging study of the architect, Reimä Pietilä, Roger Connah says of National Romanticism that, 'it was not a mass aesthetic but did in more ways than we seem to understand (or even accept) enable those tangible signs of art and culture to enter the emerging political soul of the Finnish people'.[42] Frosterus was quite correct when he observed that the Finns' livelihood no longer depended on hunting and fishing, although at that time, ninety per cent of the population still lived in the countryside and worked in agriculture and forestry, and hunting and fishing remained a constituent part of life for most. The life lived close to nature, which the artists of the turn of the century idealized and in several cases tried to re-enact, remains for the Finns today an ideal which they live out in their summer cottages. As Aalto's contemporary Hilding Ekelund put it: 'the townsman . . . gives up all these necessary conveniences as often as he can to take refuge in the simplicity of his summer cottage and the uncomplicated way of life there'.[43]

A sophisticated delight in the pleasures of a simpler, more natural life

25, 26 Lars Sonck, Stock Exchange, Helsinki, exterior, and interior courtyard: these buildings exemplify the return to a more restrained, classically-based style following the exuberant Romanticism of the turn of the century. **27** Herman Gesellius and Eliel Saarinen, Helsinki Railway Station, 1908–13, exterior view: the influence of Viennese architecture is apparent throughout; the figures holding lamps are derived from an interior by J. M. Olbrich. **28** Lars Sonck, Finnish Building Society, Helsinki. **29** Sauna, summer-house, Muuratsalo, 1953: a sophisticated play on vernacular forms, the sauna has a mono-pitch roof, created by exploiting the natural tapering of the unworked timber.

without running water or electricity, is hardly confined to Finland or to the twentieth century, but its institutionalization within, and importance to, the general Finnish culture is surely unique. Consult any popular book on Finnish design and you will find the same familiar images: a land of lakes and forests adorned by buildings and artefacts designed and made with a special feel for 'natural materials' by people whose 'hundreds of years of virtual isolation had taught [them] to trust their senses, to rely on the work of their hands, to accept and appreciate the ways of nature'.[44] And inevitably the unique rituals of the ubiquitous sauna, 'as common as a cup of coffee and as special as a holiday feast', are evoked: making fire, dowsing stones in water, stimulating the body's circulation with the birch twigs of the *vihta*, and plunging into a nearby lake or snow bank, only serve to confirm the Finns' deep roots in the natural world.[45]

Although the romance of it all tends to be played up by foreigners, this is an image which the Finns themselves are generally happy to reinforce: 'Ethnologists have not only confirmed this relationship with nature but have gone to show that it is unlike that of any other European nation. Our attitude is close to that of the Japanese.'[46] In a recent article, Johanna Jääsaari, a Research Fellow of the Academy of Finland, argues that 'the romanticization of the rural way of life continues to have direct economic and political consequences no longer found elsewhere'.[47] In part, this affinity with nature and the rural way of life – not necessarily the same thing, of course – can be explained by the fact that industrialization was slow to reach Finland: Jääsaari notes that as recently as 1960, over thirty per cent of the population still earned their income from agriculture, forestry and fishing, and we might conjecture that a relatively traditional rural life survived long enough to overlap with the contemporary search for roots and widespread yearning to return to the land.[48]

Recent Finnish writing on architecture and design has taken a phenomenological turn and tends to read the affinity with nature as a fundamental manifestation of the Finnish way of 'being'. Helander, for example, quotes Kirmo Mikkola to the effect that in National Romanticism, 'forests and wood, rocks and natural stone, wilderness and fire made their presence known as the timeless fundaments of Finnish living'.[49] The Seventieth Anniversary of Finnish Independence was marked with a decidedly phenomenological exhibition on the theme of

31

'The Language of Wood'. In the catalogue, Juhani Pallasmaa, the most influential theorist of his generation, writes that, 'the memory of the protective embrace of woods and trees lies deep in the collective Finnish soul, even this generation', and points out that, 'the main thread that runs through the history of our architecture is the conversion of stylistic features that have developed in more southern climes and more urban cultures into a form of building peculiar to our forest culture. This development is equally visible in the wooden churches of our eighteenth-century "folk builders" as in the Post-Modern regionalism to be found in Finland today.'[50]

For Mikkola, the artists of National Romanticism were merely the vehicle through which 'the timeless fundaments' revealed themselves, and for Pallasmaa a 'forest culture' is somehow inscribed in the Finnish soul. His general characterization of the history of Finnish architecture is surely accurate. Though it glosses over the radical differences between the heyday of timber church-building in the eighteenth century, when virtuoso master carpenters translated the forms of southern Baroque into timber as part of a living forest culture, and architecture since the turn of this century by which time 'nature' and the 'forest' had become complex social constructs. Their expression as timeless fundaments was to be repeatedly challenged, most systematically so in the 1950s by Aulis Blomstedt and his circle and designers (such as Tapio Wirkkala and Kaj Franck) determined to project an image of abstract precision as a sign of modernity.[51] But even for Blomstedt, in love with geometry

and systems of proportion, nature remained the inescapable touchstone: 'A long time ago I said that the themes of urbanism and architecture have all been derived from the motifs of nature – the landscape. This is especially true of the new conception of space. Continuing space, "l'espace continue", simply means the consideration of the stimulating variation of nature as the basis of architectural composition'; 'create a landscape, an interesting scenic detail, and you are creating good architecture'; 'architecture is love applied to nature'.[52] Similar, if not always as evocative, statements could be cited for almost every Finnish architect whose words one encounters in print.

The continuing feeling for landscape as a component of national identity is confirmed by the publication in 1994 of *Kansallismaisema* by the Ministry of the Environment – a collection of photographs and texts about twenty official 'National Landscapes'. And with the emergence of a resurgent Russian nationalism many of the debates and anxieties of the turn of the twentieth century look set to be repeated, albeit in a radically different context, at the turn of the twenty-first century. Throughout the 150 years during which a Finnish culture has been consciously cultivated, the tension between the national and the international, the romantic and the rational, has been a marked and recurring feature: it is a measure of Aalto's genius that he was able to embrace both these poles of the national culture and synthesize them into compelling architectural form.

Throughout this chapter, I have emphasized the culturally distinctive features of Finnish art and architecture, but it must always be remembered that alongside the innovative buildings of National Romanticism ran an unbroken mainstream of classical design, which provided the bedrock for architectural education and practice – a tradition within which Alvar Aalto learnt his craft, and which, as with the other masters of Modern architecture, provided the foundation for his radical innovations. The remaining chapters of this study are organized thematically rather than chronologically and there is inevitably some movement back and forward in time between them. I have none the less attempted to weave through them a sequential account of the major phases of Aalto's career. Above all, my aim has been to situate his work in its Finnish context: all accounts of Aalto's architecture attempt this to a greater or lesser extent, but none, to my mind, has sufficiently stressed how deeply his work is rooted in a national culture.

Classical
Foundations

Now we are setting our own course. And when we see how in times past one succeeded in being international, free of prejudices and at the same time true to oneself, we can with full awareness receive currents from ancient Italy, from Spain, and from modern America. Our ancestors will continue to be our masters. ALVAR AALTO [1]

3   4

DURING the summer of 1920, while still a student, Aalto took his first trip abroad. He travelled to Gothenburg via Stockholm, where he saw the most talked-about building in Scandinavia – the new City Hall (1911–23) by Ragnar Östberg, a *gesamtkunstwerk* still under construction. In Gothenburg, a friend helped him find work as a draughtsman for Arvid Bjerke who was busy with preparations for the Gothenburg Exhibition of 1923; it was one of the major showcases for the new classically-based architecture of which Aalto was to become a leading Finnish exponent. He returned home via Copenhagen where he seems to have particularly admired the rather ponderous Neo-Medieval City Hall, designed by Martin Nyrop and completed in 1892. When Stockholm City Hall was finally opened in 1923, Aalto observed in a newspaper article that 'young architects of the North, who dream of a cool, classical, linear beauty, may not always approve of Östberg's Venetian magnificence, but we must always admire him never the less. He is the only man who, in the midst of our chaotic era, has succeeded in producing something complete. Martin Nyrop and Ragnar Östberg – these are the men who represent the first phase of the early Nordic Renaissance.'[2] The implication presumably is here that the baton had now been passed to the 'young architects'.

The idea of a 'Nordic Renaissance' seems to have preoccupied the young Aalto, and its seed may well have been sown by Armas Lindgren. Writing in 1901, at the height of the National Romantic movement, Lindgren asked 'when shall we in the North experience a similar awakening, a similar enthusiasm to that which took hold of the Italians . . . Let our Renaissance come soon to renew the ties between the past and the future.'[3] Aalto's first recorded reference to the theme of a dawning Nordic Renaissance was in a lecture given in September 1921 to mark the opening of an exhibition of Finnish art in the Estonian city of Riga;[4] it seems, in his mind, to have been based on a compound of the demonstrable achievements of the art at the turn of the century – of which Östberg's Stockholm City Hall was a glorious after-glow – and the emergence of a distinctive classical style in Nordic architecture. Variously referred to as 'Romantic Classicism', 'Swedish Grace', 'Modern Classicism', 'Light Classicism', 'Doricism' and – the term I will use – 'Nordic Classicism',[5] this episode in the architecture of the Nordic countries was for many years seen as an unfortunate disturbance in the neat and familiar story of the development of Modern architecture; from the radical innovations of *Art Nouveau* – which struck the death-knell for nineteenth-century eclecticism – to the

triumph of the rational, socially-motivated Functionalism, which finally made its 'breakthrough' in Scandinavia around 1927.

When the first volume of his collected works was published in 1963, Aalto almost completely suppressed this phase of his work; three small photographs on the index page represented over a hundred projects produced before his adoption of Functionalism.[6] Göran Schildt has suggested that their omission was motivated in part by the desire to 'obliterate everything in his life which contrasted with the lofty role of master he had gradually come to assume'.[7] While it is true, and hardly surprising, that few of these early projects are as resolved as the work from the later 1920s onwards, they are the source of several of the major themes and formal ideas which recur throughout his mature work. Aalto's enthusiasm for the Italian Renaissance blossomed in the 1920s, but remained central both to his architectural thinking and to his conception of an ideal society of free individuals. In 1954 he wrote that: 'in my mind there is always a journey to Italy: it may be a past journey that still lives on in my memories; it may be a journey I am making or perhaps a journey I am planning. Be that as it may, such a journey is a *conditio sine qua non* of my architectural work.'[8]

Before exploring the architectural development of Nordic Classicism and Aalto's early work, a brief reference to the social context in which it flourished during the 1920s is necessary. Scandinavia remained neutral during the First World War and was somewhat insulated from the massive economic, political and cultural upheavals that followed in its wake: neither the great hope of a new beginning, which the re-stabilization of capitalism seemed to promise, nor the extreme degradation experienced elsewhere in Europe were felt as intensely as in the North. Despite this, considerable internal tensions built up in Scandinavian society, and wartime profiteering led to the emergence of a *nouveau riche* minority able to enjoy a luxurious lifestyle in sharp contrast to the steady deterioration in general living standards. Due to its close links with Russia, Finland was involved in the First World War fighting; the birth of the USSR and the socially divisive civil war, which followed in its aftermath, made the government acutely aware that the country's social problems were a political time-bomb. A general strike back in 1905 had confirmed the growing class-consciousness. The population of Helsinki all but trebled between 1890 and 1914, and almost three-quarters of the citizens were housed in small one-room flats: solving the housing problem inevitably became a major issue after the war. Culturally, the postwar climate was conservative and inward-

5

6

looking; the language conflict flared up again and the ardent pro-Finnish movement promoted cultural isolation. Although superficially the classicism of the 1920s may appear conservative, even nostalgic, in the political and cultural context of the time it was a radical, outward-looking movement opposed to the dominant nationalist ideology.

In the postwar period, architects were confronted with a disparate range of commissions: from opulent private villas to workers' housing and the related social provisions of schools and community centres; from industrial and agricultural buildings to cultural facilities such as museums, concert halls and libraries. The architect's task, Henrik Andersson has argued, 'was to create some kind of aesthetic order out of these vastly different buildings; to give shape to housing projects on the scale involved when the municipalities and housing co-operatives stepped in; to give legitimacy to the private luxury of the *nouveau riche* by adding tasteful refinement; to endow cultural buildings with dignity and democratic universality; to raise industrial environments from a rationalism that was too brutal'.[9] Nordic Classicism was highly adaptable in tackling this range of challenges, and cast a unifying veil over 'the all too bitter contrasts of the age' as the Scandinavian societies moved from privilege towards social democracy, from craft to industrial production, from predominantly rural-agrarian to increasingly industrial-urban economies.[10]

New building techniques and materials were coming into use, and demanded different handling and design. By 1920, wood construction was based entirely on machine-sawn timbers, new panelling materials such as plywood and fibreboard were available, and windows, doors and other items of joinery were increasingly pre-fabricated, necessitating the introduction of standards and dimensional controls. Steel windows were coming on to the market and new concrete building blocks were suited to straight, regular walls, for which a range of plastering techniques was available to provide even, rendered surfaces and a variety of colour effects. The Dane, Pedar Clason, observed of these developments that: 'modern working techniques with their standardization requirements reject all concepts of Medieval individualism. There is more and more accordance between the classic and the contemporary';[11] and a Finnish master-builder, Yrjö Simila, argued that housing 'should be organized on a mass scale with machine-like methods', and that therefore, 'in the design of buildings we should keep to forms that are as simple as possible'.[12]

As early as 1916, Gregor Paulsson, the influential director of the Swedish

7

Arts and Crafts Association, *Svenska Slöjdföreningen* (now known as *Svensk Form*), had identified the apartment building as 'the most crucial problem in modern architecture', and argued that, 'we should no longer accept that an entire profession is occupied with monumental buildings and houses for selected individuals while the majority of the town's inhabitants live in buildings that have no coherence whatsoever'.[13] Inspired by the *Deutsche Werkbund*, Paulsson initiated several housing exhibitions, culminating in the great Stockholm exhibition of 1930, the major manifesto of Functionalism.[14] Paulsson also coined the alliterative phrase *Vackrare vardagsvara* ('More beautiful everyday goods'), which became a popular slogan among progressive designers concerned with raising the standards of the domestic environment by developing housing, furniture and utensils appropriate to industrialized mass-production. However, it has to be said that the 'Swedish Grace', which attracted praise at the Paris Exhibition of Decorative Arts in 1925, was still confined to luxury rather than social production. A similar situation prevailed in Finland, where the slogan was often quoted but, as Igor Herler has observed, 'usually while at the same time deploring the lack of support in this country for the ideal'.[15]

8

There were, however, considerable successes in the field of social housing, to which architects applied the principles of both the traditional European city-block – as for example in Armas Lindgren's 'Vallila' development in Helsinki – and the newer garden-city ideas, which were introduced into Finland at the turn of the century. An outstanding example of the latter was the Puu-Käpylä housing development designed by Martti Välikangas on the northern edge of Helsinki, which was hailed at the time primarily as a pioneering example of rationalization and standardization on account of its pre-fabricated timber construction.[16] Despite the limited successes, Asko Salokorpi has observed that, 'the nostalgic classicism of the 1920s appears to display a more conscious sense of social responsibility than Functionalism'.[17]

The nationalist fervour of the turn of the century had given way to a desire for greater solidarity among the Scandinavian countries as a culturally distinctive part of Europe, and with Europe as a whole; but in Finland ardent nationalists still wished to assert a separate, non-Scandinavian identity. For its advocates, classicism served both these ends: it could be seen to be building upon well-established, domestic classical traditions, while at the same time re-connecting architecture with the mainstream of European culture. Indeed, for an academic architect such as J. S. Sirén it represented simply, 'a profound desire to guide developments back into the channel from which they had diverged [after] a long period of chaos'.[18] As such, it was hardly an isolated phenomenon, but related to the revival of interest in classicism apparent throughout Europe before and after the First World War. In France, for example, this manifested itself in the stripped classical style of Auguste Perret's Greco-Gothic reinforced concrete constructions and of Charles Garnier's *Cité Industrielle*. By the time Otto Wagner's Post Office Savings Bank opened in 1912, the classicization of the Viennese *Sezession* was more or less complete, and in Finland a shift towards classicism was apparent in the work of architects such as Lars Sonck, Eliel Saarinen and Armas Lindgren.

In Germany, the outlines of a modern classical style were clearly visible in many of the pavilions at the great Werkbund Exhibition held in Cologne in 1914. Although largely ignored by historians – who prefer Van de Velde's late-*Jugendstil* theatre, Walter Gropius's proto-Modern model factory and offices, and Bruno Taut's expressionist Glass Pavilion to express the supposed mainstream of architectural development – the dominant style at the Exhibition was classical, albeit spiced with a surprising amount of Nationalistic Romanticism.[19] Particularly important for developments in the Nordic countries, where German was widely spoken and read, were the publication in 1908 of Paul Mebes's re-evaluation of the *Biedermeier* period, *Um 1800*, and the four volumes of Paul Schultze-

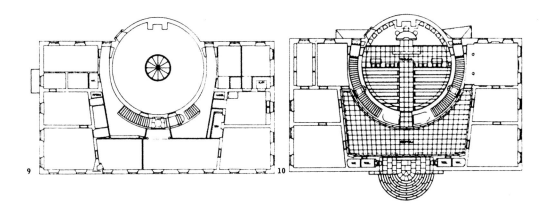

Naumburg's *Kulturarbeiten*, published between 1906 and 1908. Their advocacy of a simplified classical style for ordinary buildings was given compelling expression in Heinrich Tessenow's book *Hausbau und dergleichen*, which re-interpreted German vernacular building. It proved highly influential, partly due to its seemingly artless drawings and photographs.[20] These evoked a simple, healthy everyday life and gave, as Simo Paavilainen has pointed out, 'a social content to the new aesthetic striving'.[21]

The lead in the development of a distinctive modern classicism in the Nordic countries came from Denmark, where an outstanding neo-classical tradition flourished during the first half of the nineteenth century in the work of architects such as C. F. Hansen and M. G. Bindesbøll. In 1907, the art historian Vilhelm Wanscher published the first of several articles in the Danish review *Architekten*, in which he embarked upon a comprehensive re-consideration and popularization of the classical tradition. Interest in Hansen's work was rekindled by a proposal in 1909 from the Carlsberg Breweries to add a Baroque spire to his *Vor Frue* church. This was strongly opposed by a group of young architects, led by Carl Petersen, who

organized an exhibition of Hansen's drawings. Petersen's Fåborg Museum of 1912–15 is generally recognized as the first building in the new style, and he articulated the ideas behind his work in a series of three lectures on 'Textures', 'Contrasts' and 'Colours', which were widely read, following their publication in *Architekten* between 1919 and 1923.[22] Swedish architects, such as Sigurd Lewerentz and Gunnar Asplund, were quick to respond to the new spirit. Lewerentz's project for Bergaliden Crematorium in Helsingborg — a long, narrow, lightly coloured volume, forming a bridge over a stream, which disappeared under the building as the River Styx and emerged to fall over a cascade as the Waters of Life — suggested the means towards a new architecture that combined formal restraint with emotional resonance. The proposal was exhibited at the Baltic exhibition held in Malmö in 1914, where it was seen by two Finnish architecture students, Erik Bryggman and Hilding Ekelund, and prompted Asplund to suggest that he and Lewerentz collaborate on the competition (which they duly won) for the new crematorium and cemetery for Stockholm.[23]

The foundations for the development of Nordic Classicism were

11–14

15–18

19, 20 Workers' Club, Jyväskylä, 1924, ground- and first-floor plans: the idea of a circular auditorium, embedded within a rectilinear mass entered via an 'inside-outside' foyer, was derived from Asplund's Lister County Courthouse (p. 23). On the ground floor of the Workers' Club, a round coffee shop supported the auditorium above, with densely populated columns.

established before the First World War and reached Finland from Germany, Denmark and Sweden. The renewed interest in classicism prompted a re-evaluation of the domestic classical tradition of Engel, and, more interestingly, of the lighter style of Carlo Bassi and eighteenth-century Swedish manor houses. However, it was to Italy that the younger generation turned for inspiration. The curriculum at the polytechnic in Helsinki emphasized Italian Renaissance and Baroque architecture, and the desire to experience the buildings at first hand was doubtless overwhelming for the classically-minded young architects. In 1920, Bryggman received a grant for a study tour of Italy from the State Architectural Commission,[24] and in 1921–2 Ekelund and his wife Eva spent eight months travelling from Verona to Palermo. On their return, Hilding Ekelund wrote an impressionistic article entitled 'Italia la bella' for the Finnish architectural review *Arkkitehti*.

Aalto sought a travel grant in 1924, indicating in his application that, 'a special subject of study will be the architecture and town plans of Italian cities and towns, and their special architectural "naturalness"'.[25] In the event he had to finance his own visit, and combined it with his honeymoon in the autumn of that year, setting off in dramatic fashion with a hydroplane flight to Tallinn and then on by air to Vienna – modernity and classicism were clearly not incompatible![26] Interest in the 'naturalness' of Italian architecture was general, and although they visited the major monuments, the anonymous *architettura minore* of the Italian towns seems to have engaged the young architects' interest more than the formal set-pieces. Erik Bryggman noted in his journal that, 'much more worthwhile than to fill one's bag with innumerable details would be to study plans and locations';[27] and Ekelund summed up Vicenza as follows: 'Palladio, Palladio in dress uniform on every street corner, with columns, architraves, cornices and the whole arsenal of forms. Impressive, but boring. Between them plain, simple houses, just walls and apertures, but with distinct, harmonious proportions.'[28]

Aalto's enthusiasm for Italy was unbounded – he named his first daughter Johanna Flora Maria Annunziata – and it was above all the classical landscape of 'the holy land of Tuscany' which enthralled him: 'Whoever has once been bewitched by the magic of small Italian towns, who has but once experienced that feeling of perfection – aroused in me, at least, when memories of the hills of Cagnes, Bergamo, Fiesole emerge from the shadows of my mind – he will be left with a strange bacillus forever circulating in

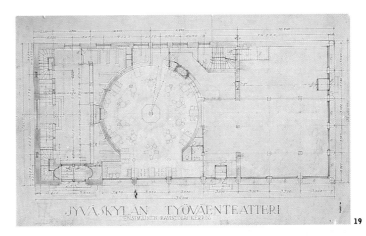

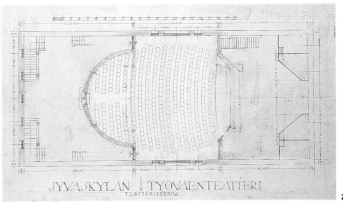

his veins, and the disease caused by it is incurable . . . For me, "the rising town" has become a religion, a disease, a madness, call it what you will: the city of hills, that curving, living, unpredictable line which runs in dimensions unknown to mathematicians, is for me the incarnation of everything that forms a contrast in the modern world between brutal mechanicalness and religious beauty in life . . . The town on the hill . . . is the purest, most individual and most natural form in urban design. Above all it has a natural beauty in that it reaches full stature when seen from the level of the human eye, that is, from ground level. A vision the senses receive whole and undisrupted, adapted to human size and sensory limitations.'[29] Although written around 1926, intimations of several aspects of his mature work are already apparent: the love of a 'curving, living, unpredictable

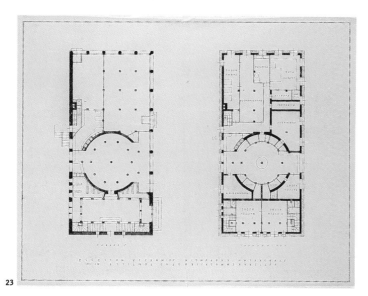

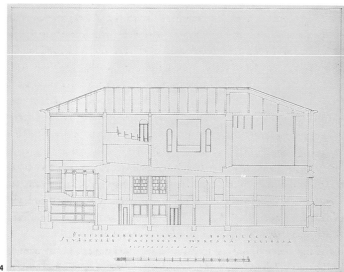

line'; the contrast between 'brutal mechanicalness' and 'religious beauty', which anticipates his critique of Functionalism; and the adaptation of the environment to the size and senses of human beings that emerged more generally with the individual human subject as the basis of architecture. Above all, what Aalto absorbed from Italy was a vision of a living urban culture: his love for Italian towns was without a trace of nostalgia – they were 'towns rooted in the earth'[30], which lived in the present.

Returning from Italy, Finnish architects saw their own country in a new light. Unlike the artists of the National Romantic period, it was not the natural wilderness that attracted them, but the agricultural landscape with its echoes of the harmonious combination of buildings and topography they so admired in Italy. In a newspaper article written in 1925, the year after his Italian journey, Aalto observed that: 'Central Finland frequently reminds one of Tuscany, the homeland of towns built on hills, which should provide an indication of how beautiful our province could be if built up properly,' and went on to suggest a few architectural additions to the surroundings of Jyväskylä which could 'make the whole landscape classical'.[31] It is interesting to speculate what the citizens of Jyväskylä made of the young architect's rhetoric, but if they were familiar with his ideas for turning their city into a Florence of the North already published in other newspapers, they would hardly be surprised at the unlikely comparison. Aalto's ideas included grandly conceived new market and church squares, and, most extraordinary of all, a 'Renaissance of the Finnish sauna' to be celebrated in a vast public building modelled on a Roman bath![32] In the event he built one or two small petrol stations and a little building for inspecting meat.

The experience of Italy confirmed the young Nordic architects' belief in the timeless qualities of geometry and proportion, and this emphasis on basic architectural values provided a framework within which both classical architecture and vernacular buildings could be understood – Scandinavian timber buildings could readily be assimilated by classically-minded architects as part of a stylistic continuum. Such a reading entailed, as Alan Colquhoun has written of the Abbé Laugier's primitive hut, 'not the discovery of vernacular building, but the *revernacularization* of classicism with which to substantiate a myth of origins',[33] and it is in this light that we must understand Demetri Porphyrios's assertion that 'classicism and vernacular, as understood and practised in Scandinavia, were of the same kind . . . an act of building sustained by a logic of construction and a

25 Lamp in the auditorium, Workers' Club, Jyväskylä, 1924. **26** Defence Corps Building, Seinäjoki, 1924–9.

25

mythology of rootedness to land'.[34] Although their work gained strength from the domestic traditions of classical architecture, the Nordic Classicists were not engaged in a stylistic revival, but with the renewal of architecture through a search for its foundations in classicism's 'ontology of construction'.[35] This was a belief that, 'the highest virtues of architecture are still to be found in proportions', as Kay Fisker observed in a lecture in 1927.[36]

An influential, and charming – a quality the Nordic Classicists valued – precedent for the marriage of vernacular and classical forms was found in the hunting lodge 'Hytten' on the Rococo Liselund estate in Denmark, published in 1918 in a small monograph produced by Aage Rafn and a group of other Danish architecture students. The classical body of the lodge – white-rendered walls and a simple Tuscan colonnade – was covered with a rustic, steep-pitched roof. This artful juxtaposition inspired Gunnar Asplund to change the design of his Woodland Chapel for the new Stockholm cemetery,[37] and finds an echo in the Aaltos' summer cottage, Villa Flora (1926), by lake Alajärvi. Although family tradition attributes the design to Aalto's wife, Aino Marsio-Aalto,[38] the influence of Liselund may well have been mediated by Asplund's Chapel, which Aalto considered representative of 'the best architecture one can hope to see in the Nordic countries'.[39] Asplund, thirteen years Aalto's senior, became a lifelong friend and major source of inspiration. Nils Erik Wickberg has pointed out that: 'in the 1920s Asplund was the inspiring personality in the Nordic countries. Only those who themselves were part of the era could possibly fully understand what he meant at the time for architecture in Scandinavia, how each new project by him was an event, and what a sensation his determined conversion to the so-called Functionalism involved.'[40]

Given the eagerness with which developments in Sweden were studied, it seems almost certain that the Aaltos would have known of Liselund from an article Asplund wrote for the Swedish magazine *Arkitektur* in 1919.[41] If so, it would help explain the similar, but altogether more startling contrast in one of the first buildings designed by Alvar Aalto, the Exhibition Hall at the Tampere Industrial Exposition of 1922. This featured a thatched roof and modular timber-framed and panelled walls, which were clearly intended to suggest the potential of standardized, machine production.[42] The roof of Villa Flora is turfed, and a shallow barrel-vaulted colonnade, supported on timber columns, forms a verandah facing the lake. The end elevations reveal the roof to be asymmetrical, and

26

the perspective drawing includes three cows who have come to the lake to drink, emphasizing that the building is part of an agricultural landscape, not a wilderness retreat.

Despite its modest scale, Villa Flora exemplifies many of the features we encounter in Nordic Classicism: the combination of classical and vernacular modes; a mixture of forms that may be constructionally explicit, such as the timber columns, or non-tectonic as in the wooden barrel-vault, a timber transcription of a masonry form familiar in Finland's wooden churches.[43] There is a sparing use of stylistic motifs: the slight entasis of the columns, and a tiny pediment on the door; and a preference for smooth, unassertive materials and finishes emphasizing form and space. The walls were rendered white, and the entire interior lined with smooth spruce boards – not the more durable pine which is visually more assertive. Finally, there is an apparent simplicity and conventionality heightened by subtle, often seemingly adventitious, deviations from the norm: the asymmetry of the roof and casual placing of the entrance door as opposed to the window, which is centred in its bay, and the classically incorrect, even number of four structural bays. Such deliberate 'errors' were much enjoyed by the Nordic Classicists: the garden facade of Asplund's Villa Snellman of 1917–18 is a classic of the genre, with its progressively displaced ground-floor windows and a single lunette seemingly misplaced amongst an otherwise regular array of rectangular openings in the attic.

Turning to one of Aalto's first major completed projects of the period, the Workers' Club in Jyväskylä designed and built in 1924, we find similar

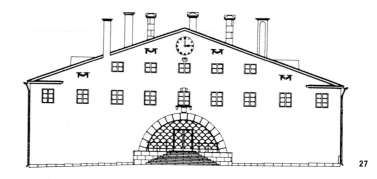

27

subtleties. The Club was organized as a solid, two-storey building containing an upper-level theatre above a glazed colonnade, which fronted a restaurant and two coffee-shops; one of these was circular and densely populated with columns supporting the semi-cylindrical drum above, which housed the rear of the auditorium. The idea of a mainly closed volume poised above a colonnade may well have been inspired by the Doge's Palace in Venice, and the theme of a cylindrical drum within a rectangular building seems very likely to have been derived from Asplund, who employed it in both the Stockholm Public Library and, the more likely inspiration, the Lister County Courthouse of 1917–21, where the cylinder – only two-thirds embedded in the main body of the building – generates a similar foyer.

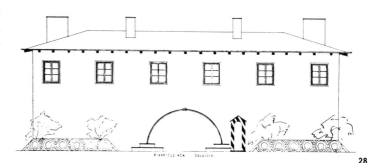

28

The main rectangular body of the auditorium is lit by a pair of centrally placed windows of an idiosyncratic 'Palladian' form; one of these, replete with balcony, forms the principal feature of the main elevation, where it appears randomly placed, off-centre and unrelated to the column bay below. Some critics have seen this as unresolved.[44] Though within the Nordic Classical syntax it can be read as an 'error', which adds tension to the composition. A recurring feature of Aalto's work, it helps to assert the individuality of each facade.[45] The plain, rendered walls are capped by a blade-like cornice projecting out over the pavement, its thin, attenuated form contrasting with the slightly squat, Tuscan columns and ample, timber balusters of the balcony. The canopy above the main entrance is appropriately theatrical, taking the form of a *baldacchino* made from iron sheet, its underside painted with stripes and rosettes – originally highlighted with 'a small amount of metallic gold' – to resemble fabric.[46] It is held aloft on a pair of lance-like poles, their ends finished with spiral stripes, perhaps to suggest furled flags, and tiny urns; the guards on the door handles reflect the military theme.

29

The entrance establishes a cross-axis, subsequently repeated by the Palladian windows, against which a symmetrical staircase marks the central long-axis of the theatre above. The first, short flight of stairs arrives at a landing lit by a half-round window that extends across the first two steps to either side in an arrangement reminiscent of the *external* aspect of the main entrance to the Lister courthouse. We know that Aalto was familiar with the Lister design because the main elevation of the rear building of his Defense Corps Building in Seinäjoki is directly derived from it, as in all probability was the half-embedded, circular assembly hall, leading into the

main building. What is interesting here about the likely debts to Asplund is not the formal motifs, but the narrative present in both buildings. The entrance hall of the Lister Courthouse is paved in stone; the door surrounds are also of stone and the enclosing walls carry a bulky cornice, again of natural stone – unlike the painted timber cornices used externally. Asplund confounds our expectations, creating an 'outside' space inside the building, in a manner involving a subtle shift in the familiar *internal* use in classical architecture of *external* motifs.[47] This offers the possibility of seeing partition walls either as the enclosing surfaces of rooms or as facades – at Lister, he clearly wishes to suggest the latter.[48] Aalto plays the same outside-inside game in the Workers' Club, where, arriving in the first-

30

31

floor foyer, you are confronted by the half-round exterior of the auditorium: painted with square white panels set in a slate-grey matrix, it seems to glow against the recessive dark walls and ceiling that visually almost disappear. The decoration recalls a Romanesque marble revetment, which encourages you to see it as an external wall, like the apse of a basilica swelling into a diminutive piazza.[49] This intention is readily apparent in an early perspective study, realized at a scale evoking the playful atmosphere of a doll's house.[50]

Rendering an interior space as if it were 'outdoors' became a favourite device of 1920s classicism, and Aalto had personal experience of one of the most complex and celebrated examples – Asplund's Skandia Cinema (1922–3) – not long before designing the Workers' Club. In his obituary for Asplund, written in 1940, he recalled their first meeting, 'in Scandia's [sic.] indigo coloured theatre a few days before it was completed'.[51] In response to his client's request that the design reflect, 'the public's desire for a festive, unreal pomp as a setting for the film world of fantasy',[52] Asplund contrived a sophisticated sequence of virtual outdoor spaces.[53] This culminated in the auditorium conceived as a festival in a courtyard beneath a starlit night sky and back in Jyväskylä, Aalto designed the light-fittings in the theatre as literal, six-pointed stars. Although used in the cinema as a playful means of creating a suspension of reality, the theme was central to Asplund's work. Elias Cornell has written that in the Mediterranean he discovered architecture in the, 'partnership with what was built on the ground or the ground itself and the sky which is stretched above it – timeless, simple and vast'.[54] Aalto relates in his obituary that Asplund told him, when he was designing the cinema, he 'thought of autumn evenings and yellow leaves', and observes that, 'this contact with nature, man included, was clearly discernible in all of Asplund's projects . . . one will always find this underlying direct contact with nature'. Aalto could equally well have been writing about himself, because a determination to establish a 'direct contact with nature' came so clearly to the fore in his work from the 1930s onwards; its origins, however, are firmly established during his neo-classical phase, as is clear in an article of exceptional insight written in 1926 for the pilot issue of the house-and-garden magazine *Aitta*, entitled 'From Doorstep to Living Room'.[55]

Aalto introduces the idea of 'entering a room' with a reproduction of Fra Angelico's *Annunciation* in which, 'the trinity of *man, room and garden* . . . makes it an ideal image of the home' (emphasis in original).[56] He goes

on to describe a photograph of the terrace of Le Corbusier's *Pavillon de l'Esprit Nouveau* for the 1925 Paris exhibition as follows: 'Latter-day Classicism. A brilliant example of the affinity of the home interior and garden. Is it a hall, beautifully open to the exterior and taking its dominating character from the trees, or is it a garden built into the house, a garden room?' Despite the climatic differences, he argues that even in Finland a garden or courtyard should belong to the home just as much as any of the rooms: 'to neglect the potential offered here by courtyards is repulsive Americanism'. He then discusses the English hall 'with an open fireplace [and] a rustic floor' which, he suggests, '*symbolizes the open air under the home roof*' and is distantly related to the atrium of a Pompeian patrician's house. 'The idea of *the hall as an open-air space* can', he states, 'form a piece of

32

33–35 Defence Corps Building, Seinäjoki, 1924–9, detailing beneath roof and around door, and view of exterior: the choice of architectural elements and the arrangement of the service wings make it stylistically one of the most classical of Aalto's build-

ings. **36** Project for Casa Väino Aalto, 1926: the atrium-like hall of the house is completed with a 'Neapolitan' washing-line. **37–41** Sketches for the League of Nations international competition, 1926–7: designed as an artificial acropolis.

philosopher's stone, if correctly used. I hand it to my reader in a locked casket, and ask his pardon if I should fail to provide him with the key. For the same reason as I previously wished to turn your garden itno an interior, I now wish to make your hall into an "open air space".' In a sense, one could say that a substantial part of Aalto's creative efforts were applied to opening the 'locked casket' of creating a sense of open-air space within his buildings, from the theatrical *piazzetta* of the Workers' Club to the interior 'landscape' of the foyers of Finlandia Hall.

We encounter outside-inside spaces in other projects of the 1920s, such as the Defence Corps Building in Seinäjoki (1924–9), where some of the walls were painted to suggest coursed masonry, and the complex stairs – symmetrical pairs of flights leading down to the assembly hall and up to offices – suggest a garden terrace.[57] In Casa Väinö Aalto, the project Alvar designed for his brother and used to illustrate the *Aitta* article, the central hall assumes the form of a Roman atrium, and the perspective drawing suggests that it is open to the sky, with a line of washing drying in the sun. The washing is actually suspended between the open galleries of the bedroom floor above, and its inclusion is every bit as deliberate as Aino's cows in front of the Villa Flora; as Aalto says, it represents 'the commonplace as a crucial architectural element, a piece of the Neapolitan street in a Finnish home interior!'[58] On a much larger scale, Aalto experimented with a 'squared-up' classical theatre as an internal spatial form, using it as a library in the 1924 entry for the Finnish Parliament House competition and, vastly enlarged, as a five-level assembly hall in the sketches for the League of Nations competition of 1926–7.

We have already seen how Aalto's enthusiasm for Italian towns encouraged him into flights of fantasy envisaging the 'Tuscanization' of the landscape and townscape of Jyväskylä. A more realistic, and, again in the long term, crucially important result of the love of Italian urban milieus was the transformation of buildings into picturesque, townscape compositions. This involved breaking the programme down into discrete volumes, and, where possible, treating these as separate buildings. Not surprisingly, Aalto took this approach to the enormous accommodation required by the League of Nations. Though the project does not exist in a definitive form, the basic idea is clear. An artificial acropolis is surmounted by a 'temple', which acts as a clerestory to the assembly hall, capturing a panorama of the Alps.

In common with several of the other classicists, he applied the same

approach to smaller projects, such as the early 1927 scheme for Töölö Church sited on a steeply sloping, granite outcrop in Helsinki. Aalto divided the required accommodation between three separate buildings – the basilican church itself, the parish halls, and the vicarage and office – which were organized asymmetrically on a level platform around a tall, free-standing bell-tower, under which one passed to find one of the two church entrances. The buildings defined a small square, a courtyard and a large terrace, and a section of arcade overlooked the park; seen from a distance they evoke memories of Italian hill towns – 'a small Finnish San Gimignano or Orvieto'[59] – but the perspective sketch with the imposing statue of an apostle, arm raised in welcome, suggests that Aalto had also been looking at the drawing of the Athenian Acropolis, which Le Corbusier borrowed from Choisy's *Histoire de l'Architecture* and published in *Vers Une Architecture*.[60]

It may be that the steeply sloping site provoked thoughts of the Acropolis – the parish building was originally envisaged as a classical temple – a monumental Pallas Athene-like figure had already appeared in the League of Nations sketches, and would feature again in the competitions for the Viinikka and Taulumäki churches. What is certain is that the Athenian Acropolis, just as much as Italian hill towns, would have appealed to Aalto as an example of 'natural' composition. Choisy's description cannot be bettered: 'Each architectural motif, on its own, is symmetrical, but every group is treated like a landscape where the masses balance out . . . So proceeds Nature . . . symmetry reigns in each part, but the whole is subject only to those laws of equilibrium for which the word "balance" is at once the physical expression and the mental image.'[61] These were also Aalto's aspirations in compositions like those of Töölö Church and Viinikka Church in Tampere, submitted a month later. The overall composition of Viinikka is again Italianate, as the perspective sketch makes clear, but whereas in Töölö the separate buildings were sited on a level platform, here they are organized more tightly around a raised courtyard of slightly different levels, on what is in fact an almost flat site: the various volumes reduce in height as they step down the slope to emphasize the subtle differences in level. The internal planning, in which the parish hall is linked to the main church by a sliding partition, hints at the spatial continuities to come later in 1927, when Aalto began to explore the Functionalist syntax. We shall also see in the next chapter how his preference for compositions based on discrete volumes informs the functional

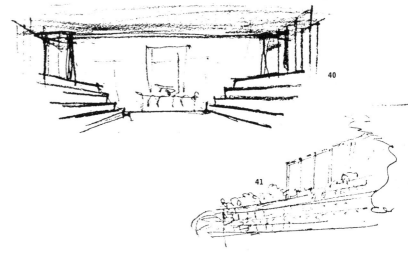

42

42 Sketch for the Finnish Parliament House competition, 1924: this project featured an external staircase that was adjacent to the library; it was an idea derived from Italian precedents, which Aalto developed and used in several later buildings, most notably Säynätsalo Town Hall (p. 122).

zoning of a building like the Paimio Sanatorium.

The only church project of this period Aalto had the opportunity to realize was on a smaller scale. It was for the village of Muurame a few miles west of Jyväskylä, and was designed slightly earlier, in 1926. Beautifully sited on a wooded ridge, its clear, white-rendered forms capture the spirit of his dream of re-creating classical landscapes in the north. The massing is a balanced composition of a long main hall, lower administrative wing and a tall square campanile, and the design is decidedly Italianate – the front elevation of the hall suggests an abstraction of Alberti's San Andrea in Mantua, while the Brunelleschian arcade at the corner of the wing is like a quotation of Fra Angelico's *Annunciation* featured in the *Aitta* article. Internally, the feeling is more reminiscent of a Finnish rural church with bare walls, simple wooden furniture, and a timber barrel vault above exposed wooden ties.

Free-standing churches offered ideal opportunities to explore the potential of combining basic geometric volumes, but the classicists were equally interested in the manipulation of solid urban blocks out of which spaces could, as it were, be carved. The Police Headquarters in Copenhagen (1919–24), filling an entire, irregularly shaped block out of which a large circular court and rectangular atrium were cut, exemplified the approach.[62] Its severe, repetitive elevations also typified the reductive, stripped down aesthetic that became increasingly popular. Aalto praised Asplund's similarly severe Stockholm Public Library because it was, 'simpler in feature than any other product of Nordic architecture up to now'.[63] He made this comment not long before beginning work on a project that was to mark a key turning point in his career, the South-Western Finland Agricultural Co-operative Building in Turku of 1926–28. This was by far the largest building he had yet tackled and in June 1927 he decided to move his office to Turku. Although motivated by the need to be near the site as construction got under way, the move to the former capital was to prove invaluable as Aalto began to explore the new ideas emanating from Continental Europe: Turku offered easy access to the ferries to Stockholm, which acted as the gateway to the Continent, and the opportunity to collaborate with Erik Bryggman.

Despite his professed admiration for the austerity of Asplund's library, Aalto won the Agricultural Co-operative Building competition with a richly decorated design, which was only later simplified by removing almost all the surface ornament to reveal a 'pure' architecture of plain surfaces and abstract geometric volumes. Externally, the building is articulated into two stages: four identical storeys of regularly spaced, square windows above a substantial rectangular cornice, which projects almost two metres, and a ground storey of larger, square shop-windows set within slightly projecting plain surrounds. The whole is capped by a thin cornice, below which runs a frieze, consisting of the building's name in tall, delicately incised letters, framed by a low-relief acanthus wreath, taken almost unchanged from the Skandia cinema's balcony rail. The elevations echo those of Asplund's Stockholm library, and use the same Dutch-manufactured *Crittal-Braat* steel windows, deeply set within their openings, in keeping with the treatment of space, which is 'hollowed out' from the solid; this was opposed to the *Biedermeier*-like preference for placing the windows flush with the wall surface typical of Nordic Classicism in its lighter mode. The main entrance is in the form of a half-cube, cut out of the building mass up to the level of the heads of the second-storey windows, into which the large cornice is returned – the arrangement is similar to the Alberti-inspired recess at the Muurame church and also recalls Olbrich's Secession Building in Vienna in a highly abstracted form.

The austere, regular facade belies the programmatic complexity within: the multi-purpose building originally contained the Turku Finnish Theatre, a hotel, restaurant, bank, shops, offices and a few apartments (the largest occupied by Aalto as a combined home and office). It is reflected in the pure geometry of the auditorium, reached via a long rectangular 'tube' containing an unbroken flight of twenty-eight steps. The solid containment and perspectival compression of the stairs brings to mind the entrance sequence to the Stockholm library, which Aalto greatly admired and emulated in his Viipuri Library; the idea of treating the stairway as a 'room' between the different worlds of the foyer and the auditorium would become a recurring feature of his later work. The auditorium was painted dark blue, like the Skandia cinema, and lit by 'PH' lamps, an early emblem of Functionalist design which Aalto modified for wall mounting.[64] When the building opened it was hailed by journalists as 'the first Functionalist theatre in the North'.[65] Aalto featured it as the first project in the collection of his work published in 1963.[66]

He introduced another sign of the new style in the form of detailing, such as the tubular steel handrails and the cantilevered balconies, which overlook the utilitarian inner courtyard. While Malcolm Quantrill acknowledges that the forms themselves are part of the classical canon, he

43 Le Corbusier, sketch of the Acropolis of Athens, *Vers une Architecture*, 1923. **44, 45** Sketches for Töölo Church scheme, 1927: this project was described by Aalto as 'a small Finnish San Gimignano or Orvieto'. **46** Perspective of Muurame Church, near Jyväskylä, 1926–9: the only one of Aalto's classical church designs to be built.

43

44

46

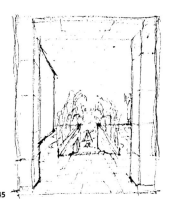

45

47–49 Muurame Church, near
Jyväskylä, 1926–9, interior and exterior
views: the nave originally had a black
ceiling; the Modernist 'PH' lamps
shown here were designed by Aalto's
friend, the Dane, Poul Henningsen.

47

48

49

50, 51 Competition project for Viinikka
Church, Tampere, 1927, perspective
and plan: Italianate, the church is
organized around a raised courtyard on slightly different levels.

50

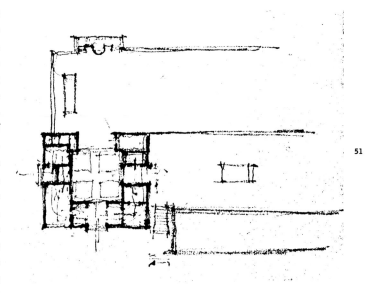

51

detects 'a new elemental purity that is decidedly nautical' in the handling
of features like the ticket booth. This consisted of a cubic plastered block
surmounted by a half-cylinder of glass, and Quantrill suggests that the
studding to the corners of the base is 'reminiscent of ships' detailing – the
riveting used to join steel plates'.[67] He may be right – we cannot be sure
what was in Aalto's mind – but the supposed rivets are square, and to my
eyes, closer to the restrained decorative enrichment found in the work of
Otto Wagner, Josef Hoffmann and other members of the *Wienerschule*. (The
three narrow stripes of dark paint, which originally ran between the shop
windows at door-head height, suggest another Viennese touch.)[68] What is
undeniable, however, is that while the building contains hints of the shift
to Functionalism which took place in 1927, the severity and geometric
purity of its major spaces, and the insistent regularity of the street elevations, are the definitive statement in Aalto's work of the reductive, essen-
tialist strain that runs through the Nordic Classicists' renewal of
architecture. He brilliantly combined this mode with Asplund's sophisticated play of nuance and mood in the project that marks the culmination
of his neo-classical period – the competition project for Viipuri City Library.

Aalto organized the library in a three-storey rectangular block, with the
main space to the rear at first-floor level. The ground level was rusticated,
and had a continuous frieze of classical motifs running beneath a cornice
that formed the sills of the first-floor windows; the rustication and frieze
returned around the ends, where they were stopped by deep-glazed indents
running the full height of the building and containing secondary escape
doors – a proto-Modern feature of an otherwise classical design. The main
entrance was formed by a lofty rectangular portal, projecting out to the
pavement. Despite the differences in plan – a linear as opposed to central-
ized configuration – the inspiration for the scheme was clearly Asplund's
Stockholm library: the elevational composition is almost identical and the
entrance is in effect formed by excising the inner portal and contained
staircase through which Asplund's reading room was entered, and trans-
planting it to form a free-standing volume. The walls either side of the
stairs were to have been painted dark, and decorated with elaborate classical frescos or reliefs: the doors were not reached until you arrived at the
first floor, so what Aalto was creating here was a novel inversion of the
outside-inside theme – a decorated 'internal' room outside.[69]

Passing through the doors, the game continued. You entered a dimly-lit,
cubic entrance hall – perhaps intended to be seen as a high court – and
then a gloomy lobby, which ran around the cella of a free-standing temple:
just the kind of arrangement Asplund had contrived for the Skandia
cinema, where the auditorium resembled a white temple standing in the
dark green foyer. A further set of doors straight ahead led into the 'temple',
which turned out to be roofless and bathed in light from roof-glazing over
the whole of the triple-height library space. Once inside the library you
found yourself surrounded by books, but metaphorically 'outside' again;

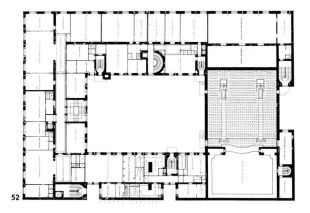

52, 53 South-Western Finland
Agricultural Co-operative Building,
Turku, 1926–8, ground-floor plan
and exterior view: the original,
richly decorated design, Aalto
later simplified to reveal a 'pure'
architecture of plain surfaces.

54

55

56

54–56 South-Western Finland Agricultural Co-operative Building, Turku, 1926–8, view of the tubular staircase that leads into the main auditorium, the *Wienerschule*-influenced ticket booth, and the cubic auditorium: the theatre was hailed in the press as 'the first Functionalist theatre in the North'.

the space opening on all sides to an upper level of books reached via a broad flight of stairs to the left, towards which you were deflected by the narrow staircase down to the bookstore. Simo Paavilainen has tantalizingly suggested a possible classical source for the 'temple' – that of Apollo at Didyma, so wide that it was originally roofless and featured a similar flight of steps at the end of its cella.[70] The recessed cistern of a Roman courthouse might equally well have been the inspiration for this depressed central space; another possible source is the stepped *impluvium*, which formed the focus of the Swedish Arts and Crafts Association's highly regarded pavilion, designed by Hakon Ahlberg, at the 1923 Gothenburg Exhibition, which Aalto would undoubtedly have studied carefully during his visit. Whatever its derivation, Aalto was to make use of the idea in all his subsequent libraries.

The experience of architecture, 'as a process comparable to the life cycle' is, as Kirmo Mikkola has pointed out, 'an important concept that Aalto learned from the Swedish Classicists of the 1920s'.[71] Ahlberg's beautiful plan was replete with the subtle spatial sequences, axial shifts, false perspectives and asymmetries in which the classicists delighted, and took the visitor on a journey from the columned hall, with its water-filled impluvium, via a long, enclosed 'Jacob's ladder' staircase to a mysterious place of light beneath an open-topped cone: the route then continued up the hillside to Lewerentz's cremation exhibit. Within the geometrically lucid, static forms of the Viipuri Library, Aalto likewise explored a vision of architecture as a richly nuanced projection of life. Simo Paavilainen concludes an exemplary analysis of the competition project as follows: 'In the Viipuri Library Aalto gave ultimate sophistication to the ideas of Twenties' Classicism – going even further than Asplund. He no longer dreamed of whole temples, but rather played with fragments and ambiences: with lighting, shadows – the interplay of dusk and dawn, darkness and brightness. This was carried so far in the Viipuri Library that it is doubtful whether even Aalto could have developed the genre much further. To do so it was necessary to change direction. The new fascination was Functionalism, whose uncharted lands lured those in quest of new discoveries.'[72] Aalto had indeed already begun his exploration of the uncharted lands of Functionalism by the time the Viipuri project was submitted on 1 October 1927, as the full-height glazed indents suggest: he took with him a rigorous foundation in classical design and a range of thematic ideas to which he would return throughout his career.

Functionalism and Beyond

The only possible factors and motives with which one can replace the old criteria are scientific studies of what people and society unconditionally need in order to remain, or better yet, to develop into a healthy organism.
ALVAR AALTO [1]

ALTO'S first forays into the uncharted lands of Functionalism began around the time of his move to Turku in June 1927. With its ferries to Stockholm and outward-looking Swedish-speaking community, the former capital was a much better base at the time than conservative Helsinki. Erik Bryggman was already well-established there and his friendship with Aalto deepened through their mutual exploration of the latest ideas emanating from the Continent. Bryggman was seven years Aalto's senior and his tour of Italy had been considerably more extensive; he had also studied at first-hand the most recent Viennese architecture and, as Schildt notes, 'actually seen real-life Functionalist buildings'.[2] Le Corbusier, not surprisingly, was the first of the European Modernists to become well known in Finland; Uno Åhren's article 'On the Way to Architecture', published in *Byggmästeren* in 1926, disseminated Le Corbusier's ideas widely. *Vers une Architecture* was reviewed towards the end of 1926 in *Arkkitehti*, but it seems reasonable to surmise from the article that Aalto wrote for *Aitta* the same year, and from his sudden enthusiasm for incorporating a Pallas Athene-like figure in his competition projects, that he was already familiar with the text. Raija-Liisa Heinonen has pointed out that Aalto's arguments about linking inside and outside spaces closely follow part of Le Corbusier's discussion of 'The Illusion of Plans'[3]. Though Aalto, it must be said, drew very different conclusions from apparently similar starting points. Le Corbusier's enthusiasm for Mediterranean culture would have found a ready echo in Aalto, who did not at first seem to feel the need to come to terms with the radically different formal expression maturing on the Continent; nor, as we shall see, did he hesitate to 'Modernize' the neo-classical projects in his office when a fascination for the new vocabulary took hold.

The first Functionalist building in the Nordic countries was designed in Norway in 1925 – Lars Backer's Skansen restaurant; but it was Sweden again that provided the stimulus for developments in Finland, and after settling in Turku, Aalto was a regular visitor. He discussed developments with his fellow architect Sven Markelius, who undertook an extensive European study tour in the summer of 1927, including the Weissenhof Exhibition in Stuttgart and the new Bauhaus in Dessau.[4] Once Aalto became familiar with the ideals and forms of the new architecture, he brought to them the same enthusiastic commitment hitherto expressed for his beloved Italy. He wrote two substantial newspaper articles advocating the Functionalist cause: the first, published in December 1927 in *Sosialisti*,

discussed housing problems and included illustrations of Le Corbusier's *Ville Contemporaine*, and J. J. P. Oud's row housing at the Weissenhof; the second was illustrated with pictures from *Vers une Architecture* and appeared in a local paper on the first day of the new year.

At Aalto's suggestion, Markelius was invited to address the annual meeting of SAFA, the Finnish architectural association, held in Turku in the Spring of 1928. His lecture, entitled 'Rationalization Trends in Modern Housing Design', reflected his recent experience of the socially-orientated strand within Modern architecture represented by Walter Gropius, and was heard by forty architects who travelled from Helsinki, Viipuri and Tampere, as well as the local association.[5] The lecture provoked considerable interest and discussion, and brought Functionalism to the attention of many of the leading architects in Finland.[6] After the building boom of the first half of the 1920s Finland was languishing in economic recession, and the time was ripe for an injection of new European ideas, especially ones whose emphasis on standardization and factory-production offered the prospects of reduced costs and new markets for Finnish industry.[7]

Almost simultaneously with Markelius's lecture, an article appeared in *Arkkitehti* by one of the youngest classicists, Pauli Blomstedt, who had also caught the Functionalist fire. Entitled 'Architectural Anaemia? A nation examines itself',[8] its tone was surprisingly nationalistic. Blomstedt

castigated his colleagues' dependence on Swedish models gleaned from various architectural reviews. He observed that, 'the fashionable style is very "uniform"; windows on the wall surface – (that probably indicates a correct understanding of the building cube) – except for the top storey, where they can be sunk in and framed (i.e. an artistic rilievo effect)', and suggested that as a result, 'the shift to the "Corbusier style" [is] unlikely to prove very difficult for us. We have already learned thin forms and asymmetry will soon be one of the orthodox dogmas – it's just away with meanders and palmettes and let's have some more horizontal lines in the facade . . . Now is the age of "machine culture": all we need is to put electric lamps, radiators, WCs and spiral staircases in our perspectives and we are keeping pace with fashion again!' He did point out that a commitment to solving social problems was integral to Le Corbusier's ideas and that, 'it really cannot be healthy for the future of our country's architecture if Functionalism is only adopted as a style and fashion without serious consideration of its real and lasting values. For those formal features and surface details of a new idiom which spread fastest and most easily are by no means always its essence. The core of "Neo-rationalism" – a term as good as the other – contains so many ideas that are positive and important for our century, even from the most prejudiced point of view, that we cannot afford to sacrifice their vital force to fashions discarded in a couple of years' time as antiquated. And this is the fate in store for the "modern view" too, unless it also contains the architect's whole philosophy of life and his basic ideas about architecture.'

The relative ease, in formal terms, with which many of the leading classicists made the transition to Functionalism confirmed Blomstedt's ironic observations on the superficial similarities between the two 'styles'. But while his caricature of Nordic Classicism was good rhetoric, it did less than justice to its radical aspects. As Erik Bryggman pointed out in a newspaper article explaining the latest, more overtly radical, ideas to the general public: 'All good architecture . . . has always been functionalistic. This applies especially to the best works of the so-called classicistic period in Scandinavia, notably in Sweden. Classicism signified the beginning of Modern thought. Its aim was to present things as clearly and precisely as possible. In its striving to be matter-of-fact it stressed [artistic] frugality and regularity, corresponding well to practical requirements such as economy and standardization.'9 Similarly, Blomstedt's fears that Functionalism would be another short-lasting fashion proved groundless,

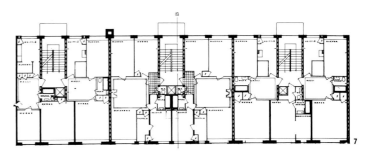

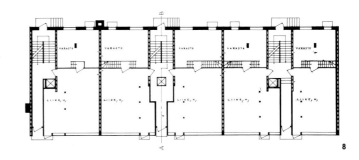

for the new architecture took hold in Finland and the rest of Scandinavia more firmly than almost anywhere in Europe, with the possible exception of The Netherlands. In Sweden it was adopted as an instrument of social policy – with, it has to be said, a gradual deterioration in aesthetic terms. While in Finland it served to present the image of a young, progressive country, particularly through tourist and sports facilities and commercial and industrial buildings; several of the more progressive companies favoured Modernism as an expression of their belief in Finland's international future as a trading nation. With the building of Bryggman's pavilion at the 1930 Antwerp Universal Exposition, Functionalism became the official expression of 'creative Finland' for the outside world.[10] However, the cultural climate at home remained deeply conservative and, as was common throughout Europe, the social ideals of the new architecture – focused around the problem of low-income housing – were realized only in isolated experiments where superficial 'Functionalist' trappings were added to the stripped-classical bones of what Aalto called, 'a rental barracks industry, whether private or co-operative'.[11]

So much has been made of Aalto's role as the 'humanizer' of a coldly rational Modernism that, before considering his architectural production during these crucial years, it is important to review briefly the Functionalist ideals he initially wholeheartedly embraced; many aspects of which remained fundamental to his conception of the architect's task. Aalto's friendship with Asplund and Markelius brought him into the circle engaged in the preparations for the 1930 Stockholm Exhibition. As we noted in the previous chapter, this was instigated by Gregor Paulsson, the long-standing advocate of socially-committed design, and became the major public manifesto for the new architecture in Scandinavia. Markelius represented Sweden in the international group of architects who formed CIAM in 1928 – the *Congrès Internationaux d'Architecture Moderne* – and through him Aalto was invited to become a member. He attended the Second Congress held in Frankfurt in 1929 on the theme of *Die Wohnung für das Existenzminimum* ('The Low Cost Dwelling' or 'Housing for Low-Income Earners') and was elected to the inner circle of the steering committee, CIRPAC.[12]

Aalto returned full of enthusiasm for the ideas discussed and new acquaintances made, commenting appreciatively to the press that the names of the architects were not even mentioned in the exhibition of projects.[13] Addressing a Nordic congress in Trondheim the following year, he declared

that: 'the Functionalist architect is an entirely different professional type from the old-style architect. In fact he is not an architect at all; he is a social administrator.'[14] Such an attitude reflected the ideals of many of the participants in CIAM, and in particular the circle around Walter Gropius, whose programme for the Bauhaus was grounded in a collectivist vision based on a commitment to craft rather than the individualistic pursuit of art; it received its most extreme expression in the ideas of his successor as head of the school, Hannes Meyer.[15] The Bauhaus designers believed that thorough analysis of problems should replace outmoded style-based design; that space should no longer be squandered through the perpetuation of outmoded building types; that architecture should be linked to the general economy and embrace machine production; and that biological and psychological constants offered a universal basis for the rational design of Modern buildings, furniture and equipment.

Involvement with these new ideas immediately led Aalto to refute key aspects of 1920s classicism. 'The unified cityscape', he wrote, was 'the product of a false formalism [involving] a denial of progress,'[16] against

10

12

11

13

14

15

16

14–16 *Turun Sanomat* Building, Turku, 1927–9, views of courtyard with staircase tower, and of interior, looking down and up the main entrance stairs: a similar arrangement of landings appear later, on a grand scale, in the main building of Jyväskylä University, 1952–7 (p. 190).

which, 'there will develop a functional architecture, which implies no special value in ornamentation, but in which the exterior faithfully corresponds with the interior.'[17] He rejected a 'striving for personal monumentality, bound by tradition', and allied himself to the 'search for an ideological, attitudinal, and technical basis for an organic architecture'.[18] In 1930, he offered a thorough exposition of the principles of designing for the *Existenzminimum* in an article entitled 'The Dwelling as a Problem',[19] which will be considered in more detail in the following chapter. Here we should note that it confirmed his commitment to the principles of Functionalist design: consideration of the 'biodynamic functions' of eating, sleep, work and play provided the basis for the 'minimal dwelling', which could be psychologically enlarged to arrive at a 'universal dwelling', designed after careful 'research based on human similarities'. All this was in line with Bauhaus thinking, and aspects of the article recall the most radical statement of such principles by Hannes Meyer in his 1928 manifesto entitled 'Building'.[20] However, Aalto distanced himself from Le Corbusier's 'machine aesthetic'. He explained his idea of culture by comparing a ship's engineer, at ease with his instruments in 'a typical totality of organic work', with 'Lady Astor with lady in waiting and retinue on her way back from Paris', where she had acquired the latest fashions in clothes, ideas and manners: 'I do not mean by the word *culture* any machine symbolism but rather the balanced mentality generated by work, organization, and an uncomplicated everyday life in which irrelevant elements essentially appear silly.'

Throughout his life, Aalto remained sceptical about the conception of architecture as 'art'. He invariably confined his discussion of projects to their resolution of practical requirements, and his understanding of culture stayed substantially unchanged. Addressing his former high school in 1958, he observed that culture 'is not an isolated phenomenon that can be divorced from life. There should not exist so-called cultural divisions among people and special decorative elements in our environment, as culture is the thread that runs through all things. Even the most modest everyday task is of such a nature that it can be humanised and given cultural harmony.'[21] The basis for that view was present in his youthful commitment to a cultural renaissance based on his experience of the urban culture of Italy, but it gained new impetus from his immersion in Modernism, as his comments on the Stockholm Exhibition make clear: '[Modernism] applies a scalpel to the deeply entrenched inclination to link

17 (Previous page), **18** Paimio Sanatorium, Paimio, 1929–33, views from balconies: the dramatically cantilevered balconies and rooftop sundeck allowed spectacular views over the surrounding countryside; their orientation south was determined by a dedication to the supposed healing powers of the sun. **19** The dining room of the sanatorium: an enclosed mezzanine is suspended from above by steel hangers.

18

19

the concept of art with an elegant lifestyle and custom-made objects', and 'is not a composition in stone, glass, and steel, as the Functionalist-hating exhibition visitor might imagine, but rather a composition in houses, flags, searchlights, flowers, fireworks, happy people, and clean tablecloths', which demonstrated 'a whole new kind of joy'[22]. This was all exemplified by a caption to an illustration in Poul Henningsen's *Kritisk Revy*: 'a picture of Tivoli: paper lanterns in the leafy branches above a café table. The heading was "Eternal Values"'.[23]

Given Aalto's enthusiasm for the new ideas, and his understanding that Functionalism was not a fashionable set of clothes, but a way of conceiving a building as an 'organic' whole, the presence of several neo-classical projects in his office at various stages of design and construction clearly presented him with a dilemma. As we noted in the last chapter, he introduced Functionalist features into the courtyard of the Turku Agricultural Co-operative Building, where their incorporation was eased by the superficial similarities between the two styles. He did not hesitate, however, to effect radical changes to the stylistically more traditional Muurame church: the window above the arcade, which originally had a small balcony and classical frieze, was replaced by a square-gridded metal screen; the bell-tower acquired a spiral staircase; the vestry was furnished in semi-Functionalist style; the choir and organ loft was detached from the walls to float free on independent columns; and, as in the Turku theatre, the church was lit by 'PH' fittings.

The project for the Kinkomaa Tuberculosis Sanatorium, an invited competition entry submitted in June 1927, combines the Italian hill-town compositions of his churches with a Functionalist zoning of the plan around a central entrance hall. The tower was clearly contrived for picturesque effect, fulfilling a similar compositional role to the church *campanili*, while the long wing of patients' wards supported a dramatic stack of cantilevered sun-balconies: the elevations were predominantly classical, but the balconies show Aalto hovering uncertainly on the brink of something new. He did not win the competition, but the basic organization of the scheme would reappear in the design of the Paimio Sanatorium.

Aalto and Bryggman collaborated in the latter half of 1927 on a competition project for a commercial and residential building in Vaasa, which shows them jointly trying to come to terms with the new vocabulary. The ground floor consists of shop windows framed by columns, and the first floor features a ribbon window sandwiched, somewhat uneasily, between

decorated spandrels and a continuous frieze of lettering; the windows of the upper floors, although still individual, were moved together to form continuous bands. The tall, rectangular opening cut through the lower two storeys to form a deeply recessed entrance, decorative frieze, and tiny step-back of the upper stories above the lettering, still gave the facade a distinctly classical air, but in their subsequent designs both Aalto and Bryggman eliminated these hangovers from their earlier work.

In November the same year, Aalto received an ideal commission on which to sharpen his skills – the Standard Apartment Block – in which he used his client's 'Tapani' system of precast concrete floor- and wall-units, first introduced in 1913. Aalto exploited the system's flexibility to the full, varying the structural bays to create six apartments on each floor, only two of which were the same size – he had doubtless heard from Markelius about the flexible accommodation Mies van der Rohe created in his block of flats at the Weissenhof, and may well have been seeking to emulate his example. The larger units were organized around a multi-purpose hall with fireplace, which formed a room in its own right or could be opened up to more than double the living area. Though it can also be seen as an attempt to provide the kind of entrance space in the heart of the dwelling he discussed in the *Aitta* article 'From Doorstep to Living Room'.[24] Elevationally, the apartment building was a direct expression of the plan, with modular steel windows of uniform height sized to suit the rooms behind; to the rear, slender cantilevered balconies were provided at the half-landings of the staircase to look out over a nearby park. The block has recently been renovated and is generally accorded the honour of being Finland's first Functionalist building.

Aalto's enthusiastic advocacy of the latest thinking on architecture commended him to Arvo Ketonen, the progressive owner of Turku's main newspaper, the *Turun Sanomat*.[25] Ketonen had decided to give the paper a more modern look by changing from Gothic to Latin typography, and wanted to match this in the design of a new office and production building. Aalto was a gifted and active journalist, and the newspaper appealed to him as a symbol of the free, international communication of ideas he believed was vital to establishing Finland's place in the world. A thoroughly modern image was clearly required and from the front elevation it is clear that he turned to Le Corbusier for inspiration, the design amounting to a demonstration of 'The 5 Points of a New Architecture'.[26] Its composition was also a development of the Vaasa project, with the

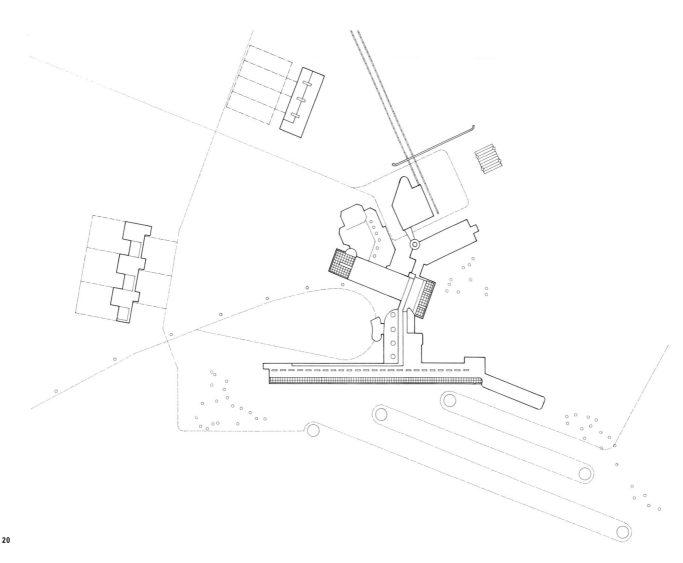

20

double-height entrance repositioned on the side of the building to form a public entrance and two-storey display window, originally intended to be filled with a vast projection of the newspaper's front-page – an idea almost certainly taken from the Vesnin Brothers' Pravda offices project of 1924.

The office entrance is accommodated within a vertical slot, in which Aalto placed louvres to carry the names of the other firms occupying the building. It leads into a long, straight flight of stairs marching back into the depth of the plan, with the porter's desk conveniently placed adjacent to the first landing. The staircase walls are painted in grey-blue with a high gloss finish, and the handrail is a thin metal rod, painted black and with contrasting offset supports of chrome-plated steel; a continuous black cove follows the profile of the treads and risers – a feature typical of vernacular timber detailing, already used by Aalto on the stairs in the Jyväskylä Workers' Club, and subsequently throughout his career. The effect is clean and hygienic, yet, as Simo Paavilainen has pointed out, an almost identical glossy colour-scheme was employed slightly earlier by Bryggman to create the illusion of a night sky in the restaurant of the nearby Seurahuone Hotel.[27]

The elegant, asymmetrical tapering columns in the basement press room, which seem to anticipate the organic forms of Aalto's later work, are perhaps the most innovative feature in the building and have been the subject of much speculation. Malcolm Quantrill and the Swedish critic Gotthard Johansson associate them with cathedrals; Raija-Liisa Heinonen argues that the consulting engineer, Arne Henriksson, brought them from Germany; and Quantrill, eager to pursue his nautical metaphors, additionally proposes 'the influence of a ship's engine room', accounting for the taper on the grounds of leaving as much room as possible for the machines, and suggests a debt to 'Maillart's mushroom construction'.[28] The reality, as Schildt has pointed out, is surely rather more prosaic.[29] The forms can be readily explained as the outcome of a fruitful collaboration between a technically innovative engineer and an architect with an instinctive feeling for form. The taper and modified bell capitals are a direct response to the need when using reinforced concrete to gather the loads and thicken the columns at points of maximum shear, and the asymmetry is a response to the much greater span of the central space. Associations with cathedrals and ships' engine rooms are not inappropriate in evoking the spirit of the result, but are out of place as explanations in considering the work of the Functionalist Aalto – although, as we shall see, his later non-structural

20 Site plan for Paimio Sanatorium, Paimio, 1929–33: the doctors' houses can be seen to the west and the staff flats to the north. **21** The staff housing of Paimio Sanatorium. **22, 23** Ground- and first-floor plans of Paimio Sanatorium: the plan was meant to be functionally-zoned and 'biodynamically' aligned to the compass so that the direction of each wing was defined according to its requirements for sunshine and view.

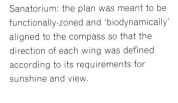

21

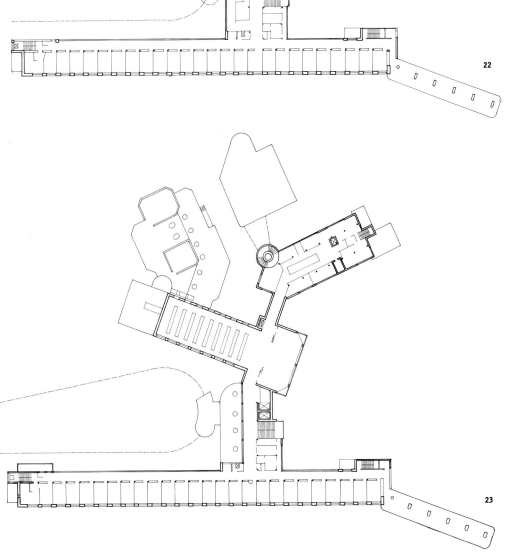

22

23

24, 25 Paimio Sanatorium, Paimio,
1929–33, cross sections of hospital
wing and balconies. 26 View of hospital
wing, Paimio Sanatorium: each wing
was given a position in the landscape
according to the demands of the rooms.

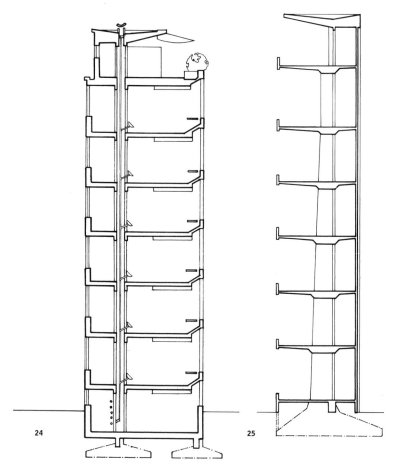

24   25

adaptations of columns do engage with just such an iconographic approach to design. Aalto also used, for the first time, what became a favourite device – the so-called 'lens' rooflights. Here, however, they were merely a pragmatic solution to lighting the linotype room.

During the summer of 1928, Aalto was hard at work on several major projects, but none the less he and Aino decided to use a travel grant, awarded the previous year, to undertake a study tour of the Continent to see at first hand examples of the new style in which they were now working. The pressures on time gave Aalto the excuse to indulge his love of flying, and the trip took them from Copenhagen via Amsterdam to Paris.[30] They visited several houses by Le Corbusier – who was away at the time in Moscow, working on the Centrosoyus building – and formed a friendship with André Lurçat. In the Netherlands, they saw some of the new housing by J. J. P. Oud and visited Hilversum; there, Willem Dudok's early buildings were completed, and they almost certainly saw Johannes Duiker's Zonnestraal Sanatorium, which was all but finished. This was to prove a timely experience because, less than three months after their return to Turku, the competition was announced for the Paimio Sanatorium.

A sanatorium provided an ideal project on which to demonstrate the principles of Functionalism. The accepted treatment for tuberculosis – isolation from urban pollution in natural surroundings, and optimum exposure to sun and fresh air – was first put forward by a Swiss doctor in 1901.[31] Numerous sanatoria were built, notably in Germany and Switzerland, where, in centres such as Davos, their provision became the basis of the local economy. The characteristic buildings – known as *Terrassenbau* – were organized as a step-back section of south-facing terraces on to which patients could be wheeled out from their rooms while still in bed: a notable example was built by Richard Döcker at Waiblingen, in Germany, in 1926. This therapeutic regime happily coincided with the Modern Movement's beliefs about a healthy environment, which was eventually enshrined in *The Athens Charter*: 'the health of every person depends to a great extent on his submission to the "conditions of nature". The sun, which governs all growth, should penetrate the interior of every dwelling, there to diffuse its rays, without which life withers and fades.'[32] It may well be that the new treatment for tuberculosis, the plague of crowded, polluted inner cities, was one of the contributory factors behind this faith; Le Corbusier made the connection explicit in his *Radiant City* when he extolled the virtues of *soleil, espace* and *verdure* as solutions to the

26

problems of 'tubercular Paris'.[33]

Aalto's introduction to the project is characteristically straightforward: 'The Sanatorium's shape of plan derives from the attempt to handle separately each dissimilar part in this kind of establishment, so that similar rooms and spaces are grouped together to form a wing. The wings are then linked to each other by the central part of the building, where common functions, like stairs, lifts etc. are grouped. Each different wing has been given a special position in the landscape, according to the demands of the rooms. Wherever possible each wing contains only "one kind of room" (or groups of rooms, where the requirements of sunshine and view etc. are similar). Consequently, the direction of each wing has been exactly defined.'[34] In other words, a functionally-zoned plan, 'biodynamically' aligned to the compass. The brief, in line with normal practice in Finland, differed from that of the *Terrassenbau* because the doctors favoured collective sun-terraces, which allowed the patients to take the air in groups of their own choice. Aalto organized these as a seven-storey stack of terraces, providing twenty-four places at the end of each floor of wards intended for the 'weaker and psychically sensitive patients' – a refinement which, he said, 'it is perhaps hardly necessary to add was an architect's not a doctor's. The Doctors fail to understand. Whether the medical profession will end by adopting it remains to be seen.'[35] The top floor linked with the flat roof of the patients' wing to form a heroic roof-top terrace running the full length of the building. Designed for the healthier patients, it afforded spectacular views of the landscape above the surrounding tree-tops and was protected with a reinforced concrete canopy to reduce solar gain;[36] sub-division with glazed screens avoided the danger of wind being channelled along its considerable length. The complex also included two blocks of houses: they were independent of the main building and will be considered as part of Aalto's approach to domestic design in the following chapter.

The patients' wing looked out over uninhabited forest and was orientated south, south-east to capture more morning sun, and reduce solar gains in the afternoon, whereas the sun-terraces faced due south, creating a slight angle at the junction with the main wing. At the opposite end, it terminated with rooms for nurses opening onto cantilevered balconies – the end elevation bears a striking resemblance to a hotel-sanatorium in the Caucasus of 1927–8 by Alexei Shchusev, but we cannot be certain whether or not Aalto knew of the project – although he was certainly aware of

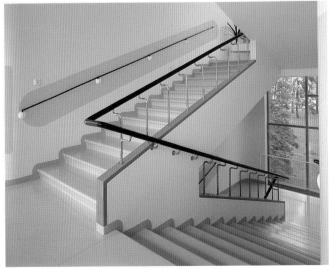

32

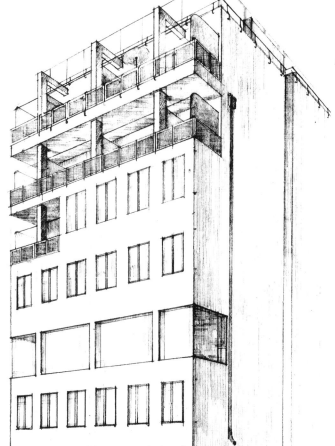

31

developments in the Soviet Union. The communal block followed the alignment of the sun-terraces, and originally contained medical care and treatment wards on the ground floor, and a range of facilities for patients, including a large double-height dining room at first floor level, with a mezzanine library and cinema running along its north side, and a terrace to the west – the mezzanine itself was hung on circular steel sections. The south-facing elevation was equipped with external roller-blinds, while the one to the east suggested a detached pavilion and contained the patients' main recreation room and offices for doctors, complete with private balconies. The technical and service facilities were accommodated in a single-storey extension on the north side of the communal block, and in a separate three-storey wing, angled, according to Aalto, to receive sun on both elevations. The boiler room was in a single-storey block to the north, its dramatic flue forming a pivot at the corner of the service wing.

It has become generally accepted that the Paimio plan, with its angular inflections towards the sun – as well as specific features such as the boiler-flue/water-tower, and detailing of the cantilevered balconies – is based on Duiker's Zonnestraal Sanatorium.[37] The specific formal derivations are convincingly argued by Paul David Pearson, and it may well be that the Zonnestraal plan motivated Aalto to introduce the splayed geometry. But if we look back at the Kinkomaa Sanatorium project of the previous year, we find essentially the same functional zoning and disposition of accommodation: the wards were arranged in a long wing, which slid past the central entrance block and ended with a stack of south-facing cantilevered terraces, with a continuous roof terrace above. The parallels are obvious and cast serious doubt on Pearson's assertion that, 'Paimio is a takeoff of Zonnestraal in terms of planning'.[38] It further discredits Quantrill's elaboration that, 'Aalto's adaptation of the Duiker plan consisted simply of compressing two of the patients' wings on the Zonnestraal design into one long one', and that he 'cleverly disguised the considerable length of his own patients' wing from the entry court by placing the nursing access at the mid-point rather than at the end as in Duiker's design'.[39] More likely by far is that Aalto began with his own earlier scheme and developed it in the light of his clearer understanding of Functionalist design – in which case the debt to Duiker appears more modest. The Zonnestraal's pavilions were virtuoso demonstrations of the aesthetic potential of reinforced concrete construction and must have left their mark, but the plan surely smelled too much of the drawing-board for Aalto. Also, the splays were at forty-five degrees and the pavilions repeated mechanically in a unified, axial arrangement, which retains distinct hints of *Beaux Arts* formality – a very different compositional approach from that of Paimio.

Aalto exploited functional/programmatic reasons to develop the particularity of the various volumes. These with minor exceptions, follow the principle that 'the exterior faithfully corresponds with the interior',[40] leading to a 'transparent' expression of the inner organization, which is a hallmark of his mature style. On the patients' wing, for example, the ribbon windows echo the continuity of the corridors behind, whereas the rooms are provided with individual windows – unlike Le Corbusier's use of the *fenêtre en longueur* that could, on occasion, run indiscriminately across a variety of internal spaces. The double-height dining room and large recreation room are readily legible from their fenestration. In addition, the lift shaft on the end of the patients' wing is glazed to reveal its contents. Aalto explained its unusual position on the grounds that it was placed beyond the nurses' rooms to keep the noise away from patients.[41] However, it is difficult not to see it as a gentle declaration of the 'machine age', which, like the proposed newspaper projection in the *Turun Sanomat*, may well have been prompted by the exposed lift in the Vesnin Brothers' Pravda building. As notable as the determination to express each part, is the refusal of any consistent handling of elements such as staircases – at the arrival end of the patients' wing the stair is internalized, whereas at the other it is articulated as a tower – and the willingness variously to crash the

33

34

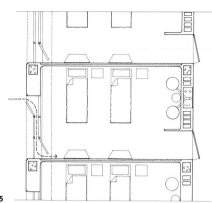

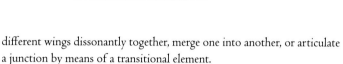

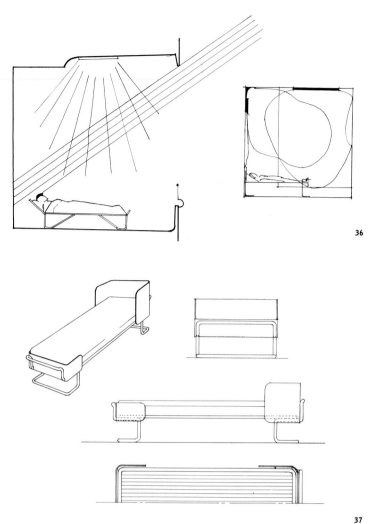

different wings dissonantly together, merge one into another, or articulate a junction by means of a transitional element.

Functional zoning provided the rationale for the design, but the building was also a composition of considerable visual and spatial sophistication. Consider, for example, the alignments of the patients' wing and sun-terraces, which Aalto explained on grounds of orientation. Facing the terraces due south is more symbolic of their dedication to the supposed healing powers of the sun than a strict functional necessity, and is used to explain a splay that serves several architectural purposes: it evokes the idea of the building as an organism that can respond to its environment – turning its head, as it were, to catch the sun; it reinforces the individuality of the two pieces, introducing a palpable tension between them; it suggests the capture of a section of the surrounding landscape where paths were arranged for the healthier patients to take exercise; and it provides a visual closure to a linear block and roof terrace that threatened to disappear disconcertingly off into infinity. Andres Duany has drawn attention to the latter as one of many examples in Aalto's work in which elements are slipped or rotated 'to correct perspectives that would otherwise be disturbingly oblique'.[42] Similarly, the angle formed between the patients' wing and the communal block means that they open up to welcome the visitor, and, through the heightened perspective, emphasize the main entrance. Simo Paavilainen has suggested that, in this respect, the Paimio plan might owe something to the splays and false perspectives that were familiar perceptual devices in 1920s classicism.[43] The internalized staircase on the patients' wing was expressed as a tower in the competition scheme, and as such would have significantly impaired the perspectival effect – hence its later incorporation within the wing – whereas the stair-tower at the other end forms an effective visual termination and articulates the junction with the sun-terraces. Such subtle responses to the experience of the perceiving human subject became a hallmark of Aalto's architecture.

The 'motto' on the competition entry was an internal perspective of the L-shaped window of the patients' rooms.[44] It was a form inspired by a project for a Mediterranean Resort Hotel that André Lurçat had shown Aalto in Paris when they met in the summer.[45] The window was eventually squared-up to save costs and, in any case, lost its *raison d'être* when the radiator was eliminated. It was clearly chosen to emphasize that the design started from consideration of the patient, and Aalto later related that: 'when I received the assignment I was myself ill and therefore had the opportunity to make a few experiments and found out what it really felt like to be sick'.[46] The illness was probably apocryphal, but his reflections on the fact that, 'the ordinary room is a room for a vertical person [whereas] a patient's room is a room for a horizontal human being, and colours, lighting, heating and so on must be designed with that in mind',[47] and his concern for the long-stay patients' individual and collective needs led to numerous innovations developed in consultation with doctors and medical psychologists. The two-bed patients' rooms were thought through from first principles: the ceiling was painted darker than the walls, so as to be more restful to the gaze; the room-light was mounted out of sight on the wall above the patients' heads, and shone upwards, light being reflected off the wall and ceiling on which a white semi-circle was painted above the lamp; heating was from a ceiling-mounted radiant panel located beyond the patients' feet; and, at an early stage in the design, the structural slabs were canted up to admit more light into the depth of the room and provide a sense of visual release – an attractive idea which presumably proved too expensive.

Each patient had his or her own wash-basin, specially designed to reduce the sound of splashing when the taps were run so as not to disturb the other occupant (an idea which did not work in practice); draught-free fresh air was admitted by opening lights positioned at opposite ends of the

35–37 Paimio Sanatorium, Paimio, 1929–33, design for a patient's ward, sketches showing effect of overhead heating on a patient, and a design for a patient's bed. 38 Sketch for a light-fitting at Paimio Sanatorium, 1931: the external lamps from Paimio established a pattern that Aalto varied throughout his career. 39, 40 Armchair and sketch from Paimio Sanatorium: the celebrated bent-wood chair was intended to encourage better breathing. 41 Lamp in patient's room of Paimio Sanatorium: lamps were placed close to the wall above the beds, so as not to shine directly in patients' eyes. 42 Wash-basin from Paimio Sanatorium: designed to be splash-free and silent; an inten-tion which did not work in practice. 43 Wardrobes in Paimio Sanatorium: built-in and made out of plywood, they are raised off the floor for ease of cleaning; however, they bear an unfortunate resemblance to a coffin.

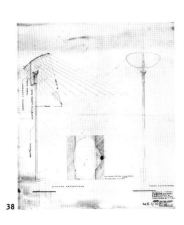

38

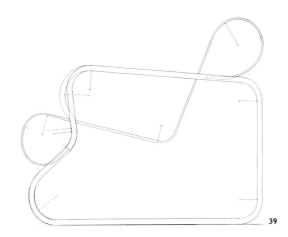

39

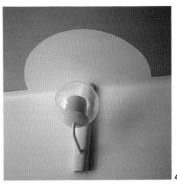

41

40

42

43

44 Paimio Sanatorium, Paimio, 1929–33: the sun balconies join the patient's wing at a slight angle and are dramatically cantilevered in reinforced concrete; above them a continuous sundeck, which is protected with a reinforced concrete canopy to reduce solar gain, runs across the roofs of both wings. **45** The sundecks of Paimio Sanatorium, in the foreground, are now glazed to form additional wards. **46** Door handle from the sanatorium: even the door handles were thought out with their users in mind, Aalto designed them in a shape that would prevent coat sleeves or pockets being caught in them. **47** Aalto's corridor lamps for the Paimio Sanatorium had elaborate fins to prevent glare.

44

45

46

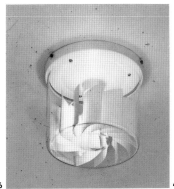

47

window, and drawn through the gap between the double-glazing, where it was pre-heated. The services were designed to be maintained from the corridor, away from the patients, and one wall was lined with absorbent insulation to make the acoustics more restful; and the wardrobes were made of bent plywood and hung from the wall to ease cleaning – their shape, it has to be said, bears a slightly unfortunate resemblance to a coffin, as is pointed out to visitors to the preserved 'museum ward'. For the patients' rooms, Aalto used timber window frame, which, compared with the steel frames elsewhere in the building, not only reduced condensation but were also warmer to the touch.

The communal areas were designed with similar attention to detail, with aspect and colour schemes varied to stimulate and soothe as appropriate: a small greenhouse was created in the corner of the recreation room; and the entrance hall floor had broad grey stripes inlaid into its bright yellow linoleum to indicate the main circulation routes with stripes continuing up the main staircase as a painted band framing the handrail. However, this reception area was substantially altered in the mid-1950s, when the free-form glazed kiosk was added. The building was furnished largely with Aalto-designed furniture, some specially made for it, such as a stacking stool, the reclining chaise-longue for the terraces, and the patients' beds, all of which used tubular metal. The acclaimed Paimio armchair was developed in conjunction with the manufacturer-craftsman Otto Korhonen, and represented one of the major landmarks in Aalto's furniture designs.[48] It was designed to be springy, with the angle of its back supposedly calculated to improve breathing: in fact it is not particularly comfortable, but the visual compensations have ensured that it continues to be in demand as a Modern classic.

Light fittings received the same attention: for the corridors he designed a fitting with curved fins to prevent glare, and in the dining room the spherical globes have an opalescent lower half and a clear upper part, where light is reflected out from a shallow recessed copper dome. The lamp standards outside are similarly inventive: a concrete base holding a steel pole from which a thinner tube rises to support a lamp and curved reflector, forming an elegant arrangement in which each part is clearly designed to do a particular job – Aalto was to produce variants on this theme throughout his career. Several of the items of furniture and fittings were envisaged as standard types suitable for manufacture and use elsewhere. Recent research has revealed that he developed almost a hundred such 'standards',

for everything ranging from windows, doors, staircases and railings, to chairs, lamps and an alphabet[49]. Of course, one of the key concepts of the movement was the evolution of 'typeforms' appropriate to serial production, so that Aalto's work in this area can be viewed as further confirmation of his commitment to functionalist ideals.[50]

The detailed innovations, designed around the patients' needs, were matched by bolder technical innovations such as a novel, zoned system of mechanical ventilation for the kitchen, and the structure of the sun terraces. The severe Finnish climate limits the opportunities for the direct expression of structure – columns in the wall plane, as in the Zonnestraal for example, would lead to unacceptable cold-bridges – but the open terraces held no such constraint and Aalto, possibly with help from Arne Henriksson again (although he was not the engineer recorded for the project), created a dramatic cantilever structure supported by tapering reinforced concrete piers, which rest on a massive triangular foundation: the weight of the construction and width of the foundation resisted the considerable overturning moment, which wind blowing against the solid rear wall would have generated. For the date, it was a structural *tour de force*, the drama of which has sadly been lost as the terraces were glazed in 1963 to provide additional wards, drugs having long since replaced the sun in the treatment of tuberculosis, and the sanatorium having become a general hospital.[51]

One of the last features to be developed was the distinctive, curved entrance canopy. Finished in black, it is known to the nurses as 'Aalto's lung' (although any reference to tuberculosis was surely unintentional!). Its curved shape clearly anticipates Aalto's personal language of forms, which matured later in the 1930s. The inspiration behind such forms has been the subject of more speculation than any other aspect of Aalto's work, and we will review some of the ideas in a later chapter. It is sufficient to say here that, by this time, curved forms as visual counterpoints in predominantly rectilinear buildings were a commonplace part of the Modernist vocabulary, and the likeliest inspiration – if there was a specific one – is the curved *porte-cochère* that Le Corbusier included in his League of Nations and Centrosoyus projects.[52] The inner curves of both Aalto's and Corbu's canopies follow the turning circle of an arriving car, but Aalto rounded-off one end and introduced a slight taper to give the Paimio canopy its distinctive biomorphic quality, which is very different from Le Corbusier's regular, classically-centred form.

Following its completion early in 1933, the Sanatorium was widely published and established Aalto's international reputation;[53] Giedion later ranked it with the Bauhaus and Le Corbusier's League of Nations project as 'one of three institutional buildings inseparably linked to the rise of contemporary architecture'.[54] Paimio was sufficiently close to the principles and aesthetic canon of Modernism, which Henry-Russell Hitchcock and Philip Johnson christened 'The International Style' in 1932[55], to gain acceptance as one of its major achievements, but the resemblance is superficial. Aalto's thoroughgoing commitment to genuinely functional design, which embraces subtle psychological and social factors as well as technical performance, and refusal to accept the rationale of the structural grid and free plan, and any attempt at stylistic codification, are the grounds for his subsequent rejection of Functionalism with a capital 'F' as part of 'a formalist front that stands in opposition to a rational view of life and art'.[56] Despite the considerable sophistication we have noted in the building's formal composition, there remains a casual, ad hoc, quality which suggests the accretional growth he so admired in Italian towns. The additive planning, asymmetry and volumetric sub-division are also akin to the rational principles of *Jugendstil*, and Aalto's determination to design every aspect of the environment has clear affinities with the ideal of the *gesamtkunstwerk*. But his aim is less an aesthetic totality, which can all too easily become an aesthetic tyranny[57], than a complex social organism designed in every aspect to make the patients' confinement tolerable and to assist their healing: Aalto even had the idea of putting out a flag on the sun-terrace to celebrate each patient who recovered. The pine forest entered into the contract, acquiring new meaning as a source of healing for the community – a discourse Aalto soon generalized beyond the specific therapeutic regime – and it is difficult to imagine the impact that the sanatorium must have had on its early patients. The dedication to serving their needs manifested in every detail, and the optimistic, uplifting quality of its light-filled spaces were far beyond anything that they could have experienced. It must have contributed in great measure to the prospects of recovery, which, before the advent of antibiotics, depended more on morale than on medical prescriptions. In Paimio, the emerging welfare state acquired a potent emblem of a new architecture in the service of its people.

While working on the sanatorium, Aalto entered a dozen other competitions without success; he also designed a Minimum Apartment for an exhibition in Helsinki (which we will review in the next chapter), pro-

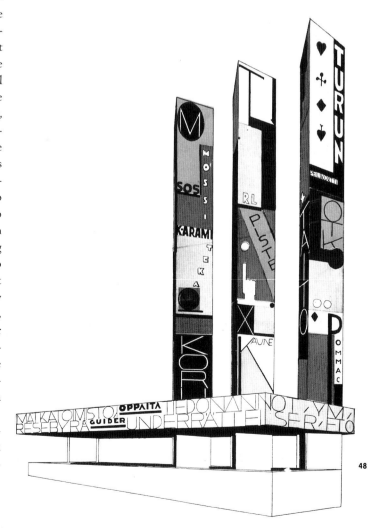

48

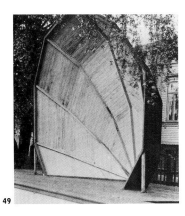

49

48 Alvar Aalto and Erik Bryggman, Pavilion for the Turku 700th Anniversary Exhibition, Turku, 1929: the bold graphics were inspired by the precedents of the Russian Constructivists and the German Bauhaus. **49** Industrial Exhibition Bandstand, Tampere, 1922: the choir-shell design was Aalto's first experiment with an acoustically-inspired form – an idea he refined for the bandstand at the Turku Exhibition. **50–52** Alvar Aalto and Erik Bryggman, Turku Exhibition, 1929. **53** Bandstand at the Turku Exhibition.

50

52

51

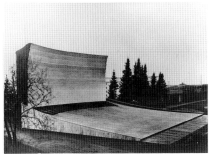

53

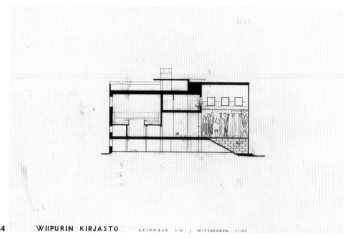

54   WIIPURIN KIRJASTO   LEIKKAUS C-D / MITTAKAAVA 1:100

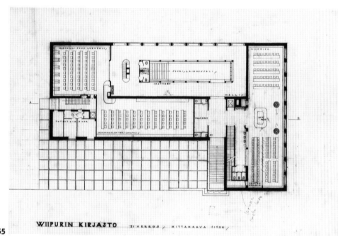

WIIPURIN KIRJASTO   2:KERROS / MITTAKAAVA 1:100

55

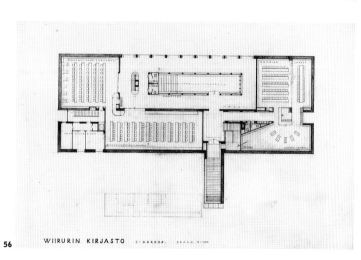

56   WIIRURIN KIRJASTO   2:KERROS.   SKALA 1:100

duced two revised designs for the Viipuri Library and, in 1929, collaborated with Bryggman on the City of Turku's 700th Anniversary Exhibition, which doubled that year as the Finnish Fair for industrial products. This was an altogether more modest undertaking than the great 1930 Stockholm Exhibition, but none the less offered an opportunity to make a significant public statement about the virtues of Functionalism. The Finnish Fair Corporation was founded in 1920 to oversee such events. Its function was to promote trade – Russia no longer being the principal trading partner after the Revolution – and an international outlook in a climate still hostile to foreign culture. Although the Turku Fair was held a year before Stockholm, Aalto was familiar with the designs being prepared by Asplund and his colleagues, and they clearly provided a source of inspiration; he confirmed this point for future researchers by placing a postcard of the Stockholm Exhibition amongst the drawings in his office archive[58]. However, as Elina Standertskjöld has demonstrated, the influence of recent German exhibition design is also conspicuous in the emphasis on advertising and typography.[59]

As the senior of the two architects, Bryggman seems to have been largely responsible for the overall site plan, also designing the major pavilions and restaurant, while Aalto organized the entrance area, smaller row pavilions and advertising stands. He also co-ordinated the innovative typography, to which all the exhibitors had to conform, much to their annoyance. This reflected the principles developed at the Bauhaus, notably by László Moholy-Nagy. It was also no doubt partly inspired by his experience of working for the Turun Sanomat. Aalto treated the whole exhibition as an exercise in communication. A letter to exhibitors from the organizers explained that visiting the fair would be like 'reading a newspaper', and that 'after the visitor has walked a few dozen metres, a new page will be turned with new advertisements'. The pavilions were cheaply constructed using a standardized timber system developed by the architects, and in the presentation of the project in *Arkkitehti* Aalto stressed that the buildings, like a modern newspaper page, did not follow a specified form but were free variations which shared 'a similar tone'.[60] As in the Paimio Sanatorium, he wanted to allow the parts a life of their own within a chosen formal, constructional language. This refusal to impose what he saw as an 'artificial synthesis' on form, and implicitly life, gradually asserted itself as a key motivation of all his work, although he reserved the right to suppress the vulgar (and stylistically outmoded) commercial imagery,

57

which would have resulted from allowing the exhibitors total freedom. Aalto also designed the well-known choir platform, which, like the earlier choir shell and bandstand for the 1922 Industrial Exhibition in Tampere, was an organic form inspired by acoustic requirements; in retrospect, the double-curved reflector with its subtly stepped profile seems almost to prefigure the articulation of his auditoria.

The final project normally assigned to Aalto's Functionalist phase, the Viipuri Public Library, underwent a series of transformations from the classical scheme we examined in the last chapter.[61] Aalto received instructions to proceed with the design at the end of February 1928, by when he had completed the Paimio competition and was firmly committed to the new architecture. The jury had criticized the external stair hall and suggested that the glazed roof be replaced by side-lighting 'for climatic reasons', thereby effectively negating his elaborate outside-inside game. In his first revision, Aalto glazed the stair hall, eliminated the roof-lighting, and effected various planning changes, including the introduction of a radiating arrangement of shelves in the children's library, which hints at the fan-shaped plan that became a feature of his later libraries. The Building Committee were still unhappy with the projecting stair hall and Aalto responded by incorporating it as the inner face of an L-shaped plan; despite the Functionalist clothing of the fenestration, the volumes and planning remained essentially classical in spirit – a fact emphasized by the projected inclusion of a two-storey high relief or fresco of classical figures and Corinthian columns in the entrance hall. Aalto was saved from building this unhappy compromise by numerous delays and a change of site, and eventually, in 1933, he was instructed to prepare a scheme for a completely new location.

The building sits in a park. In fact it is still there – the reports of its destruction having been greatly exaggerated.[62] It contains the public library and a lecture room originally planned for meetings of the local cultural society. The major spaces are accommodated in two distinct volumes, which, in good Modernist fashion, slide dynamically past each other: the composition could have been suggested by De Stijl or Suprematism, or might have been prompted by the adjacent roads approaching each other from opposite directions without meeting.[63] The larger volume contained all the strictly library functions (book stacks, reading areas, children's library), while the offices and lecture room were placed in a slightly lower, and much longer and thinner block. In germinal form, this is the 'head and

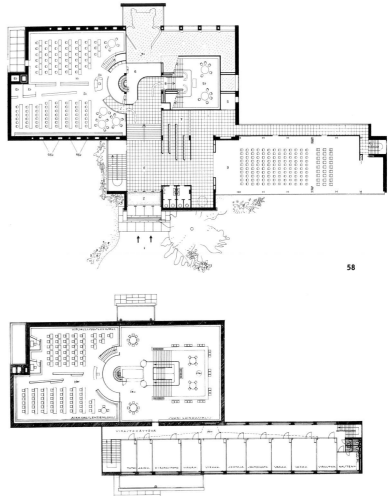

58

59

60

tail' plan type Aalto used frequently as a means of organizing a programme into a mass containing the principal activity (books and reading areas, a council chamber, or church nave). It later assumed various non-rectilinear forms, and an orthogonally planned 'tail' of secondary spaces, which was capable of extension and could be manipulated to define external spaces.

Aalto drove an axis through the two blocks: at one end the main entrance was located in a projecting vestibule, while at the other was a smaller projection for the separate entrance to the children's library. The main stair to the upper floor of the 'tail' was adjacent to the main entrance and enclosed by square-gridded glazed screens — an idea retained from the earlier revised schemes. In the library itself, Aalto developed an ingenious stair arrangement that enabled visitors to pass through a sunken area, from which they were divided by a handrail, before reaching the central control desk. The handrail is like a line floating in space, a trace of the comings and goings of people through the building; while the balustrade around the sunken well is a broad, hovering plane forming a continuous surface for casual study. The main reading room at ground level is reached around a half-cylinder, which forms an apse-like balcony for the library above and lies on the cross-axis along which the stairs, stacks and desks are disposed. The presence of these two axes, and the symmetry of the library space, are surprising in what initially appears to be a 'free' volumetric organization. Furhtermore the porches on either end are unresolved in relation to the main masses, and the internal access arrangements feel slightly awkward at entry level.

Once into the library, however, these minor problems are quickly forgotten, for here Aalto unfolds a beautifully-proportioned interior, suffused by a gentle, shadowless light filtered down from a grid of conical lens roof-lights, which are 1.8 metres in diameter; the reinforced concrete beams span 17.6 metres and the depth of the roof structure ensures that no direct sun is allowed to disturb the reader's concentration.[64] In a celebrated passage, Aalto recalled the origins of the design as follows: 'For long periods I pursued the solution with the help of primitive sketches. From some kind of fantastic mountain landscapes with cliffs lit up by suns in different positions I gradually arrived at the concept for the library building. The library's architectural core consists of reading and lending areas at different levels and plateaus, while the centre and control area forms the high point above the different levels. The childish sketches have only an indirect connection with the architectural conception, but they tied

together the section and the plan with each other and created a kind of unity of horizontal and vertical structures'.[65]

The article was written in 1947, and Aalto's memory may have worked some tricks, but surviving sketches confirm the existence of a 'mountain landscape with cliffs lit up by suns'. The passage is interesting, both for the light it sheds on his creative process, and for the doubt it casts on unduly simplified lines of influence and derivation. Aalto perhaps exaggerates how radical a re-think he undertook in developing the final design from the earlier versions. For instance, the sunken reading/stack area clearly derives from the original classical scheme, re-capturing the idea of a space opening out to the sky. In his mind this was transformed into an abstract landscape, with its 'cliff' walls, and 'plateau' floors. With this landscape metaphor in mind one notices, for example, how the stairs and library floor have the same finishes, so that the stairs are like an adaptation of the earth/floor, which enables people to ascend, rather than a separate element in the space.[66] The complex stairs and changes of level repeatedly evoke that feeling of promontory and haven, prospect and refuge, which is a basic experience of landscape.[67]

It is tempting to speculate that Aalto's 'suns' were a sub-conscious re-working of Asplund's first scheme for the Stockholm library, which consisted of a literal sky-vault in the form of a Pantheon-like dome in which the coffers were cut through and glazed to form a veritable galaxy of suns. Such speculation is fascinating, but inevitably inconclusive: Aalto's reticence about the sources of his ideas was motivated in part by a desire to promulgate the myth of the natural designer above all influences, but also reflects an understandable suspicion about attempts to rationalize and explain the inner workings of the mind. That said, he is unlikely to have arrived at such a conception had the exploration of these themes in Nordic Classicism not pre-disposed him to think in terms of creating architectural illusions and metaphors. It may be that it is 'this concern with lighting . . . that makes the Viipuri Library a truly modern building', as Quantrill suggests, but Viipuri's is a nuanced light, which not only illuminates and provides contact with the outside in a climate where daylight is precious, but is also a key term in a narrative in which the natural world is metaphorically re-created. As such, it transcends the criteria of rational illumination — of which it is, none the less, a superb example. In the Mediterranean, Asplund discovered a vision of architecture as a partnership between the ground and the clear dome of the southern sky, which he attempted to re-

60 Sketch for Viipuri Public Library, c.1929: these drawings of a 'fantastic mountain' were Aalto's point of departure for the library's layered organization into a series of plateaus.

61 Main library, Viipuri Public Library, Viipuri, 1933–5: the book stacks and reading rooms are organized around a staircase that channels the flow of visitors past the control desk; the grid of deeply recessed roof-lights creates a diffuse, overall illumination, ideal for reading; these roof-lights appeared in Aalto's initial sketches as cliffs being lit up by suns in different positions.

61

62

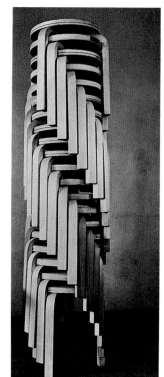

64

63

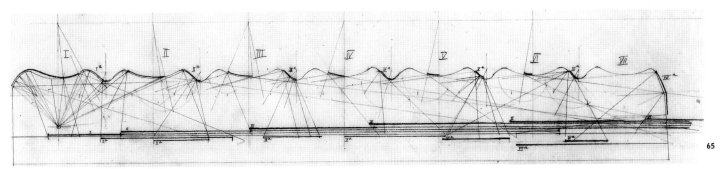

65

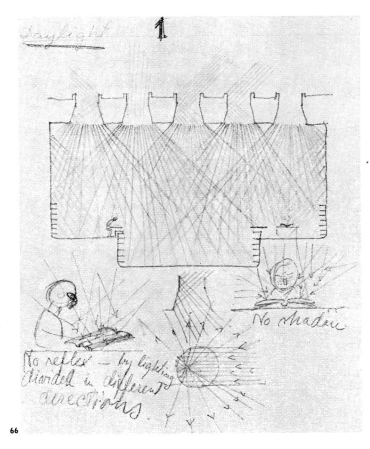

66

create in the North, whereas the diffused ceiling of light in Viipuri materialises the atmospheric northern sky as a low, misty veil hovering above the encircling horizon of books.

The other major space in the building, the lecture theatre, was lit by a continuous run of full-height glazing overlooking the park. The space Aalto assigned for it was, in acoustic terms, far from ideal – a triple-square in plan – and this prompted another of his most important innovations, the undulating acoustic timber ceiling made of 30,000 strips of knot-free Karelian pine. The room was intended for debates as well as lectures, and the ceiling was designed to overcome the acoustical problems caused by downstand beams to ensure that speakers anywhere in the room could be heard equally well – Aalto claimed it was 'ninety-nine per cent acoustically perfect',[68] but the rationale still rather begs the question why he designed it so long in the first place. Quite apart from the acoustical problems, the furthest members of the audience are a very long way from the principal speaker. One must assume that it was either overall compositional reasons that led him to compromise the proportions in order to preserve the contrast between the two main volumes, or, more positively, that he wished to stress the link with the park by maximising the length of glazed wall. Whatever the explanation, what emerged was the first original motif in Finnish architecture since the heyday of National Romanticism: the counterpoint between a free, undulating line and a firm, melodic base, which became the ground of the archetypal Aalto space. And further, by positing the radical separation of inner and outer surfaces, he overturned that paralysis of the section, which was a consequence of the plan's liberation by the structural frame. The multiple levels Aalto deployed in the library rejected the rationale of layered floor slabs, and came closer to the volumetric play of the Loosian *raumplan*.

The idea of the ceiling as an independent structure is hardly new: Gothic vaults and, much closer to the way Aalto later employs the idea, the double-skins of the Baroque are obvious precedents, but Aalto would later exploit it with unprecedented freedom. Likewise, the use of timber as a lining was something he had already essayed in the Muurame church and, as we noted in discussing the building, is a familiar feature of timber churches that imitated stone vaults. As for the undulating line, its possible origins and ramifications must await a more detailed discussion in Chapter 5. In Viipuri, the line is not as 'free' as it first appears, the seven bays being related rhythmically to the glazing, with alternate troughs always

67

68

69

occurring on the line of a mullion, and the curves themselves being constructed from just two radii. Aalto's interest in such geometry first emerged in his bent-wood furniture and related 'wood-experiments', and the affinity between the ceiling and the original furniture (including the three-legged stackable stool that continues to sell in enormous quantities) is readily apparent. Despite the 'rational' explanation of the long room and its acoustic ceiling as a space for debates, the layout of furniture, with armchairs in the first two rows, several rows of stools with backs followed by five rows of plain stools, was calculated to encourage people to sit near the speaker. The acoustic rationale of the ceiling was questionable – our ears are on the sides, not the tops of our heads and lateral reflections are crucial – but architecturally it was pregnant with possibilities.

The major technical innovation Aalto introduced at Viipuri was a mechanical ventilation system that provided fresh air via ducts buried in the walls, throughout what was effectively, a sealed building. This was surprisingly advanced for the time. At the detailed level, the building is notable for the extensive use of timber finishes, a decided novelty to which his friend, Gustaf Strengell, responded as follows: 'the interiors of the building display Japanese characteristics in many places. Observe the pale, light colouring, which gives the rooms not just their charming airy quality but actually a scent. Quite particularly the Japanese streak appears in the choice of pale wood only – birch, pine, beech – for the panelling and furnishings, and it is even more striking in the treatment of smooth surfaces: in true Japanese manner, they are not treated at all, but "left in their natural state", which is both attractive to the eye and pleasing to the touch.'[69] Strengell's attribution of what today seem quintessentially Scandinavian characteristics to Japanese influence was not merely critical speculation, as is clear from a letter Aalto wrote to the Japanese ambassador: 'There is a very special affinity between us modern architects and the well-balanced architecture of your country. I believe that it is a deeper understanding of the language of materials that unites us.'[70] Aalto used timber to mediate between the building and the people using it: its surfaces are inviting to the hands, as are the rails which form 'an elaborate network of touch'[71]. It helps protect more vulnerable finishes such as plaster or paint, as in the 'fins' added to the columns in the children's library; a practical motive once again providing the basis for an idea later elaborated for various expressive effects. This 'naturalization' of surfaces was also evident in the incorporation of a large trellis for plants up the staircase adjacent to the main entrance, which were invited to colonize the inner steel glazing grid, and in the provision of poles for climbing plants alongside the children's entrance. One of these ran past the edge of the building in a premonition of his later erosions of form.

Just as significant as the hints of innovations that Aalto would later exploit, is the residue of classical ideas. Although the massing is essentially Modernist, the volumes themselves are surprisingly solid both in construction and feeling: the walls are 750 mm thick and appear decidedly earth-bound. The main entrance porch is finished in natural stone and looks as if it would belong more happily to the classical original. Finally, and in many ways most surprising in its park setting, is the total introversion of the library itself. Aalto saw this as a functional necessity: 'reading a book involves both culturally and physically a strange kind of concentration; the duty of architecture is to eliminate all disturbing elements.'[72] However, it is in radical opposition to the spatial continuity of inside and out that the new architecture espoused. Despite the differences in form and size, the interior recalls the calm, classical world of Asplund's Stockholm Library.

Beyond its intrinsic interest, Viipuri was a key building in Aalto's development. It was the first in which he established a type-form. The organizational schema is present, with minor variations, in almost all his future libraries: the volumetric articulation of the programme into a high, introverted, figural library hall and lower, linear support facilities; a central control desk looking out over a sunken reading/stack area; and even, diffused lighting, admitted either through the roof or through a clerestory and reflected down from a specially shaped ceiling. Secondly, it stands on the threshold of his development of a personal style combining formal invention – the undulating ceiling, column 'fins', furniture, themes and motifs drawn from architectural history, evident here in the marked classical residue – and spatial ideas developed from abstractions of natural and urban spaces – the 'imaginary mountain'. The library entered the canon of Modern architecture as an exemplary Functionalist building, but the stylistic traits that justify this designation are, in the context of Aalto's trajectory, its least significant aspects; the future lay in radically functional design mediated by an interplay of invention, memory and metaphor that can already be discerned at Viipuri.

Dwelling
in the
Modern World

In this modern society it is possible, at least theoretically, for the father to
be a mason, the mother a college professor, the daughter a film star, and
the son something still worse. Obviously each would have special needs
to be allowed to work and think undisturbed. The modern dwelling must
be built in accordance with these needs. ALVAR AALTO [1]

AHOUSE for the 'common man' was, according to Le Corbusier, '*the* problem of the epoch. The balance of society comes down to a question of building . . . Architecture or Revolution'.[2] Given the opportunity to present a pavilion to 'the new spirit' at the Paris Exhibition of Decorative Arts in 1925, he chose to construct a small, standard apartment – 'a practical machine for living in'.[3] Within the German circles to which Aalto was introduced by Sven Markelius, the problem was discussed in less apocalyptic terms, but the concerns were the same: 'The Bauhaus intends', Walter Gropius announced in 1926, 'to contribute to the development of housing – from the simplest appliance to the complete dwelling – in a way which is in harmony with the spirit of the age.'[4] That Aalto shared these concerns is apparent from the article, 'The Dwelling as a Problem', we considered briefly in the last chapter, where he set out the principles of designing for 'biodynamic functions' in terms clearly influenced by the discussions at the 1929 CIAM gathering in Frankfurt on the theme of the low-cost dwelling.[5]

More interesting than the obvious similarities, however, are the different emphases in Aalto's account. He was concerned less with the possibilities of industrial production, and not at all with what he saw as a superficial 'machine aesthetic', but stressed the social and cultural factors necessitating new approaches to housing design. The dwelling had become a problem, he explained, because, 'a society based on prestige and clearly etched class distinctions belongs to the past'. The individual of the past was in thrall to the outmoded bourgeois values of 'developed taste', expressed 'in the collecting of objects, in owning things [such as] all types of unusable status furniture, factory baroque at cheap prices'; whereas the modern individual would develop a 'lovely, almost intellectual ability to grasp and enjoy the moment's and brief instant's *values*.' (Emphasis as in original). This was a truly Baudelairean engagement with 'the passing moment and all the suggestions of eternity that it contains'.[6]

Spatially, this meant the rejection of the concept of the 'room', which, 'exists in a final "proletarianised" form but continues to have the same meaning it had in the palaces from which it is a descendant. The living room in a peasant farmhouse – whose Finnish name *tupa* developed from the Lapp *kota*, in Swedish *kota* – is a combination of different functions, and was never, before its period of decline, combined with the concept "room". In the city dwelling, on the other hand, the room continues to exist in an artificial manner, as an inheritance from palace architecture.'

The new demands on the house were coming from what he called 'the decentralization of family life', following the breakdown of a patriarchal society and women's 'emancipation and subsequent rise from a subordinate position both in working life and in the home to become an equal work companion'. The need for each member of the family to have privacy within a small dwelling could not be met by traditional rooms, but demanded 'half-rooms', effective use of common areas, and the development of new means of insulation. These were ideas that he had already attempted to implement in the Standard Apartment Block discussed in the

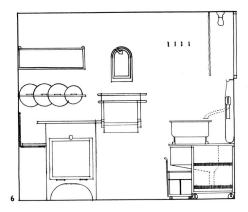

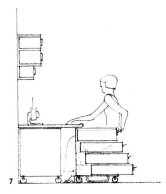

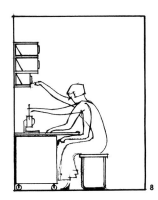

last chapter.

The analogy Aalto draws between the spatial concepts of a modern dwelling and the *tupa* of the traditional farmhouse can be explained, in part, by a desire to lessen 'the shock of the new' by relating the ideas to something familiar and essentially Finnish – he was writing as much for a general as a professional audience. But it is revealing that he should invoke such an analogy at the height of his Functionalist enthusiasms, suggesting that the determination to help bring Finland into the modern world was already matched by a desire to give a national inflection to international developments. At least that is how it appears in the light of later projects such as the Villa Mairea, for which, as we shall see, the *tupa* formed a paradigm.

In 1928, he entered a competition organized by the magazine *Aitta* for the design of prototypes for a weekend cottage and summer villa. Aalto won both, and submitted an additional entry for the cottage, which was purchased.[7] The first-prize scheme for the weekend cottage, 'Konsoli', was adapted from Aino's classical-vernacular Villa Flora: the main fireplace was changed from a square to round shape and was made the focal pivot of an open-plan; the barrel-vaulted porch became a dynamically cantilevered roof; and the kitchen chimney was expressed as a mass on the end elevation and positioned asymmetrically in plan, eliminating any suggestion of a central axis. Aalto observed of 'Konsoli' that: 'the idea of making use of ethnographic or stilted forms borrowed from old rural architecture never once came into the author's head';[8] the turf roof being, presumably, simply a functionally sound solution to the problem of waterproofing and insulation: the roof did slope back slightly from a shallow parapet, so the grass was relatively inconspicuous from the front. For 1928 it was a startlingly Modern image for a traditional building type, and in the alternative entry, 'Kumeli', he hedged his bets with a much safer, more conventional design.[9] Aalto clearly saw no disparity between Functionalism and the proximity to nature, which the Finns seek in their weekend cottages, nor between a turf roof and a building expressive of the modern world; he would not borrow the 'stilted forms' of rural architecture, but was perfectly happy to emulate its rational means where appropriate. The inclusion of a broom tucked into the corner under the porch is surely not accidental, but a Tessenow-like touch intended to evoke the virtues of an unaffected lifestyle.

The summer villa entry was called 'Merry-Go-Round' and Aalto described it as follows: 'The entry of sunlight into the rooms, the view and protection from wind suggested the round form of the building. Other

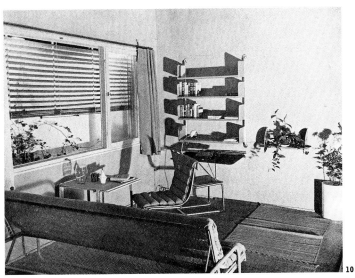

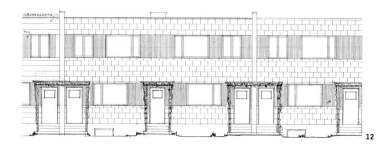

considerations included the need for concentration and the wish to spare the legs of the lady of the house for tango and jazz . . . If modern people who can read and count and speak three civilized languages spend the summer in this building, the exterior of the "villa" is not intended to conceal these facts. The author was not looking for originality or unusual effects but for a natural solution. Therefore the building may seem "original" to some.'[10] Its design reflected the ideas he had put forward two years earlier in *Aitta*, when he wrote that: 'the garden (or courtyard) belongs to our home just as much as any of the other rooms', and praised the virtues of the 'long-despised corridor'.[11] The plan was simply a conventional corridor house-plan wrapped around a circular court, whose room-like quality was reinforced by two large curtains that could be drawn across to enclose it completely. The court was both an outdoor room and a piece of captured nature, as the irregular stone paving and tree made clear. The circular geometry was slightly awkward (and one cannot help noticing that it was an enlargement of the fireplace in 'Konsoli'), but the design hinted at the dialogue between nature and culture that runs through Aalto's mature work. The design was Modernist, and Aalto explains it on typically 'functional' grounds, but the use of the court is clearly indebted to classical precedents. It would certainly have appealed to the competition judge, Oiva Kallio, who had built a masterly version of the atrium type in 1924 in his own summer house on an island in the Helsinki archipelago.

Success in the *Aitta* competition provided valuable publicity, both for Aalto and Functionalism, and in 1930 he organized an exhibit on the theme of 'The Minimum Apartment', based on the previous year's CIAM congress. Part of the Finnish Arts and Crafts Society's annual exhibition, it was held in Helsinki's Art Hall, itself a distinguished example of Nordic Classicism built in 1927. The Aaltos designed a complete interior, using the same determination to re-think every aspect of the domestic environment that had been applied to the patients' needs at Paimio.[12] Many of the ideas were developed from his experiences at the Stockholm Exhibition and knowledge of Bauhaus ideas, which had been demonstrated as early as 1923 in the experimental *Haus am Horn*;[13] in a newspaper review, Hilding Ekelund (architect of the Art Hall) pointed out that: 'Aalto sniffs out rational technical innovations from all four corners of Europe and adroitly proceeds to utilize them by recasting.'[14] The Aaltos designed everything from the overall plan through to the furniture and fittings, even a tidy-bin on wheels, a waste-grinder and a carving-board. The furniture included a

tubular settee, which folded out to form a bed, and a stackable version of the early 'hybrid chair' that combined metal legs with a bent plywood back. Here was a complete setting for modern life in which everything had been comprehensively thought through on functional grounds. The only suspicion of old-fashioned 'developed taste' was in the stackable wooden dining chairs, which still emanated a slight perfume of *Art Nouveau*. These were such a contrast to the light, tubular chairs, which 'meant less wear on rugs', but were so often 'treated as purely formal novelties'.[15]

Aalto's first opportunity to build a Modern house came with the design of the on-site accommodation for both employees and doctors at the Paimio Sanatorium, built in 1932–3. Eight flats were provided for office staff in a terrace with a continuous first-floor balcony divided by party walls. The form recalled J. J. P. Oud's row-houses in the Hook of Holland and at the Kiefhoek in Rotterdam. Internally, Aalto responded to the need for flexibility by devising a plan in which one bedroom could be used by either one of two adjacent flats, depending on the family's requirements. The larger houses for the doctors offered the opportunity to develop an open-plan with sliding partition-doors, and were organized in an L-shape around a patio, with additional private outdoor space on a first-floor balcony. Although they formed a short terrace of three units, the spatial arrangement suggests a debt to Gropius's free-standing houses for the Bauhaus Masters built in Dessau in 1925-6, to which Aalto returned for inspiration in the design of his own house and studio in 1935. Before acquiring a site for this, he began preparing a housing plan for an area of Munkkiniemi, west of Helsinki, which was to be of a hitherto unprecedented scale for Aalto.

Inspired by the sea-view, Aalto proposed four high-rise buildings, ranging from a point-block to a vast fourteen-storey slab a full 200 metres long. The blocks were arranged in an open fan, anticipating some of his later site plans, but the heroic scale was clearly indebted to Le Corbusier, as a comparison of Aalto's perspective with a view of the *Ville Contemporaine* of 1922 confirms[16]; the inclusion of a terrace and table in the foreground with an aircraft flying perilously between the blocks above a canopy of trees are surely derived from the Corbusian prototype. Although the scale and relentless repetition of the Munkkiniemi scheme seem like aberrations in his work, Aalto maintained throughout his career a relatively straightforward 'rationalist' approach to the design of housing as opposed to individual houses.

11 Perspective of tower block
for Munkkiniemi, Helsinki, 1934.
12 Elevation for EKA ROT row house,
Karhula, 1937: these houses were
designed for staff at the Sunila Pulp
Mill, the entrances feature wooden
pergolas inspired by the vernacular.
13, 14 Sunila Pulp Mill, Sunila, Kotka,
1936–7/1950–4, site plan and exterior
view: Aalto acted as aesthetic consultant for the mill, and also designed
extensive areas of housing for workers.

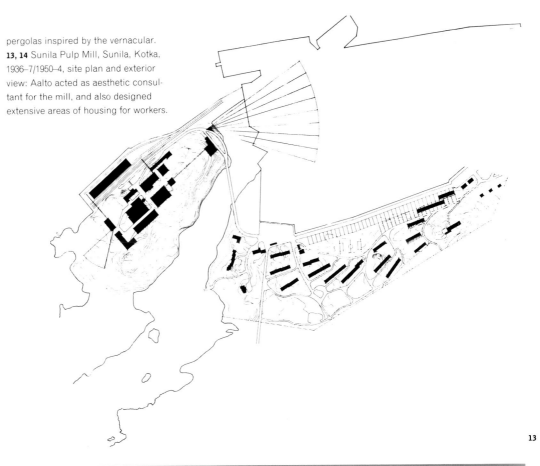

13

14

15, 16 Sunila Pulp Mill, Sunila, Kotka, 1937, plan and exterior view: the splayed terrace of five dwellings for the engineering staff at the Sunila

Pulp Mill was the most interesting and individual of Aalto's housing designs for the site. 17 Stepped terrace of houses at Kauttua, completed in 1939.

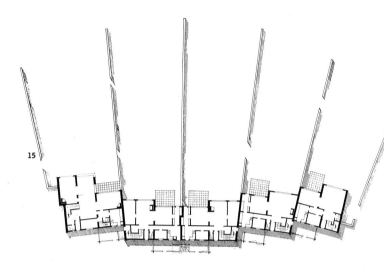

15

16

Following the completion of the Paimio Sanatorium, the Aaltos had no work to keep them in Turku and moved to Helsinki. In 1935, Aalto was introduced by his friend Nils Gustav Hahl to Harry and Maire Gullichsen, who were to prove his salvation during the economically difficult years of the 1930s. Maire was the daughter of Walter Ahlström, director of the vast Ahlström timber and paper company. She studied painting in Paris during the early 1920s, and in 1928 married the businessman Harry Gullichsen, who, four years later, became managing director of the Ahlström company. Maire and Hahl wanted to start an avant-garde art gallery in Helsinki that would act as a focus of progressive culture; in due course this became Artek, the manufacturers and distributors of Aalto's furniture and glassware. Artek was founded in 1935, amidst general celebrations for the hundredth anniversary of the *Kalevala* – the sharp contrast between the progressive and conservative elements in Finnish culture during the 1930s could hardly be better illustrated. The Gullichsens shared Aalto's belief in the possibility of a social utopia based on reason and technological progress. Under Harry's persuasion, the Ahlström board commissioned plans for the company town in Varkaus and the vast Sunila pulp mill with its related housing; work on these projects continued well into the 1950s.

Aalto's role in the design of the mill itself was essentially that of 'aesthetic consultant' to the engineer. The collaboration resulted in one of the most impressive industrial complexes built anywhere in the 1930s. However, Aalto had sole charge of the housing, which was built in several stages and carefully integrated into the surrounding forest forming, in effect, a prototype for his later idea of the 'forest town'[17]. The most interesting of the various schemes was designed in 1936 for the engineering staff, and consisted of a terrace of five houses with splayed and staggered party walls extending into the landscape. Two houses were handed, while the end ones had parallel walls and differed in size from the three intermediate units, one larger and the other smaller than the rest. The steps and staggers enhanced the privacy of the garden terraces and gave individuality to each house. This is an example of the kind of 'flexible standardization' that Aalto advocated: 'the purpose is not to aim at identical types, rather to aim at change and creative richness which in the ideal situation is to be compared with the inexhaustible gift for nuances possessed by nature'.[18] Nature was invited to add further nuances in the form of climbing plants trailing over trellises, which defined small forecourts on the entry side.

17

18, 19 Hansaviertel Apartment Building
for the Berlin Interbau Exhibition,
1955–7, view and plan: the apartment
block features a pinwheel plan and
deeply inset balconies; the balconies
led off a multi-purpose living space,
which was a Modern, open-plan type.

20–22 Aino and Alvar Aalto, Villa Aalto,
Munkkiniemi, Helsinki, 1934–5, front
and rear view, and ground-floor plan:
this house and studio that the Aaltos
designed for themselves in a suburb of
Helsinki, remained Alvar's home
throughout his life; the studio occupied the small, narrow wing and the
first floor included a roof terrace.

18

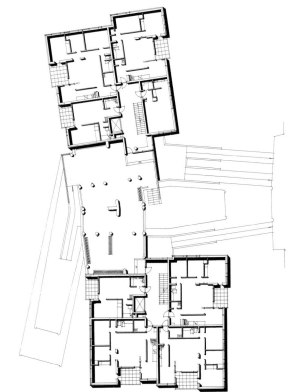

19

These trellises were made from the unstripped trunks of slender saplings
in emulation of vernacular practice, and were also used to create balcony
rails and pergolas in the superb stepped terrace of houses built in Kauttua
(1937–9).

Throughout his career, Aalto's multiple housing schemes adhered to an
essentially rationalist approach, although he almost always devised spatial
ideas to individualize the units; this is clearly the intention behind the fan
configuration of the Neue Vahr Apartment Building in Bremen (1959–62).
In the Hansaviertel Block built for the 1957 *Interbau* exhibition in Berlin,
deep balconies were inset into the apartments, whose plans were rotated
around a common stair. The balconies led off a central multi-purpose
living/circulation space: a Modern, open-plan type which none the less
recalls the atrium form of Aalto's Casa Väino, designed in 1926, which was
used to illustrate the idea of re-creating a sense of the outdoors within the
dwelling discussed in an article for *Aitta*.

Individual dwellings offered greater opportunities for architectural
innovation than multiple housing schemes, but they also posed the socially-motivated Modernists with a dilemma: how to reconcile a commitment
to the mass-produced small dwelling with the individually designed one-
off residence. Like Le Corbusier before him, Aalto argued that there need
not be any conflict because the one-off house could be used as 'a kind of
experimental laboratory, where one can realize that which is not possible
for the present mass production, but out of which these experimental cases
gradually spread . . . to become an objective available for everyone.'[19] In
retrospect this may seem slightly disingenuous or politically naive, but one
should not doubt the conviction with which such views were held at the
time. Aalto's first 'experiments' were in the design of his own combined
house and studio on which he started work in 1934.

The scheme was developed using a two-storey L-shaped volume, from
which he managed to carve a surprisingly complex building. One wing of
the 'L' was occupied by the double-height studio, which had a large mezzanine, and was linked directly to both the living room and master-
bedroom, but set a few steps up from both to establish a psychological
distance between living and work. At the opposite end of the house, a
covered terrace was hollowed out under the children's bedrooms; these
shared a small hall/play area with its own fireplace, and this upper hall
opened on to a large roof-terrace running across to the studio. The bedrooms were contained in a timber-framed and clad 'box' overhanging the

20

21

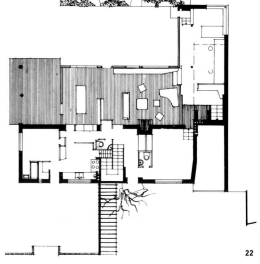

22

23, 26 Villa Mairea, 1938–41, sketch and plan: in Aalto's earliest versions of the villa, an art gallery occupies the place later taken by the sauna wing. **24** Niemelä's cottage, Konginkangas, Seurasaari Open Air Museum: the courtyard of the Villa Mairea was inspired by the organization of vernacular farmsteads. **25** Frank Lloyd Wright, Fallingwater, Pennsylvania, USA, 1936: Aalto's massing of Villa Mairea was influenced by Fallingwater, which he discovered through publications in early 1938. **27** Elevation for the 'Proto-Mairea': the distinguishing features of this early design are a soapstone clad studio to the left, a grand-piano vault, roof-lights in the art gallery to the right, and a main entrance that is tucked away under the projecting studio.

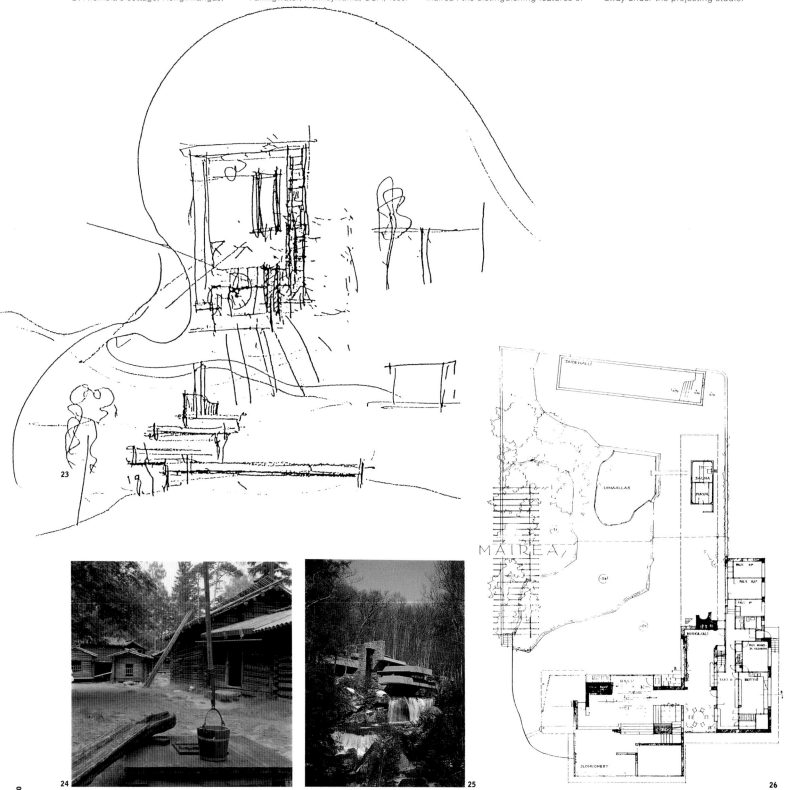

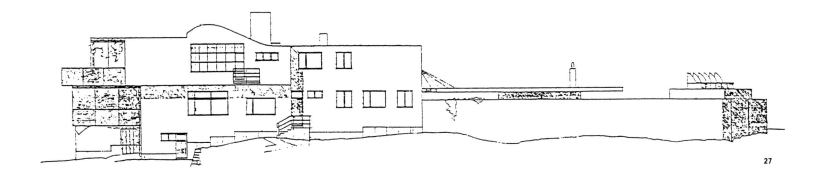

lower floor of white, lime-washed brickwork; at Viipuri, Aalto had plastered the brick walls in good Functionalist fashion, but from now on he favoured lime-washing which brought out the texture of the brickwork and combined Modernity with memories of the Mediterranean vernacular. The timber boarding had a deep groove cut into the 'tongue' edge to enhance the textural effect. (This was clearly important to Aalto as he published the full-size detail.)[20] In addition the circular steel column supporting the bedrooms above the terrace acquired timber slats.

Göran Schildt has pointed out that the volumetric organization recalls the Bauhaus Masters' houses, both feature an L-shaped volume wrapped around a roof-garden and projecting over a ground-floor terrace.[21] However, Aalto has moved decisively away from the crisp, pristine forms of Gropius's design. The general direction of that move is confirmed by a tragic anecdote: in the summer of 1937 his old friend, the distinguished critic Gustaf Strengell, visited the Finnish folk museum on Seurasaari Island to see the celebrated Niemelä farmstead, and then made the short journey to Munkkiniemi, where he explained that he had come to see the 'modern Niemelä farmstead' for the last time; shortly afterwards he shot himself.[22] Niemelä Farm was moved from central Finland and exemplified the accretional growth of traditional farmsteads built around a courtyard, with each building serving one function, and Schildt says that Aalto considered this the finest criticism he ever received of his home.

Sketches prepared in 1932 for a competition to design a winter house included one inspired by Norwegian vernacular buildings. In spite of his earlier unwillingness to make use of 'ethnographic or stilted forms borrowed from old rural architecture', by the early 1930s he clearly had these forms in mind as potential exemplars. In his own house, a low stone wall, akin to those around Medieval churches, mediated the transition to the garden. Was Strengell, one wonders, referring simply to the general atmosphere created by the use of wood and the new rapprochement with nature, which this implied, or did he discern in the building's spatial organization and collage of materials a hint both of the archetypal courtyard form and a simulation of growth over time? If so, it was a remarkably prescient observation, for precisely these themes came to the fore in the design of the house upon which Aalto was about to embark – the Villa Mairea.[23]

Harry and Maire Gullichsen owned an estate at Noormarkku, a few miles inland from Pori on Finland's west coast, north of Turku. In 1877, the founder of the Ahlström Company, Maire's grandfather Antti Ahlström, built an imposing wooden house there, and at the turn of the century her father, Walter, commissioned an *Art Nouveau* dwelling on a nearby site. Each typified the values of the time in which they were built: the first a castle-like expression of semi-feudal authority organized around a highly formalized style of living, the latter an embodiment of the turn of the century's vision of bourgeois domesticity. The new villa – to be used as a summer house – was intended to express the Gullichsens' vision of modern life. Aalto began work on the project towards the end of 1937, and was given an almost free hand by his clients: 'We told him that he should regard it as an experimental house; if it didn't work out, we wouldn't blame him for it,' Maire Gullichsen recalled. His first proposal was a rustic hut modelled on vernacular farmhouses, which prompted her to exclaim, 'Well, we asked you to make something Finnish but in the spirit of today.'[24] Early in 1938, however, inspiration came from a radically different source. Frank Lloyd Wright's 'Fallingwater' had just received international acclaim thanks to an exhibition at the Museum of Modern Art in New York and publication in *Life* and *Time* magazines as well as in architectural journals. Such was Aalto's enthusiasm for the design, Schildt tells us, that he even tried to persuade the Gullichsens to build their home over a stream on Ahlström land a few miles out of Noormarkku![25]

The influence of Fallingwater is evident in several sheets of studies showing boldly cantilevered balconies and an undulating basement storey, intended as a substitute for the natural forms of the stream and rocks.[26] Later, the free-form basement appears as an upper-floor studio whose serpentine wall is sunk into a one-and-a-half storey entrance hall, forming a drop-ceiling around the fire. Early in spring 1938, the Gullichsens approved a design which Schildt has called the 'Proto-Mairea', on the basis of which construction began in the summer. The L-shaped plan established the basic disposition of accommodation found in the finished house, but Aalto's analysis of the activities to be accommodated produced a schedule of reception rooms that included an entrance, hall with open fireplace, living room, gentlemen's room, ladies' room, library, music room, winter garden, ping-pong room and separate art gallery. It reads more like the programme for a Victorian country house than a demonstration of the social-democratic dwelling of the future, and was based on the bourgeois concept of the 'room', which he had condemned as outmoded in his article on 'The Dwelling as a Problem'. Aalto was still far from satisfied with the design, and after the foundations had been excavated he had a new idea and

28

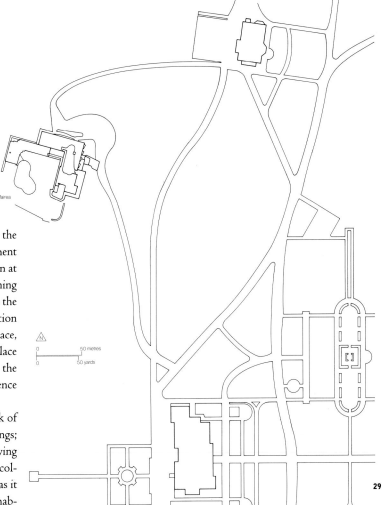

Villa Mairea

persuaded the Gullichsens to accept a radical re-design in which only the footprint and servants' wing remained more or less intact. The basement was greatly reduced, the main entrance moved from its curious position at the side and rear to a much more obvious location in front of the dining room, and Maire's studio was re-positioned to occupy the place above the former entrance canopy, whose shape it echoes. The various reception 'functions' were accommodated in a large fourteen-metre-square space, the art gallery removed – art would be integrated with life – and its place taken by the sauna, which nestled against a low L-shaped stone wall; the remainder of the original wall and trellis being replaced by a short fence and earth mound.

Harry Gullichsen's only objection to the revised design was the lack of a separate library where he could hold confidential business meetings; Aalto, in response, proposed a small room screened by movable shelving units, which, he suggested, could also be used for storing Maire's art collection – an idea that, he pointed out, should be 'socially supportable as it could be realized in a small, even single room, dwelling', where the inhabitant has 'a personal relationship to the phenomena of art'.[27] Not surprisingly this arrangement did not offer the necessary acoustic privacy and the shelving units were permanently located (although not actually fixed), with one angled to suggest frozen movement, and the gap between the units and the ceiling later filled in with an undulating glazed screen.

Although the revised plan followed the existing foundations, the transformation achieves a compression and coherence almost entirely lacking in the 'Proto-Mairea'. The entrance opens into a small, top-lit lobby, from which another door straight ahead leads into an open hall positioned four steps below the main level. One enters on axis with the dining table beyond, but the axiality is undermined by the asymmetry of a screen of wooden poles and a free-standing, angled wall, which together define an informal ante-room between the living space and dining room. The angle of the low wall is set from the corner of the white-plastered fireplace diagonally opposite, which becomes the natural focal point as one ascends the steps into the living room. Similar diagonal relationships are established between Harry Gullichsen's private library/study and the winter garden (Maire used this for flower arranging, and an adjacent staircase led directly up into her studio), and between the main stairs and open sun-lit part of the living room, into which your eye is drawn as you emerge from behind the vertical poles screening the stairs.

The open living room is planned around a rectilinear structural grid whose dimensions are adjusted to suit the disposition of rooms above. This contrasts with the conventional Modernist practice exemplified by the work of Le Corbusier and Mies van der Rohe, in which the structural grid was conceived as a regular counterpoint to the independent spatial disposition of the 'free plan'. Aalto does everything he can to avoid what he called 'artificial architectural rhythms in the building': not only does he vary the dimensions of the grid in both directions, but the circular steel columns are randomly doubled, and, in one case, tripled, and clad with wooden strips or bound with rattan; and, in the library, one of the three columns is arbitrarily changed to concrete – early sketches also show it as free-form in plan. Aalto is at such pains to subvert any clear geometric reading of the structural and spatial organization, that it comes as something of a surprise to discover that the whole plan is in fact regulated by a series of squares.

Although this geometry contributes to the formal discipline underpinning the episodic spatial composition, it is only in the dining room that one can sense an underlying order. The room itself is a double-square in plan, and the triple-square of the service block is centred on it; the

30

formality is entirely appropriate to the activity of dining and entertaining and can be interpreted, as Klaus Herdeg has argued, as an architectural embodiment of the social traditions of the bourgeois family.[28] Harry Gullichsen, as head of the household, occupies the head of the table, which gives him a view towards the front of the house. From there he can see along the axis to the entrance and beyond into the pine forest through the clerestory windows above the vestibule, and also diagonally through the entire living room. Mrs Gullichsen would occupy the seat at the opposite end of the table, conveniently close to the servery and kitchen, from where, as Herdeg writes, she 'can contemplate her husband silhouetted against the dining room's asymmetrical fireplace, while through the window she can see the sauna, the pool, the garden court, and the pine forest – things natural or traditional. Most of these views the father would only see reflected in an artifice: the living room windows.'[29]

The flat roof of the dining room is extended to form a covered terrace linked to the irregular roof of the timber sauna. The terrace is served by a fire backed-up against the fireplace in the dining room and inflected towards the courtyard, above which a rustic stone staircase rises to the wooden deck on the roof. The angle of the stairs determines the line of the plaster inside, which rises diagonally up from the fire to level out above the door. The same angle is continued outside in the flue, which connects at first-floor level into the service wing. This is a typical example of the rigorous formal integration underlying Aalto's, at times seemingly wilful, manipulation of form. The rectangular pier at the end of the terrace affords another example. Viewed in isolation, it seems to be simply another instance of Aalto's desire to break the 'artificial rhythms' established by a regular grid, akin to the doubling and tripling of columns in the living room. But it also acts as a visual and formal termination to the implied band of secondary circulation running through the door between dining room and terrace, passed the servery and on to the narrow steps adjacent to the angled wall that defines the entrance hall.

By comparison with the sophisticated spatial composition of the ground floor, the first floor is a relatively straightforward assemblage of private rooms. The main stair arrives in an intimate upper hall, with its own fireplace located directly above that below. Mr and Mrs Gullichsen's bedrooms are paired either side of an *en suite* bathroom and entered under a slightly dropped ceiling, which houses vents for conditioned air and terminates in a serpentine line. The three children's bedrooms lead into a large circulation/play space, fitted with wall bars for exercise. Their windows are obliquely projecting bays, which read almost as objects on the facade, rather than openings in it, and are angled to address the line of approach to the main door. The guest bedrooms are disposed along a single-banked corridor and look out north-east into the forest; the corridor is lined with full-height cupboards and presents a blank wall to the family's private garden.

In his description of the Villa, Aalto remarks somewhat obscurely that, 'the form concept that is associated to the architecture of this special building . . . includes a deliberate connection to modern painting [which] gives the building and the home a deeper and basically more human substance.'[30] This link may in part have been prompted by Maire Gullichsen's personal involvement with modern painting, both as a student painter and collector, but, as Schildt has pointed out, painting had been a decisive influence in the formation of Aalto's ideas: 'But it all began in painting', was a frequent remark.[31] This 'connection to modern painting' can be seen in two related but distinct ways: firstly, in Aalto's conception of interior space, indebted originally to Cézanne; and secondly, in his 'painterly' rather than architectonic handling of form.

What Aalto discovered in Cézanne, Schildt argues, was a treatment of space quite unlike that in paintings governed by the conventions of linear perspective dominant in Western painting since the Renaissance: 'If we look at a painting by Cézanne . . . we see how the space grows directly out of the forms placed on the canvas; individual elements with volume spread out towards the sides from an intensely modulated central zone. There is no abstract space here, merely concrete relations between forms and volumes, surfaces forming partly overlapping solids, creating an impression of space which is neither uniform nor unambiguously coherent . . . Aalto's great discovery was that architectural interiors can be treated in the same way.'[32] In 1936, in the second-prize winning entry for the Paris World's Fair competition, called 'Tsit Tsit Pum', Aalto began to explore the development of architectural space as an abstraction of the forest; the idea is central to his mature work and will be discussed in a later chapter. For now, it is sufficient to recognize that the idea of 'forest space' provides a key to understanding his intentions in the Villa Mairea. Walking around the living room one experiences neither the containment of traditional interiors, nor the open 'flowing space' of Modern architecture, but something very much akin to the feeling of wandering through a forest in which

30 Villa Mairea, Noormarkku, 1938–41: the bedroom windows project out at an angle to address the line of approach to the house through the forest.
31 The main entrance to the Villa Mairea: the door is approached under a two-level canopy supported by compound timber columns and screened by a miniature 'forest' of timber poles.

31

32, 33 Villa Mairea, Noormarkku, 1938–41, ground- and first-floor plans.

Keys

Ground-floor plan
1 Swimming pool
2 Sauna
3 Winter garden
4 Living room
5 Library
6 Dining room
7 Entrance hall
8 Main entrance
9 Staff rooms
10 Office
11 Kitchen
12 Office

First-floor plan
1 Studio
2 Master bedroom
3 Upper hall with fireplace
4 Master bedroom
5 Terrace
6 Children's hall/playroom
7 Children's bedroom
8 Guest rooms

34 Villa Mairea: the junction of the dining room and covered terrace features an extraordinary collage of materials, creating a sophisticated play on references to vernacular buildings and the Modernist architectural vocabulary.

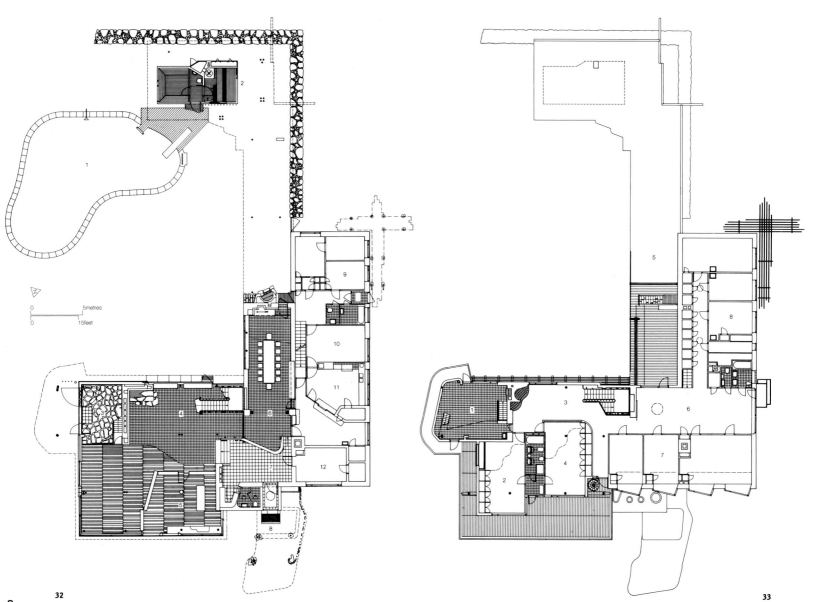

0   5metres
0   15feet

32

33

34

spaces seem to form and re-form around you; in a forest, the individual feels himself to be the moving centre of its spaces. At the time he was designing the Mairea, Aalto observed in a lecture in Norway that, 'architecture's inner nature is a fluctuation and a development suggestive of natural organic life'.[33]

In the Villa, Aalto evokes the experience of the forest in several ways: by the varied handling of the perimeter, which ranges from solid, to part-glazed, to the full-height sliding glass screen into the garden, which runs between the fireplace and main stair; by destroying the square of the living room by intruding into it the volumes of the garden room and library (the surfaces of the former read as the 'exteriors' of the rooms behind rather than as bounding planes of the living room itself, while the latter is defined by the object-like storage units which exist 'in' the space); by counter-pointing the continuous pine-strip suspended ceiling (pierced with 52,000 holes to admit conditioned air) with the varied materials and textures of the floor – the sequence from red slate in the entrance, through ceramic tiles to white beech, with natural stone in the garden room and around the fireplace, both marks out the transition from natural forest to civilized dwelling, and also asserts the presence of nature within the dwelling; and finally, by a series of subtle but unmistakable formal analogies with landscape. Most obvious are the tree-like poles, which screen the stairs, and help separate the ante-space to the dining room from the entrance below. These poles rhyme with the steel columns, further undermining any suggestion of 'artificial architectural rhythms' to which the structure might give rise, and absorbing the columns into the overall free – 'natural' – rhythmic development of the space. The columns themselves, as we noted above, are variously bound with rattan or partially clad with timber strips. The wrapping and cladding serve to 'naturalize' and 'humanize' the standard industrial products, rendering them richly tactile objects, but also evoke memories of classical and natural forms. The timber cladding can be interpreted as both an allusion to the fluting of Doric columns and as an evocation of the texture of bark, while the rattan seen against the black paint offers a vivid abstraction of the trunks of mature pine trees on which, well above ground level, the dark outer bark peels away to reveal the golden layer below.

Such evocations of natural forms and textures reinforce Aalto's naturalization of the architecture of the Villa; their 'fluctuation' is indeed 'suggestive of natural organic life', and he literally threads the trees of the

35

36   37   38

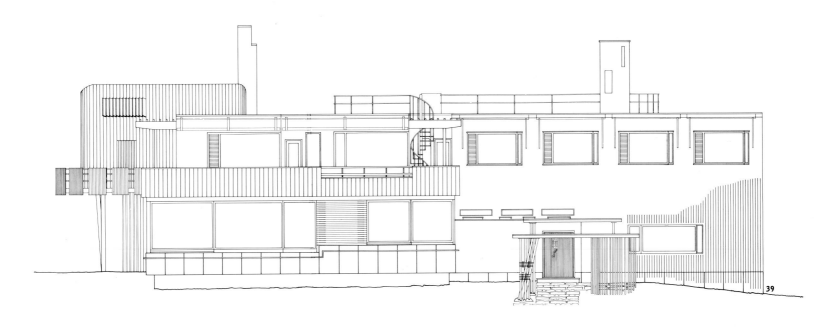

39

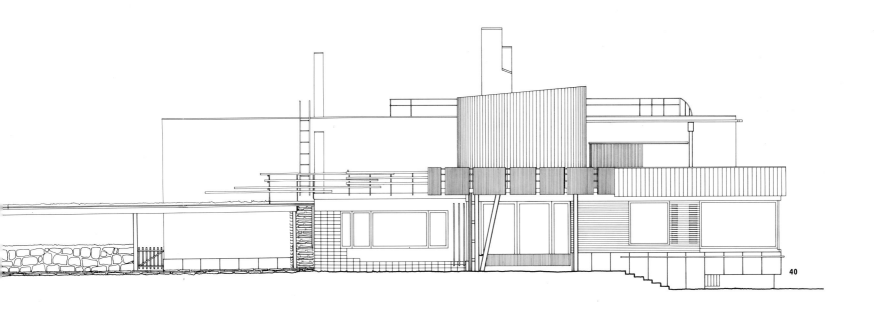

40

forest through the house, just as he interweaves its materials with those of modern industry. Once one recognizes the game he is playing the possible references begin to multiply. It is tempting, for example, to see the curious, splayed double-column, which supports the studio, as a twin-stemmed silver birch tree, a familiar sight near the edges of pine forests. This is suggested by the position it occupies here, at the edge of the building and the pine-tree columns within. The plausibility of this reading is reinforced by the fact that the splayed piece is structurally redundant: it neither connects to the beam nor bears on the foundation.[34] The white circular columns supporting the deck over the covered terrace, and the nearby timber columns of the sauna roof, similarly become visually absorbed into the forest setting; the sensuous moulding of the fireplace (known in the office at the time as 'Aalto's ear'![35]) recalls the forms of snow, wind-sculpted or melted by the fire. It is also a beautiful way of resolving a potentially awkward juxtaposition of solid masonry and glass, and avoiding too strong an edge between the house and garden, which can here be physically dissolved into each other by the sliding screen.

A further intriguing instance is provided by the glazed slot around the library. Given that Aalto wished to preserve the openness of the living room and to suggest that the partitions defining the library were notionally movable, it is suprising that he did not opt to insert a frameless glazed screen. What he did create, in fact, is a marvellous evocation of a horizontal slice of forest, through which shafts of light suggest the familiar broken sunlight of the forest edge – just such a slice of forest, incidentally, is visible between the split levels of the entrance canopy, and a similarly vivid evocation of forest light is created in the late afternoon when the sun slants through the main staircase.

The play on natural form is introduced immediately on arrival at the house by the screen of saplings adjacent to the main door, which suggest a forest-in-miniature, an arrangement almost certainly inspired by Japanese bamboo fences. An early sketch for the main staircase shows that Aalto originally thought of screening it with bamboo, and traces of this idea remain in the detailing that seems to echo the natural growth rings of bamboo. We noted Aalto's affinity for Japanese culture when discussing the Viipuri Library: he had a substantial collection of books on Japanese architecture from which he clearly derived some of the motifs in the Villa. The garden room, with its delicate glazed screen and Katsura-inspired shelves, for example, and details such as the paving and stone bases to the columns under the entrance canopy, are clearly indebted to traditional Japanese architecture. The exquisitely refined sauna likewise suggests the inspiration of tea-houses, most obviously in the elaborated entrance transition and sub-divided door. Settled by the plunge pool, it recalls both an elegant tea-house adjacent to a garden pond, and a vernacular sauna near a lake. Although we should remember that such a pool, with its shimmering blue water, was as fashionably *modern*, and American, as the jazz to which the Gullichsens' and their guests danced the nights away.

In examining the transformation of the Modern open plan into a metaphorical landscape evocative of the surrounding forest, we have already invoked the second aspect of the Villa's 'connection to modern painting', namely Aalto's painterly handling of form. Every view of the house presents a remarkable array of forms, colours and textures – abstract white planes, lime-washed brickwork, weatherboarding, teak and stone cladding, assorted poles, trellises, wooden and metal railings, blue-glazed tiles, grass roofs, a spiral staircase, fragments of structure and climbing plants. The inspiration for such an approach is surely to be found in Cubist painting, and in particular in the technique of *papier collé* or collage invented by Georges Braque one famous day in September 1912 when he pasted onto a canvas a strip of paper with simulated wood-graining.[36] Fragments of sheet-music, daily papers, even a section of chair caning, soon appeared in the work of Braque, Picasso and their followers, and it is precisely such canvases that provide the closest formal model for Aalto's radical assault on the conventional tectonic handling of architectural form. Just as the fragments chosen by the Cubists were absorbed into the formal structure of the painting, but also carried with them direct associations with aspects of everyday life – the newspapers and chairs of a café, for example – so in the Villa, Aalto's fragmentary forms and surfaces operate both visually and referentially.

In your first glimpse of the Villa through the forest, the 'white box' of an orthodox Modern house seems dominant, but as you draw closer this image is overlaid and subverted. The living room is clad in teak and stone as a mark of its importance, while above and behind it the studio is faced with vertical weather-boarding. At first-floor level a white staircase spirals up to the roof and a single column supports a fragment of beam with a tapering cantilever, over which is laid a timber trellis. The free-form, rustic structure of the entrance canopy speaks an entirely different formal language, and to the side a series of slender poles support climbing plants and

44

45

41–43 Villa Mairea, Noormarkku, 1938–41, views of the main entrance, covered terrace, and a detail of the villa's grass roof, which is laid over birch bark in a traditional way. **44, 45** Views of the north-east corner of the Villa Mairea: this area is visually eroded by a cluster of poles, over which climbing plants are invited to creep up and engulf the building; similar poles run freely across one of the kitchen windows.

describe a serpentine line across the front elevation, which wraps around, and thereby visually dissolves, the corner. In the courtyard beyond, the juxtapositions are even more startling. Consider the corner of the dining room, for example, where the white rendered volume is eroded by a seemingly random patch of blue-glazed tiles, which turn and similarly dissolve the corner to form the backdrop to the rough stone staircase and a white Corbusian *piloti*. The handrail to the stairs is circular and of polished wood, while the wooden deck over the dining room has a balustrade formed of square mild-steel uprights, which support timber poles, unworked except for the removal of the bark.

The sheer wealth of materials and motifs is astonishing. Although some, such as the blue tiles outside and brickwork inside the end wall of the dining room, appear, as Juhani Pallasmaa aptly puts it, 'only once as isolated brushstrokes'[37], and carry no obvious meaning, most are carefully calculated allusions to Finnish vernacular traditions, to the recognized forms of architectural Modernity, or, as we have seen, to nature. Amongst the former, for example, we might note the turf-roofed timber sauna and the artfully cultivated primitiveness of its surrounding structure; the low stone wall which recalls similar Medieval churchyard walls; the timber balustrade, which echoes farm fences; the weather-boarding of the studio; the timber gutters; and, to cite just one more instance, the handle on the main entrance door, which is a representation in brass of the natural wooden handles – straight-from-the-tree as it were – frequently found on traditional buildings, especially saunas.

The white-plastered fireplace suggests a particularly rich range of associations: it immediately recalls a vernacular form, but may also allude to the sculpturally elaborated fireplace that Gallén-Kallela incorporated in his studio-home 'Kalela'; its sensuous, and evocatively feminine form, was probably inspired by the reliefs of Aalto's friend Hans Arp; and comparison with the gravestone that Aalto designed for his brother-in-law, the architect Ahto Virtanen who died in 1935, may even lead one to agree with Kenneth Frampton's suggestion that it also harks back to 'the lost profiles of classical architecture'.[38] Allusions to Modernism are similarly pervasive and range from the white surfaces of the main volumes with their substantial areas of glazing, including the full-height sliding screen (used only once or twice in fifty years!) which had already appeared in Le Corbusier's Villa Savoye and Mies van der Rohe's Tugendhat House, to details such as the 'nautical' hand-rails, external spiral staircase and adjacent round-cor-

46, 47 Villa Mairea, Noormarkku, 1938–41, view and sketch of the main staircase: though its design was originally inspired by Japanese bamboo screens – as the sketch makes clear – the staircase is one of the most vivid abstractions of the forest in the house's interior.

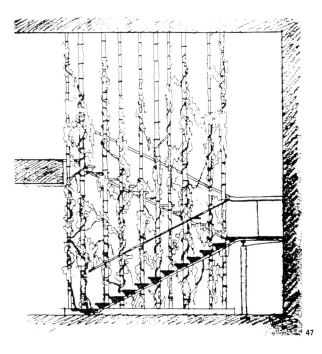

46

47

48, 49 Villa Mairea, Noormarkku, 1938–41, view of the living room, looking towards the main stairs, and the entrance hall and dining room: double square in plan, the dining room is the only room in which the underlying order can be sensed. **50** The living room of the Villa Mairea: the sculpturally elaborate fireplace forms a strong visual and symbolic focus.

48

49

50

51

52

nered ship's-door, and fragments of structure.

The painterliness of Aalto's design was also inspired by Maire Gullichsen's involvement with modern art, and her studio recalls the milieu of Paris by using timber cladding derived from Aalto's Finnish Pavilion for the Paris World's Fair of 1937. Paul Bernoulli, who worked as a site architect on the project, recalls that it was following Maire's interventions that several of the most painterly touches were included.[39] The structurally redundant, angled column under the studio, for example, appeared on the early elevations but was later eliminated by the consulting engineer, only to be reinstated at Maire's insistence. Similarly, the blue tiling around the end of the dining room was also retained following discussion with Maire: at her suggestion, Aalto envisaged painting it ultramarine, like the night sky in Asplund's Skandia Cinema, but opted for the more durable tiles that had to be brought from Denmark to achieve the desired colour.

The more one looks, the more subtle Aalto's play on these references becomes. The white surfaces, for example, are not the smooth render one would expect, but the lime-washed brickwork he first used in his own house. The weather-boarding of the studio, which appears conventional from a distance, is in fact, like the Paris Pavilion, made of subtly-profiled boards. Juxtapositions of 'traditional' and 'Modern' are repeated throughout the design: the exemplarily Modern concrete frame of the terrace supports a timber deck and turf-roof, complete with birch-bark lining and hollowed-out log gutter; the farm-fence handrail above the dining room is supported by mild steel posts; the poles of the trellises around the service wing, a vernacular device, are also miniature De Stijl constructions without any hint of how the timbers are joined. These poles are a marked contrast to the elaborately bound joints of the columns and beams supporting the sauna roof (an idea derived from African or East Asian buildings and artefacts the Aaltos saw at the Brussels World's Fair in 1935[40]). African examples may also have been the inspiration for the wrapping of the steel columns in the living room. Everywhere Aalto interweaves the natural and the man-made; nature suffuses the house, just as technology invades the garden in the form of steel lamps blossoming like exotic flowers amongst the shrubbery.

The collage technique enabled Aalto to suggest a synthesis of seemingly incompatible materials, forms and images, to express polarities such as vernacular and modern, nature and culture, free-form and geometric, romantic and rational, in the creation of an architecture both Modern and Finnish. It also recalls the vernacular practice of adding on non-integral features to emphasize particular parts of a building, such as entrances or windows. The Modern open-plan can be interpreted as a reworking of the traditional *tupa*, which Aalto praised as a space designed for 'a combination of different functions', arguing that a dwelling 'should offer protected areas for meals, sleep, work, and play'.[41] In the *tupa*, these 'protected areas' were defined by means of poles crossing the space just above head height ('rooms' were implied rather than enclosed, but the location of activities was no less clear because the patterns of use were socially codified). In a similar way, Aalto deploys changes of floor level and finish, columns and screens, walls and book-cases to establish a series of inter-linked but differentiated places, each tuned to the activities that take place there. One notices, for example, the intimacy of the area around the hearth, or the way in which the main stair, with its screen of poles and open, carpeted treads, effects a transition to the private realm of the bedrooms, further emphasized by the partial closing of the stair void by the floor slab above.

The task of the house, Christian Norberg-Schulz has written, is 'to reveal the world, not as essence but as presence, that is as material and colour, topography and vegetation, seasons, weather and light'.[42] Villa Mairea embodies a 'Finnish world' at every level, from the play with vernacular forms, through the abstractions of forest space and light, to its overall organization, which suggests the pattern of incremental growth around an implied – rather than wholly enclosed – courtyard familiar from traditional farmsteads. Here, indeed, is the fully-fledged 'modern Niemelä' which Strengell did not live to see. To dwell is to occupy a particular place in time and space, and in the Villa Mairea the forest is claimed as a place for dwelling in the modern world.

Nature
and
Culture

After all, nature is a symbol of freedom. Sometimes nature actually
gives rise to and maintains the idea of freedom. If we base our technical
plans primarily on nature we have a chance to ensure that the course of
development is once again in a direction in which our everyday work and
all its forms will increase freedom rather than decrease it. ALVAR AALTO [1]

THE Villa Mairea was completed during 1941.[2] Finland was in the throes of the Continuation War with Russia, and Aalto's thoughts were turning to the needs of reconstruction.[3] It was a challenge, he said, which 'brings to the fore the most critical problems facing architecture in our time', namely the design, not of the complete dwelling, but of 'the basic cell or unit for the dwelling, one from which the first primitive dwellings could be formed'.[4] Writing in *Arkkitehti*, he contrasted a family building its own 'primitive shelter', with the industrial process that interrupts the 'evolutionary graph'. 'Primitive shelters and single dwellings', he argued, 'were all different, the products of circumstances, local materials and individual ways of thinking. They belonged to site conditions and the topography as an animal does to the forest and surroundings. In their stead appear residential areas made up of identical buildings in which the dwelling unit does not stem from local conditions or from the people but has been generated by civilization, commerce and technology.' Against the 'short-term technology-based standardization method', which is causing 'a new variety of slum area, to wit a psychological slum', he proposed a biological model: 'the most striking of all standardization committees is nature itself . . . [generating] a richness of form that is inexhaustible and moreover in accordance with a given system'.[5]

Aalto first proposed nature as a model in an article written in 1932.[6] The 'biological' approach to form was also a major theme of a key lecture, 'Rationalism and Man', given to the Swedish Craft Society in 1935.[7] 'Nature, biology, is formally rich and luxuriant. It can with the same structure, the same intermeshing, and the same principles in its cells' inner structure, achieve a billion combinations, each of which represents a high level of form. Man's life belongs to the same family. The things surrounding him are hardly fetishes and allegories with a mystical eternal value. They are rather cells and tissues, living beings also, building elements of which human life is put together. They cannot be treated differently from biology's other elements or otherwise they run the risk of not fitting into the system; they become inhuman.' What Aalto was articulating here was an holistic – we might now say ecological – conception of architecture, whose task was to create appropriate niches for man.[8] While he was critical of a narrowly conceived technology that threatened a stultifying uniformity, he saw no necessary conflict between science, art and technology – an attitude grounded in his formative experiences as a child.

Although his family lived in Jyväskylä, the young Aalto was immersed in the practical culture of the forest. His father was a district surveyor, and his maternal grandfather was a chief forester who taught at the Evo Finnish Forestry Institute in Lammi, then a near-wilderness, sixty miles north of Helsinki. In later life, Aalto frequently reminisced about the large 'white table' at which he worked as 'an assistant cartographer' to his father.[9] He recounted 'the experience of the landscape as a functioning equilibrium . . . taught me how man ought to deal with his habitat . . . I learned in my youth that man can deal with nature both in a responsible and positive way and in an unseemly and destructive way. The white table taught me that one has to exercise tact when approaching nature, that life has to be cultivated carefully – but using technology.'[10]

Drawing at the table and assisting his father stake out the alignment of the future Jyväskylä-Pieksämäki railway, Aalto acquired a feeling for the lie of the land and its representation in topographic maps. While one hesitates to attribute too much to such early experiences, it is difficult not to see them as contributing to his later mastery of fitting buildings to the land, and, more specifically, to that fascination with line and contour, which is such a conspicuous feature of his drawings.[11] The vision of a potential harmony between the natural landscape and man's interventions – be they railways or buildings – was also informed by the ethos of the

3

1 (Previous page) sketch of hurricane, Cape Cod, USA, 1946. 2 (Previous page) one of a series of 'wood experiments' Aalto made to investigate the technical and aesthetic potential of bent-wood furniture during the 1930s. 3 Exhibition of Aalto furniture at the Museum of Modern Art in New York, 1939. 4, 7 Wood experiments, 1930s: Aalto was fascinated by the organic structure of wood, his bent-wood furniture designs and 'wood experiments' exploited the potential of bending and laminating wood in ways that reflect its internal structure. 5 The fan-shaped leg, 1954. 6 The 'bent-knee', 1933: this enabled Aalto to develop wooden counterparts of Marcel Breuer's bent-metal designs.

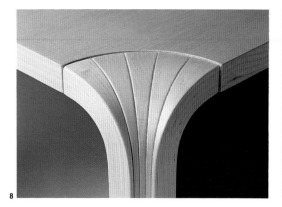
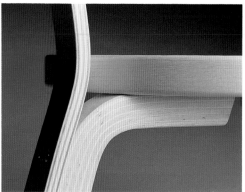

8

9

remote Forestry Institute, which, Schildt tells us, was an anachronistic survival of the classical tradition as reinterpreted by Goethe. This emphasized the Greek idea of the *kosmos* – or natural order – as a balanced system to which mankind must adapt. For Aalto, Italian hill towns offered a paradigm of such harmonious accommodation between man and nature. The town was subservient to the topography, which was in turn heightened by man's intervention – a cultural symbiosis.

Although his upbringing undoubtedly pre-disposed Aalto towards an interest in nature and biology – a lifelong fascination for natural forms and processes is evident in his sketchbooks – the use of such analogies had more immediate sources, having become common currency in CIAM circles during the 1930s.[12] Kirmo Mikkola has also drawn attention to Aalto's interest in Vitalist philosophy which sought, in the words of Ortega y Gasset, 'to bring the intellect to the services of vitality, to subdue it to the biological, and let spontaneity rule over it'.[13] Aalto had direct contact with such thinking through his friend Yrjö Hirn, a distinguished philosopher, who stressed the importance of emotion in experiencing art and the role of play in the creative process. Asplund's emphasis on psychological aspects of design and use of biological metaphors in his work pointed in a similar direction: in his obituary, Aalto wrote that Asplund had 'found a direct path to nature and its world of forms', and that archi-

tecture 'continues to have inexhaustible resources and means which flow directly from nature and the inexplicable reaction of human emotions'.[14] But as Schildt has suggested, perhaps the most direct influence on his thinking was László Moholy-Nagy.[15] He wrote the last of the 'Bauhaus books' – *von material zu architektur*, published in 1929.[16] In it, he stated that: 'in this book the word "biological" stands generally for laws of life which guarantee an organic development', and advocated 'the biological pure and simple . . . as the guide'.[17] Throughout he emphasized the importance of an experiential understanding of materials, believing that the artist or designer could produce constructions in accordance with natural principles without the direct study of a natural model.

The first fruits of Aalto's 'biological' approach to form came not in the design of buildings, but of furniture, to which he was able to apply Moholy-Nagy's precepts more directly. Having furnished the gallery of the Itämeri Restaurant, and his own flat in the Agricultural Co-operative Building in Turku, with tubular metal chairs by Marcel Breuer, Aalto characteristically set about improving them.[18] Shortly after their appearance, his ever-sceptical friend Poul Henningsen had pointed out that such metal chairs 'are so cold they give the modernly dressed woman a cramp in the thigh'.[19] Aalto clearly concurred with the judgement. In his lecture to the Swedish Craft Society he lamented the fact that Modernism had 'run amuck with the world of forms that has arisen through the analysis of materials, new working methods, new social conditions etc., and made of it a pleasant compote of chromed tubes, glass tops, cubistic forms, and astounding colour combinations'. Supposedly 'rationally' designed objects frequently lacked 'human qualities' because – and the emphasis is Aalto's – '*the rationality of the object most often applies to a few of its characteristics but not to all . . . the criticisms, too noisy, too light-reflective, and too good a heat conductor, are in reality scientific terms for things that when put together form the mystical concept of "cosy"'.[20]

Aalto's development of bent-wood furniture was as much a response to the perceived shortcomings of Breuer's prototypes, as a desire to exploit the ubiquitous Finnish material. The use of wood was not a nostalgic return to a traditional material; what mattered were its 'biological characteristics, its limited heat conductivity, its kinship with man and living nature, the pleasant sensation to the touch it gives'.[21] Nor, in my view, was it an 'attempt to ally industrial production with savage nature', as Demetri Porphyrios has suggested.[22] Aalto had no desire to suggest a sentimental

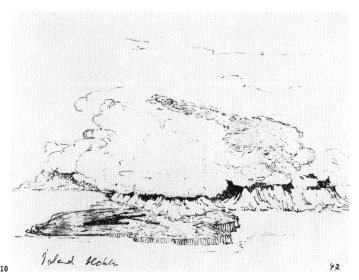

10

42

8, 9 Details of Artek furniture: the
fan-shaped leg was developed in 1954.
10 Sketch of an island, 1947: this was
made from an aeroplane as Volcano
Heklas erupted. **11, 12** Technical
University of Helsinki, Otaniemi,
1953–66, views of the Department of

Architecture and Library: the buildings
are clad with Carrara marble, which
contrasts with the dominant red brick.
13 Finlandia Hall, Helsinki, 1967–71:
marble cladding extends over most
of the hall, rising in layers above
worked and natural granite.

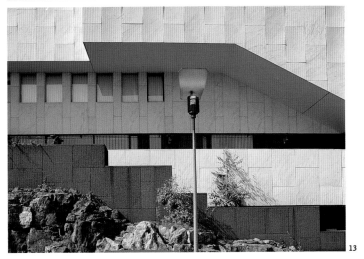

link to craft traditions, which were associated with opposing, deeply conservative elements in Finnish culture, wishing instead to turn industrial production to more fully human ends. The rationalism Functionalism professed, but soon neglected, had to be deepened to embrace psychological and emotional needs: 'the candle's yellow flame and the interior decorator lady's inclination to glorify her light composition with yellow silk rags come closer to the mark *vis-à-vis* human instincts than the electrical technician with his luxmeter and his schematic concept of "white light" – much of rational lighting is inhumane'.[23]

As we noted in connection with the Paimio chair, Aalto collaborated with the manufacturer-craftsman Otto Korhonen in the design of furniture.[24] Although they did not develop any fundamentally new techniques – Thonet had been producing bent-wood furniture since 1836, and plywood bench-seats were already a familiar sight in Finland – they were the first to apply the technique to birch, which had a greater resilience than the softer woods used previously, enabling them to develop wooden counterparts to Breuer's bent-metal designs. Aalto had Korhonen and his staff make Bauhaus-like 'wood-experiments' to explore the nature of the material. (It is uncertain whether the relief he designed in 1931 came immediately before or after the Paimio chair, but it marks the first appearance of that undulating, serpentine line which soon formed the primary motif of the lecture room ceiling at Viipuri.) The following year, Aalto and Korhonen perfected the first versions of a cantilever armchair with continuous laminated-wood frames, combining arms and legs, a bent Paimio-like plywood seat, a related dining chair and assorted stools and tables. In 1933, Fortnum and Mason hosted an exhibition of the furniture to enormous acclaim: the organizers, H. de Cronin Hastings and Morton Shand, hailed it in *The Architectural Review* as 'cheap and seemly furniture, light and easy to move . . . For England it may at last spell death to the fake Queen Anne.'[25] Artek continue to manufacture many of Aalto's designs and they are among the very few Modernist designs to have assumed the status of vernacular objects.

Aalto regarded his invention of the 'bent-knee' in 1933, as his most important innovation in furniture design. This involved cutting the solid birch along the direction of the fibres only where it needed to be bent, gluing thin pieces of timber into the grooves and then bending them at right angles; he went on to develop a two-sided 'Y leg' in 1947 and the exquisite fan-shaped leg in 1954. Aalto referred to these as 'the column's

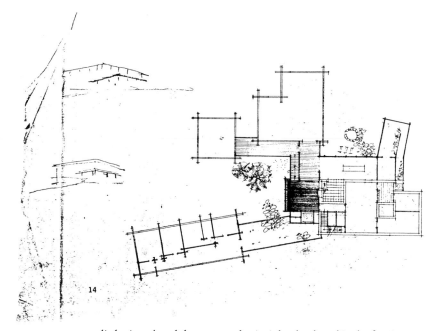

little sisters', and the structural principles developed in the furniture occasionally reappear, almost too literally, in buildings such as the Riola Church in Italy. More important than such obvious similarities across a vast shift in scale – a characteristic of Aalto's thinking – was the feel for the nature of wood he developed.[26] He was clearly fascinated by its fibrous structure and continued to experiment with wood-reliefs well into the 1950s, developing them on a large scale as interior wall decorations. The series of reliefs included a pairing of a convoluted piece of birch with an artificial bundle of fibres – a first abstraction of nature en route to the definitive form of the 'column's little sister'. Writing in 1947, Aalto attributed the origins of the Ionic capital to just such a process: 'it has its source in the sculptural shapes of wood and the release of fibres under pressure', adding that, 'the marble product is not a natural copy of this process. Its polished, crystalline shapes contain human elements that did not exist in the original form'.[27] Aalto similarly sought inspiration from natural forms and processes, but they were always subjected to the abstracting power of the human mind: as such, his approach was essentially classical, based on a mimetic rather than literal emulation of natural forms.[28]

Throughout Aalto's work we find a double movement: from nature to architecture, and from architecture to nature. The lakeside elevation of Finlandia Hall suggests both a vast geological stratification, above which the main auditorium looms like an abstract 'imaginary mountain', and that transformation of rock into abstract form, which classical architecture memorialized in the passage from *opera rustica* to pure geometric forms rendered in *stucco*. The Villa Mairea narrates a similar transformation from the natural forest, to the first hints of man's intervention in the form of an earth bank, through a rustic timber fence to the more refined construction of the sauna; the low stone wall which wraps behind the open concrete frame invades the now artificial world as a rustic stone fireplace and steps. The upper floor of the house presents itself as an abstract white volume in space, but culminates in the free-form studio, which links back to the forest through its richly textured timber boarding: natural materials and motifs are gradually turned into architecture, while architecture is invaded by nature in the form of stone, wood and plants.

The reverse movement, from architecture to nature, also exerted a peculiar attraction for Aalto, and from Viipuri Library onwards many of his buildings give the impression that time has already begun its relentless work.[29] Plants are invited to climb randomly over them, not as in Frank

Lloyd Wright's designs where they form an integral part of the 'organic' ornament. They engulf the corners of buildings, as at the Villa Mairea, and trellises and climbing poles are provided that take no account of the underlying form, sliding across windows and running past the ends of walls.[30] Materials suggest the action of the elements: blue glazed tiles erode the corner of the Mairea's dining room, and emphasize the deterioration of the adjacent white render; pristine white marble sits next to brickwork on the campus at Otaniemi; and patinated copper frequently provides a living record of the process of ageing.

Aalto returned repeatedly to the idea of nature as a model for 'flexible standardization', and the related concept of 'elasticity' yielded fruit in his large-scale planning studies[31]; the so-called 'Reindeer Plan' for Rovaniemi included some rather biological-looking sub-divisions based on hexagonal plots. He compared the 'expanded Karelian house' to a 'biological cell formation', and argued that its ability to grow organically was based on its 'main architectural principle, the fact that the roof angle isn't constant', permitting the roofs to 'adapt themselves to nature' to form 'a living, constantly changing, and unlimited architectural totality'. Studies for the unbuilt – and decidedly Karelian-looking – Villa Tvistbo show Aalto trying to apply this concept.[32] His research into the problems of reconstruction was also based on the idea of 'the growing house', which he may have derived from Gropius's project with the same title designed for the 'Sun, Air, and House for All' exhibition held in Berlin in 1932.[33] Despite these attempts at practical application, however, 'flexible standardization' remained primarily a verbal concept with which to beat the system-builders rather than a viable design strategy.[34]

A desire to simulate the 'natural variation' Aalto admired in Karelian buildings helps explain the picturesque roof compositions characteristic of several later designs, such as Säynätsalo Town Hall, and the careful adjustment of buildings to the topography is characteristic of all his work. As we shall see in considering specific buildings in detail, such adaptations could be both actual – through the adjustment of form and levels to the topography, for example – and metaphorical. Aalto employed natural metaphors at a variety of scales, from the roofs of the Rovaniemi theatre, modelled on the surrounding hills, to the 'tree'-columns of the Villa Mairea.

The emphasis on nature is clearly consistent with that affinity with nature, which, as we discussed at length in the introduction, was a well-

14 Plan for Villa Tvistbo, 1944: Aalto's additive plan for this unbuilt villa was his most explicit attempt to mirror the organic growth of Karelian vernacular buildings. **15** House at Proikkoila, Eastern Karelia: Aalto compared the 'expanded Karelian house' to a 'biolog-ical cell formation'. **16** Farmhouse, Fielisjarvi, Kuhmo. **17** Rovaniemi Theatre, Rovaniemi, 1970–5: local farmsteads were a paradigm for Aalto of architecture made close to nature; his theatre was designed to evoke the forms of the surrounding hills.

16

17

18

18 Finnish Pavilion at the Paris World's Fair, 1937: the subtly profiled boarding created a visually volatile corrugated texture, which changed dramatically according to the viewpoint or direction of the sun. **19–21** Finnish Pavilion at the Paris World's Fair, 1937, view of approach to main entrance, close-up of the entrance's bound timber columns, and plan: the timber entrance was inspired by African vernacular buildings, and the plan organized as 'a walk through the woods', making the most of the trees on the site to help evoke the experience of being in a Finnish forest.

19

20

established component of the Finnish national identity. However, Aalto's relationship to this tradition was far from straightforward. As a young classicist he was predictably critical of National Romanticism, describing its wilder manifestations as the 'absurd birch-bark culture of 1905, which believed that everything clumsy and bleak was especially Finnish'.[35] Throughout his life he professed no particular 'feeling for folklore'.[36] He had a particular loathing for the cultivation of *ryijy* rugs as cultural emblems.[37] Such attitudes are especially understandable during the 1920s and 1930s, when Aalto would have been reluctant to identify too explicitly with the nationalistic appreciation of the *Kalevala*, Karelia and love of the land. The historian Kerstin Smeds summarizes the situation as follows: 'Founded in 1922, the Academic Society of Karelia gave a clear picture of what it meant to be Finnish. It embraced not only the conflict between the "Swedish-speaking gentlefolk" and the "Finnish-speaking peasantry", but also the contradiction between town and country, worldliness and Christianity, international and national – with Finnishness representing the latter in each case. People of this stripe considered everything modern as tainted with Bolshevism. Architect Alvar Aalto was victimized this way in the 1930s.'[38]

Gradually, however, Aalto came to terms with the recognized represent ations of national – as opposed to narrowly nationalist – sentiments in Finnish culture, regretting that 'neither the cultural activity around the turn of the century nor in general the laws that organically bind tradition and influences from the past to today's creative work are particularly well known'.[39] During the Continuation War, he patriotically praised the buildings of Karelia as a 'pure forest settlement architecture' which demonstrated 'how human life and nature harmonize in the best way'.[40] Later in the less problematic atmosphere of the 1950s, he expressed admiration for the *Kalevala* which 'is woven like a textile where every element is nature, constantly alive', and suggested that, 'this closeness to nature [which] has been preserved in our literature [might provide] a common bond for the literary and material sides of culture'.[41] Whatever his reservations about too overt an identification with 'Finnish nature', it is clear from his work of the mid-1930s onwards that having initially thrown himself headlong into the international mainstream of architecture, he soon began to worry about a 'rootless, airborne internationalism', and to search instead for an architecture 'which builds upon the popular psyche and on purely geographic conditions'.[42]

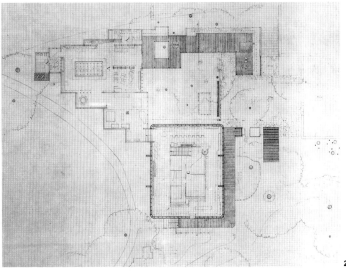

21

22

ALVAR AALTO

23

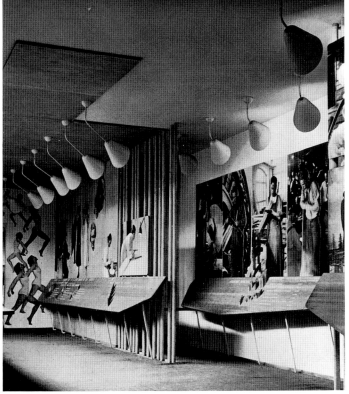

24

The Aaltos' own house signalled this new direction and in 1936, as it was nearing completion, a much more public opportunity to demonstrate his emerging vision of a modern Finnish architecture presented itself: the competition for the national pavilion at the World's Fair to be held the following year in Paris. Despite his string of competition failures, Aalto decided to participate and even took the trouble to visit the site; he duly won first and second prizes. (The second-prize scheme was spatially the more inventive of the two, and will be discussed in the following chapter.) The winning design was a development of the head-and-tail organization implicit in the Viipuri Library: the main exhibition space was a large, introverted, top-lit volume with a sunken well, reached via a circuitous route through a tail of lower buildings which stepped and staggered between the trees on the sloping, wooded site. The irregular plot it was on was regarded by many as less than ideal for an exhibition building, not least due to the prohibition on cutting down any trees.[43]

Aalto turned the difficulties brilliantly to his advantage, producing a scheme in which the external spaces were an integral part of the conception. In his account of the project, he stressed that 'the visitor hardly noticed the change from interior room to open space', and that the design of the surroundings of buildings 'to the human scale' was a difficult problem for Modern architecture, where the 'rationality of the structural frame and the building masses threaten to dominate'.[44] The spatial integration of building and site was achieved by a series of fully or partially enclosed courts, covered walks, and a staggered perimeter, which was reinforced by a promiscuous array of columns that included lashed bundles of saplings, circular columns with tapering fins, and sections of birch-trunks, complete with bark — the birch-bark culture making a literal, perhaps slightly ironic, return! The main pavilion was clad with strongly profiled timber boarding, its solid exterior in total contrast to the openness within, where, as in Viipuri, Aalto created a diffuse, northern light; the circular rooflights were provided with projecting sheet-metal shades to cut out direct sun, and the natural lighting was re-created at night by externally mounted lamps which shone both up and down.

The pavilion and its contents were seen as inextricably linked: 'I have thought of a Finland Pavilion', Aalto wrote, 'that would make up a coherent cultural demonstration, with the material and spiritual aspect consistently dovetailed to make up a *single image*. This is not just an ordinary commercial fair. I want to make it clear that a coherent, material/cultural

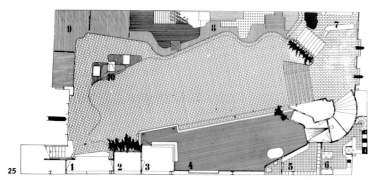

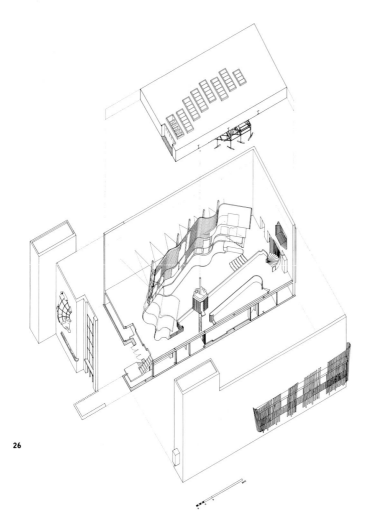

image is more useful than just a loosely organized trade fair . . . This principle of unity is not just a futile aesthetic doctrine, it has a direct practical application in that only music in a single key, a symphonic structure, has the power to strike the imagination and form a basis for new information and new influences.'[45] In practice, Aalto was not allowed the total control he sought – he was still relatively young for an architect, and his international reputation was considerably higher than his standing at home – and he had to concede on a number of points, including a display of his pet-hates, *ryijy* rugs, leading him to declare the building a mere 'shell' of his ideas.[46] The most conspicuous losses were two 'lakes', one of which was to have had wooden boats from the eastern province of Savo on its 'shores'.[47] The Paris pavilion was an enormous success with all but the captains of industry, who thought it did not promote trade sufficiently and lamented the lack of 'pretty girls in national costume'[48]. Two years later, in New York, Aalto was given the freedom to realize his 'symphonic structure'. The message was the same as in Paris, so we will delay discussion of it for a few paragraphs.

The 'shell' of the pavilion in Paris has generally been seen as 'rooted' in Finnish traditions. Malcolm Quantrill suggests that the 'informal courtyard arrangement . . . owes something to the loose organization of farm buildings in Middle Finland and the grouping of the separate houses on the Harjukatu site in Jyväskylä where the architect grew up from the age of seven'.[49] Peter B. MacKeith also says that Aalto 'filtered the forms, structures and detailing derived from Finnish vernacular buildings and constructive traditions'.[50] For my part, I would suggest that the 'informal courtyard arrangement' owes more to the staggered plans of traditional Japanese villas, which grew in a similar echelon fashion and presented open verandahs and elevations to the garden and to small internal courts. While Aalto's use of timber is clearly part of the image of Finnishness he wished to present, his handling of it is patently not derived primarily from the domestic vernacular. The lashed columns, as we noted in the case of the Villa Mairea, were based on exotic precedents seen in Brussels in 1936; those with tapered fins are modelled on the entasis of classical columns; and the cladding of the main pavilion – which MacKeith likens to a barn – was intended, Aalto said, to develop an appropriate form for timber, which could not be treated like concrete or render, but must respond to the intrinsic qualities of wood, sections of which have their optimum length and width.[51]

Aalto published a full-size detail of the cladding that featured a projecting moulding whose sole purpose was visual, not constructional, and exploited the cheapness with which such profiles could be machine-produced. The subtle interplay of concave and convex surfaces was clearly derived from classical fluting.[52] It yielded a surface of exceptional visual refinement, which would have 'rippled' visually and changed dramatically in tone as you moved past and around, varying also with the time of day and lighting conditions. The effect would have been similar to that of his later tile claddings.[53] It resulted, if photographs may be believed, in the visual dissolution of the solid mass – one also notes the rounded corners and minimal coping. The convex moulding and staggered butt-joints suggest bamboo more than normal weatherboarding; this might also be one of his many inventive transformations of Japanese construction.

The square grid of poles secured by tension wires in the interior court of the book exhibition is another example of the design's sophistication: the parallax effect as you moved past would have been in marked contrast to the decidedly 'architectural' appearance when seen on axis, suggesting that the court is both captured forest and hypostyle hall. The Paris Pavilion offered the world a vision of a contemporary Finnish architecture, which certainly evoked associations with domestic vernacular traditions, but was developed with all the sophistication of a classically-trained architect turned committed Modernist, determined to explore new means, spatial and constructional, to meet the needs and express the aspirations of his country. The cladding, like Aalto's furniture, used a traditional material and industrial manufacturing techniques to achieve distinctive, *modern* ends – an approach wholly in keeping with the overall theme of the Fair: 'Art and Technology in Modern Life'.[54] Overtly exotic features, such as the unworked birch and lashed columns, which demanded time-consuming hand-labour, would reappear in the luxurious Villa Mairea, but were later eliminated from his vocabulary. Aalto's motto for the competition design was *Le bois est en marche* (The wood is on the march).[55] Indeed it was, marching triumphantly into Paris and the modern world.

The competition for the New York World's Fair was held in the spring of 1938, and Aalto, deeply upset by the loss of a competition for the extension to the University Library to Aarne Ervi (who worked in his office on the Paris designs), initially decided not to enter.[56] But the competition brief was clearly in his head and with only three days before the submission he changed his mind and submitted two schemes; Aino decided to make an

30

30, 31 Views of Finnish landscape at Saimaa and Punkaharju. **32** Pavilion at the Agricultural Exhibition, Lapua, 1938: the undulating profiles of Aalto's native country are reflected in his work at every level, from the overall plan of a building – as here in the timber exhibition pavilion – to details, like the lamps in the National Pensions Institute Library (p. 162). **33** Aerial view of a typical Finnish landscape. **34, 35** Savoy vases, 1937: the vases were created for the Savoy Restaurant in Helsinki's Esplanade, for which the Aaltos designed a complete interior, which survives today virtually unchanged.

31

entry of her own, and the Aaltos won all three prizes – with Alvar taking first and second, and Aino third. In New York, Finland could only afford to rent a standard interior in a narrow, lofty box whose proportions posed the challenge of how to enlarge the space visually – for which, Aalto said, 'the development of a free architectural form was necessary'.[57] The first sketch in the Aalto Archive shows a roughly-drawn rectangle containing a single undulating line: that familiar line which seems to have begun its active life in the 1931 wood-relief; migrating to the ceiling of the Viipuri lecture room; appearing as a balcony front in the second-prize entry for Paris, as a small pool in the winning scheme, and in the Savoy vase exhibited there,[58] and, just before New York, as a balcony in rejected sketches for the Villa Mairea; now finally emerging as the leitmotif of a *parti* of startling simplicity and power.

The New York Pavilion has entered the history books on the strength of the iconic image of the great undulating wall. While this was undoubtedly the feature designed to make the greatest impact on visitors, the pavilion was far from a sensational one-liner – frequently adopted for such ephemeral buildings – but the 'symphonic structure' that he hoped to create in Paris. The limitations of the New York box proved to be his best friend, and following the success of Paris, Aalto was given the authority he demanded to organize the pavilion as a *gesamtkunstwerk*. He called it an 'organic exhibition'.[59] It was not only the architecture, but also the thematic content, selection and placing of virtually every exhibit, which were under his control.

The undulating wall was suspended diagonally across the length of the box, linking the off-set entrance and exit doors; it was almost as if he had unpeeled the cladding of his Paris box and allowed it to assume its 'natural' form.[60] Constructed in three stages, which stepped and inclined as they rose, making the photographs more visible, and visually compressing the space, its undulating form played against the straight diagonal of the balcony opposite. A free-form projection booth hung above the mezzanine cinema/restaurant, and additional exhibition space was created at first-floor level behind the suspended wall. Service spaces were accommodated as *poché* between the free-form inner skin and the outer wall, effectively destroying any hint of the containing box. The long straight wall above the mezzanine was visually dissolved by a vast aerial photograph of typical Finnish lake-and-island landscape, and similar images featured on the upper level of the suspended wall. The end wall opposite the

32

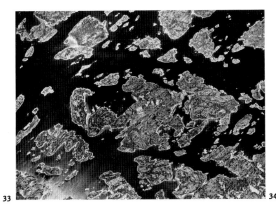
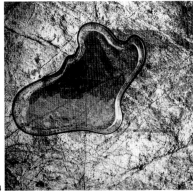
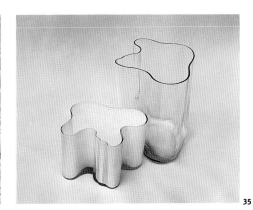

33   34   35

entrance held the main projection screen. This was deeply embedded in a recess within an acoustically absorbent mosaic of sawn wooden discs, which were like the ends of stacked logs – a familiar sight in Finland.[61]

The motto for the design – 'Land, People, Work, Products' – was translated directly into visual form as photographs mounted on the three stages of the undulating wall, and an exhibition of objects on low plinths layered below – Aalto likened it to the dense display of an old 'general store'.[62] The exhibits were mostly of wood products, both traditional, such as axes and skis, and new – aeroplane propellers (also hung below the ceiling as fans) and Artek furniture legs; even the Valio dairy-co-operative's enormous cheeses appeared in the form of wooden replicas![63] 'It was no easy work', Aalto said, 'composing the individual elements into one symphony';[64] surprisingly, the editors of *The Architectural Review* – normally amongst his most enthusiastic supporters – had difficulties seeing the symphony for the notes, and wrote that too much had 'been crammed into too small a building', creating 'a general confusion'.[65] The almost Marxian scheme was even more explicit in the economic-cultural exhibition on the first floor which was similarly stratified and presented as a 'base' of economic activity below a 'superstructure' of cultural work.[66] Aalto used the photographs metaphorically and regarded them as a modern equivalent of Gallén-Kallela's frescos which adorned the walls of the 1900 Paris pavilion; he specified their subject matter in great detail, and had massive enlargements made, some of which were cut into free-form shapes. The serpentine wall was intended to evoke the *aurora borealis*, and was clad with closely-spaced fins to enhance the optical effect of its undulating surfaces; the metaphor was made even more vivid by washes of coloured light from a battery of spot-lamps mounted on top of the projection booth.

Aalto described his intentions for the pavilion as follows: 'an exhibition is a momentary impression, a snapshot, and it can only succeed if it is backed up by a profound and penetrating analysis of the times and their spirit'.[67] He wanted to avoid 'cheap bragging' and said it was not about 'advertising', although his methods were, as Kerstin Smeds has pointed out, precisely those of modern advertising.[68] In place of the didactic, narrative structure of traditional exhibitions or, more commonly, an unstructured collection of 'stuff', Aalto applied Modernist principles to create an integrated presentation, which exploited the latest techniques – vast photographs, cinema, lighting and spatial composition – to create an illusory atmosphere, wholly appropriate to a Fair. Wood provided the unifying

factor in the 'snapshot', and the emphasis was on the products of modern industry more than the traditional icons of Finnishness: the expected fishing nets, bearskins and reindeer heads were there, but not prominent; the dreaded *ryijys* were admitted, but only as room furnishings, not objects for aesthetic contemplation; works of art were few, and carefully commissioned; and even the 'industrial arts' section – a key component of Finland's international reputation – was surprisingly modest in extent. The architecture and exhibition were inseparable, combining for a symphony of wood that created a compelling, kaleidoscopic vision of a modern Finland.

The landscape was brilliantly evoked by the undulating geometry, whose relationship to the profiles of lakes was unmistakable, due to the vast photographs, which made the connection explicit.[69] A further connection was made by the marked contrast of vertical and horizontal, and the collage of floor and plinth surfaces, which suggested the broken terrain and varied surface of the forest floor. It is tempting to see the broad expanse and shiny surface of the main, and lowest, floor level as a metaphoric 'lake' surrounded by the landscape, people and products of the forest – tempting, and to my mind, by no means far-fetched. Whatever nuances one chooses to see in the design, the message of Aalto's 'Modernist forest' was clear for all to see: Finland is a modern, creative country with deep roots in the landscape and culture of the forest.[70] His 'symphony' proclaimed a productive, harmonious symbiosis between man's intellectual and material culture, and nature, a vision of what Finland could aspire to more than what it already was – for Aalto, ever a Modernist, the world was about becoming not being. The pavilion proved a popular triumph and was acclaimed in the press. Finland was already well regarded in the USA, having been the only country fully to pay off its reconstruction loan, and this showing at the World's Fair confirmed its status as an exemplary social democracy – although the reality, of course, was still far from the ideal Aalto so convincingly conveyed.

The New York Pavilion provides an ideal opportunity to consider Aalto's use of the undulating line – a leitmotif which must have gained added piquancy for him because *aalto* is Finnish for 'wave'. Colin St John Wilson has reflected on it as follows: 'The language of his architecture followed very closely the contours of the building programme that he was studying at any one time. And it did this because of one very striking characteristic in the "structure" (abstractly speaking) of his creative attack.

36 The northern shores of Lake Päijänne: Aalto built his summer-house here on the island of Muuratsalo; it still looks much the same as it did in 1953

when Aalto built the house.
37 Summer-house, Muuratsalo, 1953: the courtyard walls were enriched by Aalto's 'brick experiments'.

This can be epitomized by drawing two forms – an ideograph of two lines – one straight, the other serpentine. We can transform the lines into planes and whether we view it as plan or section it will recall to us the archetypal Aalto space in which the juxtaposition of a strictly flat plane with a rhythmically wavelike surface seems to charge the air of the space like the beating of a giant wing. But these two forms can also be imagined as the lines of an encephalogram – an imprint of the brain's processes, in the sense that there seems always to be in the "argument" of an Aalto building a complementarity between the rigorous plane of analysis and the turbulent wavelike surge of fantasy.'[71]

There have been many suggestions for the 'source' of the motif – the Finnish landscape, the contour plans he drew with his father, his distinctive sketching style, abstract art – but they are ultimately beside the point.[72] Aalto clearly had a fascination for lines – as expressions of movement and natural processes, as the laminations of wooden furniture, as the striations of his timber and tile claddings – and as early as 1926 he praised 'that curving, living, unpredictable line which runs in dimensions unknown to mathematicians', which is 'the incarnation of everything that forms a contrast in the modern world between brutal mechanicalness and religious beauty in life'.[73] Its origins are various – Aalto's motto for the Savoy vase was 'The Eskimo girl's leather breech'.[74] Furthermore its specific 'meanings', if any, depend on the context: in New York it could clearly be read as a metaphor of the landscape, and later, at the Baker House dormitory for MIT (1947–8), it suggests the meandering form of the Charles River – although that was hardly the starting point of the design. But whatever the context, in the discourse of Aalto's work it consistently represents the presence of nature – 'freedom's symbol' – in man's world.[75] It also evokes the intuitive, creative 'surge of fantasy' within a design process grounded in, but never bound by, rational analysis of the problem at hand. The melodic, serpentine line is invariably played against a firm base, a counterpoint, which is the foundation of harmonic compositions intended to express the synthesis of nature and culture, reason and imagination – not a juxtaposition of irreconcilable opposites.

The New York Pavilion was the most public statement of that synthetic vision in Aalto's career, and we will conclude this chapter by moving forward slightly in time to consider his most personal and private meditation on the theme of nature and culture – the summer house built on the island of Muuratsalo in 1953. Muuratsalo is close to Säynätsalo, near the

northern shore of Lake Päijänne, which stretches some one hundred miles from Lahti to Jyväskylä. It can now be reached by bridges, but was then about an hour by water from Jyväskylä station. Aalto designed his own motor boat for the trip – 'like a small floating island, where one could settle comfortably and enjoy the peacefulness of the lake in the company of guests' – and pointedly christened it 'Nemo Propheta in Patria'.[76] He always described Muuratsalo as an 'experimental house', inspired by the freedom building only for himself and his new wife Elissa allowed.[77] Moreover, he believed that the tax laws in Finland would enable it to be paid for as a legitimate business expense – the authorities, however, later had to disagree.[78]

Aalto's 'experiments' were partly motivated by his philosopher-friend, Yrjö Hirn's theories of creative play, and grounded in the belief that, 'proximity to nature can give fresh inspiration' in the effort to 'find the specific character of architectural detail that our northern climate requires'.[79] They included: a building without foundations; a 'non-linear colonnade', with columns sited according to the terrain; the celebrated experimental walls, designed to test the visual effects and weathering of bricks and tiles – including a small 'free-form' section, soon developed on a large scale in the House of Culture in Helsinki; and finally an ambitious plan for solar-heating a studio that never went beyond an idea.

The figure-ground drawing captures the essence of the scheme: the main house is a perfect square, tactfully set back from the shore, as was the accepted practice for summer-houses. The living and bedroom wings define two sides of a square courtyard enclosed by free-standing walls; at its centre is a square fireplace: 'the whole complex of buildings is dominated by the fire that burns at the centre of the patio and that, from the point of view of practicality and comfort, serves the same purpose as the campfire in a winter camp, where the glow from the fire and its reflections from the surrounding snowbanks create a pleasant, almost mystical feeling of warmth'.[80] The visitors' accommodation, outbuildings and 'experimental' constructions run off the square 'head' as a 'tail' adjusted to the terrain – the precise position of the buildings was determined, as the larger scale plan makes clear, by exploiting existing rocks as foundations. The tail was gradually transformed into free-form structures – these were to have been the larger scale brick experiments, but were not completed. A wooden sauna was sited to the east, away from the house and close to the lakeside. At first glance it looks like a perfectly conventional log building, but Aalto

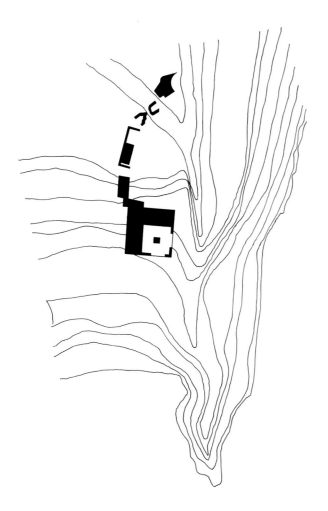

39

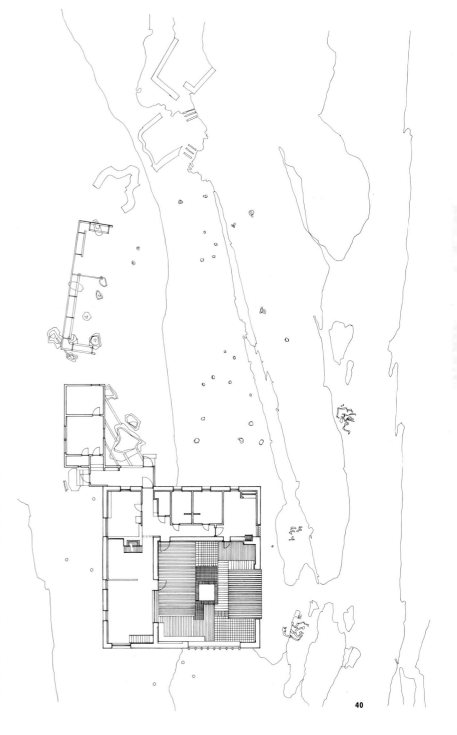

40

modernized the vernacular by stacking the tapering section of the logs so as to build up a gentle mono-pitch roof – normally, of course, they are cut to a uniform section and stacked horizontally: the effect is so subtle that it takes a while before you detect his hand at work.

By comparison with conventional summer-houses, both traditional and contemporary, the design is remarkably introverted.[81] The rooms have small windows and the normally direct relationship to nature is mediated by the courtyard, which defines a man-made place within the forest – in essence, it is a re-working of the *Aitta* summer villa project of 1928, with its circular outdoor room. The courtyard walls frame a superb view south along the lake, and to the west, the foliage of pines and slender silver-birches filter the view of the sky and water through a large opening gridded with white-painted timber 'mullions'. The brickwork is also painted white externally, while inside the courtyard the brick and tile experiments create a rich patchwork-quilt on the walls and floor, which suggest by turn De Stijl-like reliefs, or old walls with redundant door and window openings bricked-up and patched over time.

41, 42 Summer-house, Muuratsalo, 1953, views looking into courtyard and out from it: defined by the living and bedroom wings the courtyard frames the landscape, and creates a space that mediates between man and nature.

41

42

43

44

45

43–45 Summer-house, Muuratsalo, 1953, views taken at the back of the house. **46** The Sauna behind the summer-house: the sauna remains central to life in the Finnish summer-cottage; Aalto's was built as a separate structure, a short walk through the forest from the house.

46

These experiments were as much aesthetic as technical: we are in the world of metaphor again, for what are these walls if not intimations of 'ruins' – past, or perhaps to come? Is this a tiny *piazzetta*, the atrium of a Pompeian patrician's dwelling, or the (de)relict room of a large, old house, which has lost its roof and been re-colonized as a picturesque courtyard? All these possibilities come to mind: the image is too general to be pinned down to a specific interpretation – it would lapse into kitsch otherwise – and can still be contemplated simply as an abstract collage. Memories of Pompeiana probably played their part.[82] As did those of Italian piazzas.[83] I like to think Aalto intended the walls to be seen as the arch-empiricist's ironic commentary on the fate of the strict geometric compositions then coming into favour in Finland under the influence of the arch-theorist Aulis Blomstedt, with his Pythagorean fascination for number and proportion as the basis of beauty.[84]

The poetic metaphors evoke manifold associations, but the content of Aalto's main argument is clear. The summer-house presents us with an essentially *civilized* relationship with nature: this is no romantic retreat into the make-believe world of the noble savage, but a cultured outpost where architecture and nature can be experienced as one, and each on their own terms. The house memorializes man's conquest of nature: the (camp) fire at its heart; a first attempt at levelling the ground in the grass steps restrained by boards, which form the side entrance; the small buildings sited according to the dictates of rocks and trees; and finally the ideal geometry of the repeated square. But the form is fractured, and its patched walls pre-figure the ruin that it may one day become. Aalto was fascinated by ruins, and some of his most moving travel sketches are of the remains of classical Greece made in 1953. In Delphi, he captured the clear geometry of the theatre gradually being reclaimed by the surrounding hills, and at Olympia he shows us the scattered fragments of the temple of Zeus, melancholy reminders that architecture, as Aldo Rossi so beautifully expressed it, 'is made possible by the confrontation of a precise form with time and the elements, a confrontation which [lasts] until the form [is] destroyed in the process of this combat'.[85]

Demetri Porphyrios has invoked Aalto's built ruins as evidence of his partiality to 'picturesque' composition. There is no doubt that they, like many of his buildings, admirably meet Uvedale Price's definition: 'the two opposite qualities of roughness and sudden variation, joined to that of irregularity, are the most efficient causes of the picturesque', of course, the eighteenth-century cult of the ruin did develop as part of Picturesque aesthetics.[86] The parallels are intriguing, but Porphyrios demonstrates no direct link. The ideals of the Picturesque could be said to have reached Finland, at some remove, via their influence on the English Free Style, and thereby have been assimilated into National Romanticism, with which they certainly share certain aesthetic underpinnings – Aalto's church compositions of the 1920s were in this general sense 'picturesque'. But Porphyrios is eager to tie Aalto into the 'subjectivist aesthetic' of the Picturesque (with a capital 'P') because it opens him up to criticism on the same terms: hence he condemns Aalto's 'radical anti-intellectualism', the way his work 'infiltrates the senses rather than engages the mind', and his 'insistence on the lyrical transmutation of nature into sense-experience; in short, his symbolist preoccupation with nature as form'.[87] Aalto undoubtedly created some of the most lyrically sensuous forms in Modern architecture, but his preoccupation with nature was far more complex than Porphyrios can allow for the purposes of advancing his neo-rationalist case against Aalto – who, he says, was 'never a Modernist'[88] – and with it his own decided disenchantment with our difficult times.

Aalto described architecture as 'a component in the struggle between man and nature', and Muuratsalo both infiltrates the senses and engages the mind in a poetic mediation on our place in the world.[89] Aalto seems to be telling us that nature will always win out in the end: that death is the birthright of every organism – be it architectural or biological – and that as individuals, we must reconcile ourselves to the inevitably time-bound nature of existence; and as a civilization, we should renounce the hubris of victory over nature and seek a sustainable symbiosis of nature and culture. But compared with the optimistic vision he projected in New York, it is impossible not to detect, as Schildt has suggested, 'a streak of pessimism' in this melancholy love of ruins.[90] The causes may have been partly personal – the death of Aino, and dashed hopes following the indifference which greeted his grand visions for post-war reconstruction – or cultural: in the aftermath of the Second World War it was difficult to rekindle the optimism which inspired the 'Heroic Period' of the Modern Movement. Increasingly, one senses, Aalto believed that our technologically-obsessed world was in danger of becoming uncivilized. Addressing his old school in 1958, he declared that, 'if a strong, culturally orientated general will doesn't intercede and steer our lives in a better direction, the beautiful rising curve of civilization will rapidly sink to its own demise'.[91]

Sense
of
Place

Calatarao Sopsano, 57,

We may define the ideal outcome of architecture as being that a
building should serve as an instrument which mediates all the positive
influences and intercepts all the negative influences affecting man . . .
a building cannot carry out this task unless it is itself as finely nuanced
as the surroundings in which it stands. ALVAR AALTO [1]

1 (Previous page) Sketch of Catalanao, Spain, 1951. **2** (Previous page), Säynätsalo Town Hall, Säynätsalo, 1949–52. **3** A foggy morning in Aavaskana. **4** Stairs up to the internal piazza of the Rautatalo, Helsinki, 1953. **5** Staircase in foyer of main building, Jyväskylä University, 1953. **6** Windows in Vuokkseniska Church, Imatra, 1957–9. **7** External stairs of Seinäjoki Town Hall, Seinäjoki, 1961–5. **8** Staircase in foyer of Department of Architecture, Technical University of Helsinki, Otaniemi, 1955–66.

3

P RESENTING his work in Vienna in 1955, Aalto began with 'a typical picture of my country . . . to give you an idea of the landscape that surrounds the buildings I shall discuss'.[2] An intimate connection between his architecture and the Finnish landscape has been accepted as self-evident ever since Sigfried Giedion included a similar picture in *Space, Time and Architecture* and declared that, 'Finland is with Aalto wherever he goes.'[3] But beyond appreciation of his undoubted skill in site planning, and overworked analogies between the profiles of lakes and his favourite serpentine line, the nature of the connection has remained, surprisingly, little explored. More recently, Juhani Pallasmaa has invoked the powerful concept of 'forest space'.[4] This also provides an underlying theme of Göran Schildt's biography. We have already encountered the most literal of Aalto's 'forest spaces' in the Villa Mairea; in this chapter we will examine his buildings as metaphoric transformations of landscape, and his commitment to the making of an architecture that is 'not merely national but clearly has local ties in that it is rooted in the earth'.[5] It is an architecture that is concerned with the particularities of 'place' more than the generalities of 'space'.

In his celebrated essay 'Modernist Painting', Clement Greenberg wrote that: 'the essence of Modernism lies, as I see it, in the use of the characteristic methods of a discipline to criticize the discipline itself – not in order to subvert it, but to entrench it more firmly in its area of competence'.[6] Applied to architecture, that process of self-criticism led to the elimination of ornament and a focus on space as the primary 'material' of the discipline; as early as 1905, Hendrik Berlage declared that, 'the aim of our creations is the art of space, the essence of architecture'.[7] The *pilotis* grid of Le Corbusier, the 'clear structure' of Mies van der Rohe, and the floating planes of De Stijl described a new, continuous, universal space, within which partition walls, emancipated from their traditional load-bearing role, could be freely arranged. The 'free plan' represented freedom from the social, cultural and physical restraints of the old, hierarchical order – an order complacently summed up by the Victorian moralist Samuel Smiles as 'a place for everything, and everything in its place'.[8]

As Stephen Kern has demonstrated in his book *The Culture of Time and Space*, the new ideas about space were a response to the transformation of human experience wrought by developments such as telecommunications, electric lighting, new forms of transportation, and the cinema, which created the 'vast extended present of simultaneity'.[9] As traditional ties to family and land broke down, the old, rooted culture of 'place' was destroyed in a maelstrom of disintegration and renewal. The modern world was both exhilarating and frightening, and Modern architecture was an attempt to give spatial expression to the new realities and possibilities. At the scale of the individual building, Modernist space captured the excitement of the 'new spirit'; but at the level of the city it reduced buildings to objects in a formless universal space, whose radiant pleasures of *soleil*, *espace* and *verdure* all too easily became the urban wastelands familiar in new and modernized cities around the world. Aalto, as we have seen, was acutely conscious of the dangers of a 'rootless, airborne internationalism', and soon after embracing the ideals of Modernism, sought to give them a distinctive inflection in response to the Finnish landscape, and to rediscover the particularities of a culture of place.

The archetypal image of Finland is of the glaciated landscape of forests and lakes Aalto displayed liberally throughout the interior of the New York and Paris Pavilions. There are officially 187,888 lakes, and many more islands – 20,000 in the Turku archipelago alone.[10] Water covers roughly a tenth of the land area, sixty-five per cent of which is forested: vast quantities of timber can still be seen being floated to the mills, although road transport is increasingly used. The landscape is experienced as a more or less continuous forest interspersed by the network of inter-connected lakes, their outlines set in high relief by the dense surrounding trees: space

alternates between dark enclosure and sudden, light-filled release. The coniferous trees – predominantly pine and spruce – grow straight and tall, forming a rhythmic counterpoint to the surfaces of the lakes. As Gunnar Birkerts observes, 'Finland has a tremendous juxtaposition of horizontality and verticality.'[11] It is, if one may be allowed the expression, a highly architectural landscape; its regularity a counterpart to the fluidity of form and space in which Aalto excelled.[12] The birch forests create a similar but lighter, more fragile effect: their gleaming white and impossibly slender-looking trunks are one of the Finnish landscape's most distinctive sights.

Beneath the tree canopy, the forest floor is discontinuous, a broken terrain with occasional rock outcrops, varied but generally low relief, and a mix of ground cover plants and low shrubs. The more or less continuous tree-cover may be interrupted by occasional wind throws, creating small glades where the sun can penetrate. Although the summer months offer many days of continuous sunshine, the characteristic sky is modified by clouds, producing a patchwork of light and shade across the landscape or a diffuse general illumination. Sunlight is typically experienced through the filter of clouds, vapour or trees – as atmospheric lighting rather than the clear, constant light of the South[13]. In summer, the days dim imperceptibly into dusk, offering an enchanting play of subtly nuanced colours.

In the design of his own house and studio, Aalto signalled a rapprochement between the abstract white surfaces of Functionalism and the forest through the use of timber cladding, and it was in the design of the Paris Pavilion that this new interest came to the fore. The winning design, as we have seen, was built primarily of timber and closely interwoven with its wooded site. What Aalto presented there was his vision of a modern Finnish 'home' in the forest, an architecture integrated with its actual, and metaphorical, context through the extensive use of wood, inside and out, 'tree-columns', and site-responsive planning. But in the second-prize scheme, 'Tsit Tsit Pum', he developed an altogether bolder spatial idea to present a modern Finnish 'forest culture' to the world, which, as in New York, was the theme of the exhibition.[14] Like the winning entry, the plan stepped in and out between the trees, but whereas the former was akin to the loose, tatami-mat planning of Japanese houses, here the module was a structural bay and the scheme organized as stratified terraces of uniform width stepping down the site beneath a large flat roof with five northlights at its upper end. The internal levels ran out to become planted terraces, terminating at their lower end in a triangular pool, and the flat roof

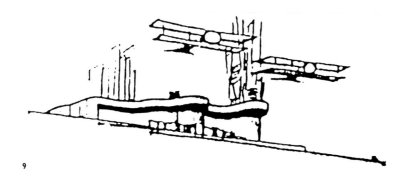

9

10

11

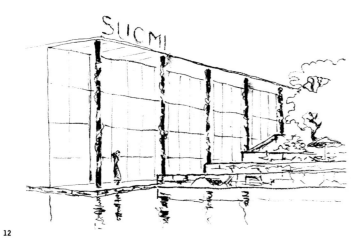

12

projected, on the entrance elevation, to cover a long colonnade of slender, vine-clad columns – an arrangement probably modelled on the Swiss Pavilion the Aaltos would have seen at the Brussels Fair in 1935.

Internally, Aalto projected the highest level forward as a free-form balcony – he had been toying with a similar freeing-up of the apsidal balcony in the Viipuri Library[15]. This would have afforded splendid views of three aeroplanes suspended in the main exhibition hall. To the north of the site, a freely arranged cluster of enormous flagpoles – the tallest almost 30-metres high, and presumably to be painted white – suggest a grove of slender birches, an emblem of Finland's most distinctive timber export, birch-ply. Although one hesitates to judge on the basis of fairly schematic drawings, it is clear that spatially this was an altogether more sophisticated proposal than the winning design: brilliantly evoking the Finnish landscape through a series of abstractions and formal metaphors. The lake is there, not as the rather literal free-form pond that sat uneasily as a 'feature' below the main pavilion in the winning design, but as a pool closely integrated with the form and experience of the building. Its shape follows the lower 'strata', the water lapping against the colonnade, and a landing stage and boats imply that it is to be understood as a fragment of a lake, not merely a decorative pond. Inside, the familiar serpentine lake-shore is evoked by the balcony, on which visitors floated above the exhibitions below. In the perspective sketch, Aalto shows the balcony front between the flying aeroplanes and the tree-flagpoles beyond, with no indication of a ceiling overhead, confirming that he intended this as an abstract landscape.

Although the spatial composition is structured by the repeating structural/spatial bay of the terraces, the overall form is amorphous and fragmentary, more like a landscape than a composed piece of architecture. In a general sense, the open, 'flowing' space the Modernists explored in the 1920s could be said to be landscape-like in contrast to the room-based compositions of traditional buildings, and it is hardly surprising that it should be interpreted this way in Finland. Aulis Blomstedt observed that, 'l'espace continue simply means the consideration of the stimulating variation of nature as the basis of architectural composition'.[16] One of its iconic manifestations – Mies van der Rohe's Barcelona Pavilion – has recently been interpreted as an architectural transformation of a picturesque garden.[17] But Aalto alone of the European masters was to develop the abstract representation of landscape as the basis of a unique, regionally-

9–12 *Tsit Tsit Pum* competition entry for the Finnish Pavilion at the Paris World's Fair, 1937: perspective with aeroplanes and the winding terrace front; facade of the exhibition hall seen from the garden; section of the exhibition hall; and perspective of the lower end of the pavilion, seen from across the pond. **13** Site plan for *Tsit Tsit Pum* competition entry: the project was organized as a descending series of platforms, weaving their way in and out between the trees. **14** National Pensions Institute, Helsinki, 1952–6: the stone plinth defines an urban garden.

inflected architecture.[18] Frank Lloyd Wright had already attempted something similar in his 'Prairie Style', using, as Neil Levine has shown, a method of abstraction based on the reciprocity between figure and ground akin to Analytical Cubism.[19]

Wright continued to explore such an approach throughout his life, and it may well be that the overwhelming impression Fallingwater made on Aalto when he was designing the Villa Mairea arose from the fact that he could see that it was, as Levine says, 'not simply a static representation of natural appearances. Rather it is an image of nature perceived in the process of growth and change'. An image in which, for example, the cantilevered balconies both echo the rocks of the waterfall and, seen through the rising mists and vapour, 'begin to look like layers of clouds floating up through the forest cover into the sky'.[20] As Aalto began the search for a modern architecture rooted in the geography of Finland, Le Corbusier in *La Ville Radieuse* declared that we could finally 'say "goodbye" to the natural site, for it is *the enemy of man*'. His reasons ostensibly had to do with health – 'the natural ground is the dispenser of rheumatisms and tuberculosis'.[21] However, they were also integral to the conception of an abstract architecture whose presiding metaphor was the machine. A chasm now separated Aalto from the mainstream of European Modernism.

As we noted in examining the Villa Mairea, Schildt has likened Aalto's conception of space to the 'suggested and partial figures' of Cézanne's paintings.[22] One can equally well relate it to the Cubists' subsequent construction of pictorial space as a dense fabric of fragments seen from a multiplicity of viewpoints – a mode of perception ideally suited for coming to terms with what Norberg-Schulz describes as the 'indefinite multitude of different places' encountered in the Nordic forest.[23] In this sense, Schildt is surely right when he says that what Aalto proposed in the Tsit Tsit Pum project was, 'literally a *forest space*, related to the spatial experience of wandering among tree trunks, rocks and bushes in the broken terrain of a Nordic forest'.[24] Having invoked memories of the Barcelona Pavilion, I am all too conscious of Juan Pablo Bonta's studies of that building, which demonstrated how critical, sometimes essentially literary as opposed to architectural, ideas take on a life of their own and become the filter through which architecture is seen – or, more alarmingly, become a substitute for seeing it at all.[25] 'Forest space' clearly has the makings of such an idea, but it seems to me to describe accurately the experience Aalto was trying to create in Paris. He achieved this using the techniques of

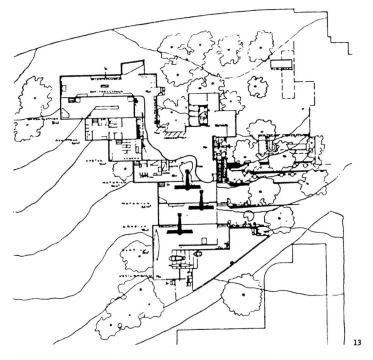

13

14

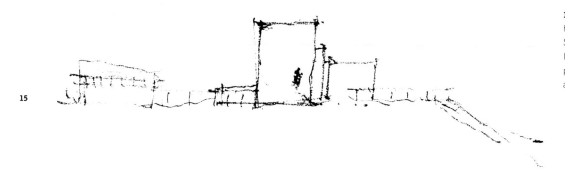

Modernist spatial composition and abstraction, and metaphorical associations – between flagpoles, columns and trees; a pool and a lake; a serpentine balcony and the Finnish landscape – in a way which clearly anticipates the unmistakable forest ambience of the Villa Mairea. It is there that 'forest space' appears at its most literal, but it remains a recurring theme throughout his work and provides one of the keys to understanding how Aalto sought to 'root' his architecture in the landscape.

Aalto's 'forest spaces' are complemented by a 'forest', or, more generally, Nordic light. The Tsit Tsit Pum drawings are not sufficiently detailed to enable us to discuss how the lighting would have been handled, but we have already noted the characteristic diffused light in Viipuri and the main exhibition hall in Paris, and the broken sunlight created by details, such as the library screen and staircase, in the Villa Mairea. Aalto typically conceived his windows and rooflights as filters mediating the transmission of light into the buildings, and developed a repertoire of devices for layering and baffling light, which recall the way, as we noted above, Nordic light is experienced as an 'atmosphere' filtered by clouds and foliage. When sunlight is admitted directly into his interiors, it frequently appears as patches which enliven, but not overwhelm, the general ambience. Many of the external finishes are designed both to evoke and respond to the volatile, ever-changing northern light. Such, one suspects, was the effect of the timber cladding on the Paris pavilion; it is certainly so with the glazed, rounded tiles used on the exteriors of buildings such as the theatre and town hall in Seinäjoki and the Rovaniemi library and theatre. The surfaces are like corduroy, their tone changing dramatically according to the time of day and relative position of sun and viewer; in sunlight they shimmer as you move past, suggesting the play of light on water. In contrast to the tiled surfaces, which contribute actively to the creation of a specific light, the white painted brickwork, render and Carrara marble used on so many of his later buildings, are wonderfully receptive, 'concretizing' the subtle nuances of the Nordic dusk and summer night.[26]

The rounded-tile claddings have been interpreted as referring to the traditional timber cladding of butt-jointed boards with narrow cover strips.[27] However, I would rather emphasize the pervasive vertical striation of Aalto's buildings as another means by which he alludes, albeit highly abstractly, to the characteristic texture of the forest. I suggested in the case of the Paris Pavilion that the timber cladding – based on the board-and-cover-strip principle – was intended through its sophisticated refinement

both to recall, and also to establish a distance from traditional weather-boarding; in doing so it created an optically responsive surface whose alternation of light and shade suggests the forest texture. This reading is reinforced by Aalto's characteristic handling of other elements such as windows and doors. In windows, the mullions are emphasized and horizontal sub-divisions either avoided or suppressed. Of course, this is precisely the reverse of what Wright did at Fallingwater to echo the horizontal stratification of the site: purpose-made doors were constructed of timber boards, alternating with either glazed slots or slightly recessed, white-painted strips; and staircases typically entered foyers screened by closely spaced vertical timbers. Aalto's handling of such elements has been widely imitated and appears so familiar as hardly to be worthy of comment. But seen in the context of the pine forest, as for example in the courtyard of Säynätsalo Town Hall, the resonance between the projecting mullions, which run across the tiled plinth, the pine-board/white-strip doors within, and the trees beyond contributes significantly – albeit subliminally – to one's sense of the unmistakable rightness of *this* building in *this* place. Similar examples could be cited throughout Aalto's work – the slender white metal screens, for example, suggest the finer grain of the birch forest – and we will note others in examining individual buildings in more detail.

The vertically grained 'micro-structure' forms a counterpoint to a marked horizontal stratification of the overall form, materializing within the buildings a sense of that 'tremendous juxtaposition of horizontality and verticality' characteristic of the landscape. Windows frequently appear as continuous bands alternating with, or capping, layers of brickwork; the latter rarely meet the ground but give way to a band of stone, which may reach out – as in the Otaniemi campus or the National Pensions Institute – to form a plinth of raised gardens or planting. The ground floor may be recessed – as on the entrance elevation of Finlandia Hall or the Enso-Gutzheit building – or transparent, as at the Festival Hall of Jyväskylä University. Abstract 'imaginary mountains' sometimes rise above the horizontal mass, as in the rock-like forms of the auditoria in Finlandia or Seinäjoki Town Hall, or the folded hills of the Rovaniemi theatre. A similar layering is apparent indoors, as in the floating balconies of the Rautatalo or the Finlandia foyers and auditorium. Almost everywhere you look, a counterpoint between strong horizontals and striated verticals is apparent. Aalto never explicitly stated that his buildings were

17

North elevation

South elevation

East elevation

West elevation

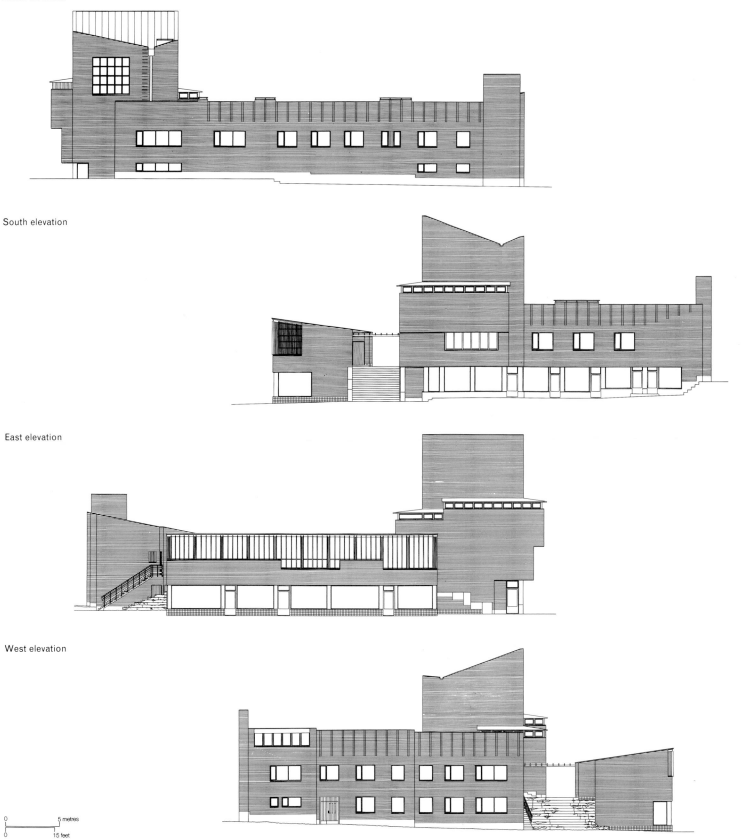

0 ___ 5 metres
0 ___ 15 feet

abstractions of the landscape, but he did talk about 'avoiding artificial architectural rhythms' in the Villa Mairea; he praised the houses of Karelia that 'adapt themselves to nature' and form 'a living, constantly changing, and unlimited architectural totality', and said that a building should be as 'finely nuanced as the surroundings in which it stands'.[28] How better to describe his consistent articulation of space and form to resonate with the dominant visual features of the Finnish landscape?

Having seen how Aalto's architecture can be interpreted as concretizing the *genius loci* of Finland, we may now examine Säynätsalo Town Hall in detail to see how he achieves that intense 'sense of place', which is such a marked characteristic of his finest buildings. Säynätsalo is a small, lightly-forested island near the northern shore of Lake Päijänne. Its 3,000 inhabitants are largely dependent upon the wood-processing factory of the government-controlled Enso-Gutzeit Company, and Aalto's involvement with the island began in 1942 when he was invited to prepare a plan for a small company town to serve the expanding factory. The plan was not fully implemented, but it was decided to build the 'municipal building' Aalto sited at the head of a triangular open space, and a competition was held to find a detailed design. Aalto duly won with a scheme he modestly called 'Curia' – the meeting place of the Roman senate, no less![29]

The brief called for administrative offices, meeting rooms, council chamber, public library and local shops, and Aalto exploited the sloping site to organize the accommodation around a raised open space, formed by using the inner walls of the ground-floor accommodation to retain the material excavated from the foundations. The raised level establishes a *piano nobile* on which all the civic functions are accommodated – the library to the south, offices to the north and east, and apartments for officials to the west. The main entrance is tucked behind the cubic mass of the elevated council chamber, which dominates the south-east corner of the building. On the ground floor, there were originally shops beneath the library, a bank under the council chamber, and service spaces for the council: it was always envisaged that the library and other civic accommodation might need to expand into the ground floor areas, which they have now done. A formal flight of stairs leads up to the main entrance at courtyard level, which can also be reached via the freely-angled grass steps in the south-west corner of the complex. The council chamber is entered via a staircase ascending in a solid block of brickwork from the entrance hall; it wraps around three sides of the chamber and terminates as a slightly raised

gallery. This is in effect, an extended version of the 'tube' leading to the auditorium in the Turku Agricultural Co-operative building.

Aalto chose a restrained palette of materials – mainly brick, stone, wood and copper – and structurally the building is straightforward, with reinforced concrete columns, floor slabs and ceilings, and black-painted circular steel columns supporting the roof around the glazed corridor. The walls are of brick and mostly load-bearing, and, characteristically, the brickwork does not rise directly from the ground, but is protected from snow and frost by being set above a low concrete plinth, clad with square, dark-grey tiles with white joints. To either side of the formal staircase, the tiles are replaced with granite, which is also used for the steps themselves. Exposed brickwork is employed extensively inside: as a wall finish, along the inner wall of the main corridor and staircase, and in the council chamber; as a floor finish, in the entrance hall and staircase to the council chamber, and along the edges of the main corridor; and as a low bench/plant-stand, which conceals the radiators and runs around the courtyard-side of the corridor. The corridor is finished in a light-coloured, polished concrete screed between the single brick-edging strip on its inner side, which is interrupted at the timber entrance screens, and the broader band of brick paving along the courtyard side.

The window mullions are of black-stained timber, their deep sections running from the tiled plinth just above the internal floor level to the ceiling; in the courtyard, some of the mullions and the rendered wall near the entrance are overlain by clusters of round poles that encourage ivy to grow over the building. The doors reflect the vertical rhythm established by the mullions, being made – as we noted above – of broad planks separated either by bands of white paint, on internal doors, or by strips of glazing at the main entrance. Around the public corridor, the doors are set in similarly constructed timber screens to create a more generous scale – and a more expansive evocation of the forest. Ceilings are mostly of white-painted concrete, but as a mark of its importance, the council chamber has a timber-boarded ceiling and floor; the latter being highly polished. The timber and varnish have yellowed with age and the room has become surprisingly dark, although it was clearly never intended to be brightly lit. The main source of natural light is a large rectangular opening through which light is filtered and reflected by a grid of slender wooden slatted screens of Japanese inspiration. The pendant light fittings in the council chamber are a mass-produced Aalto design, which was modified by

22

23–25 Säynätsalo Town Hall, Säynätsalo, 1949–52, view showing apartments on the left, the library to the right, and council chamber beyond, and the town hall as seen from the south-west and east.

26

28

27

29

26, 27 Säynätsalo Town Hall, Säynätsalo, 1949–52, views of entrance hall from courtyard and exterior: the entrance hall is a single storey volume, next to the council chamber; the courtyard is visually closed by the chimney diagonally across from the corner at which it is entered. **28–29** Exterior and interior views of the courtyard windows of Säynätsalo Town Hall. **30–32** Plans of the Town Hall at ground-floor, courtyard and council chamber level.

cutting out a small rectangular section from the shade so that the lamps throw more light onto the brick walls.

Aalto included another indirect source of natural light in the council chamber, in the form of a small niche to receive a painting by Fernand Léger, an old friend whom he met again in Paris in 1950 while working on the building. The fact that Communist workers were in the majority on the council appealed to Léger and he offered to make a painting for their new town hall. However, the rural community did not share Aalto's enthusiasm for the work, and, unwilling to hurt Léger's feelings, he paid the nominal asking price himself and kept the painting.[30] The celebrated fan-shaped roof trusses in the council chamber provide the only structural flourish, and have been the subject of much speculation. Porphyrios says they represent upturned hands.[31] While to Quantrill they recall 'great barns', an 'entirely appropriate "umbrella" for this assembly of councillors drawn from farming stock'.[32] Aalto typically offered a more prosaic explanation: faced with the necessity of providing ventilation between the ceiling and roof, he invented a structural system that enabled him to run both the primary and secondary beams parallel rather than at right angles as in a conventional roof.

In his competition report, Aalto stated that he used the courtyard form as the main motif because, 'in parliament buildings and courthouses the court has preserved its inherited value from the time of ancient Crete, Greece and Rome to the Medieval and Renaissance periods'.[33] This confirms that in designing the building he had in mind – as the 'Curia' motto suggested – Italian precedents. Any doubts on this count are dispelled by an anecdote Göran Schildt relates. Veli Paatela, an assistant in Aalto's office, recalls that when the members of the municipal board of building asked if a small and relatively poor community like theirs really needed a council chamber 17-metres high built of expensive bricks, Aalto replied: 'Gentlemen! The world's most beautiful and most famous town hall, that of Siena, has a council chamber 16-metres high. I propose that we build one that is 17 metres.' Schildt remarks: 'In [Aalto's] view, providing the citizens of Säynätsalo with a setting in which they could live like the fourteenth-century inhabitants of Siena or San Gimignano was a patriotic act ... Aalto envisaged the raised courtyard enclosed by the various buildings as a place for all citizens to assemble in the manner of Siena's Campo.'[34]

Schildt further suggests that a sketch of the towers of San Gimignano, made in 1948, may have been a direct inspiration for Säynätsalo, and his

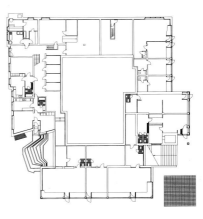

Plan at ground floor level

Plan at court yard level

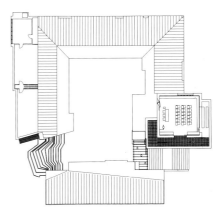

Plan at council chamber level

30–32

33

case is strengthened by Aalto's designation of the council chamber on the elevations as a 'tower': writing about the Town Hall in a student journal in 1956, he remarked that, 'the tower is not a tower at all but a culminating mass under which lies the main symbol of government, the council chamber'.[35] It is unnecessary to suppose a precise inspiration for the tower-like form: it clearly came from his beloved Italian hill towns. This is confirmed by two sketches simply designated 'Culture House' and tentatively dated '1940–' by the Aalto archivists: they almost certainly related to the earlier planning studies for Säynätsalo and envisaged a small 'acropolis' for cultural and leisure activities – an approach which, as we have seen, he explored in the mid-1920s.

In his article on Karelian buildings, Aalto suggested that their 'refined, free-roof formation' was the key to their 'living and flexible forms'.[36] He seems to have emulated this approach in the composition of Säynätsalo. The complex, asymmetrical butterfly roof of the council chamber is the most obvious example. (Aalto first used the butterfly form in his own house in Munkkiniemi, where it was intended to avoid snow falling into the garden – the combination of functional rationale and picturesquely varied profile clearly pleased him.) The staggers and angles introduced into the plan also enhance the feeling that the Town Hall is an 'organic' cluster of buildings, but they are never arbitrary formal gestures, and always serve to clarify the spatial organization. Along the western side, for example, the separate apartments are expressed by slight steps in the wall plane, the northern-most also marking the solid element of the northern wing, beyond the inner wall of the corridor. In the library, the entrance, WCs and newspaper and magazine room are expressed as a low projection, which, combined with the angled end of the western wing, helps to increase the sense of containment of the courtyard as you enter from the straight flight of steps – the diagonal view across is also held by the chimney stack, which anchors and rises above the north-west corner of the building. The main entrance is similarly expressed as a separate volume: accommodated in a single-storey space leaning against the solid mass of the 'tower', it allows the main stairs to be aligned on the corridor to emphasize the symbolic pre-eminence of the ceremonial route into the council chamber above.

The composition is enriched by subtle changes in material, and by planting intended to engulf the building – which it did to great effect, although it was cut back during a restoration undertaken shortly before the colour pictures were taken. One notes, for example, the slight step and changes in material over the roofs around the courtyard: the glazed corridor is covered in copper and the roofs above in cheaper painted galvanized steel sheet. This reinforces the idea that the corridor is akin to an arcade running around the court – another example of an 'outdoor' space created inside a building, emphasized by the brick flooring and bench, and the brick finish of the inner corridor walls. Aalto included areas of paving in the courtyard, but they have now been largely grassed over: they were made of rectangles of bricks, cobbles (which remain in place outside the main entrance), and vertically placed clay pipes, suggesting the kind of patchwork effect he soon exploited at his own house on nearby Muuratsalo.

Although the Town Hall could be described as picturesque, its form is generated by a plan of extraordinary rigour and grace, distancing it decisively from the looser compositions of the Picturesque movement. Faced with such obvious rightness, it is tempting to seek an underlying geometry, but one searches in vain for any system of proportion or modular co-ordination. It is a familiar story, of uncertain provenance, that when asked what modules he used to control dimensions, Aalto replied that he found one millimetre perfectly satisfactory![37] The overall plan is very nearly – but not quite – a square, and the council chamber almost – but not exactly – a cube. Aalto's preliminary studies frequently show regulating lines used to help organize the diagonals he often introduced as a contrast to a predominantly rectilinear order, but no such controlling lines can be discerned here – or indeed in the final versions of most of his plans. Aalto seems to have trusted entirely on his pencil and unerring eye in matters of proportion to achieve what he referred to as, 'the right sense of form and rhythm to produce something refined and exquisite'.[38]

In discussing the concept of 'flexible standardization' in the previous chapter, I suggested that it yielded no practical results at the level of actual building. Aalto seems to have regarded bricks as an example of the kind of 'cellular' standardization he advocated – which is hardly what the system-builders had in mind – and when using them was eager to emphasize their individuality. For Baker House at MIT, he found a factory, which was on the brink of bankruptcy, and offered a product defying all the requirements of normal quality control. He insisted that the bricks be used without sorting, and the resulting walls are of exceptional vitality, with occasional banana-shaped ones almost falling out, and colours ranging, as he noted with obvious pleasure, 'from black to canary yellow, though the

33 Detail of the glazing in the main corridor of Säynätsalo Town Hall, Säynätsalo, 1949–52. **34** The Library of Säynätsalo Town Hall, 1949–52, in its original condition. **35, 36** The main corridor of Säynätsalo Town Hall with its brick bench that conceals the radiators, and a view from the corridor into the courtyard. **37–39** Seating, lectern, and benches, which were specifically designed by Aalto for the council chamber of the Town Hall.

35

34

36

37

38

39

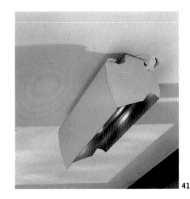

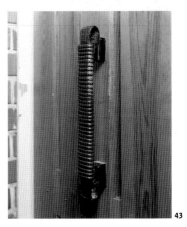

predominant shade is bright red.'[39] For Säynätsalo, he could not find such highly individualized bricks, and so, to enliven the walls, used Flemish bond and had the craftsmen lay the bricks slightly out of line to avoid any mechanical effect – when the sun rakes obliquely across the wall surfaces they appear to ripple and come alive. The upper sections of the walls are marked with narrow vertical slots: Porphyrios interprets them as an allusion to Medieval crenellations.[40] However, I think they can more convincingly seen as yet another instance of Aalto inscribing the forest in the building – unlike crenellations, they step up towards the corner of the building. He was so happy with the quality of the walls – which, of course, cut across the conventions of 'good' bricklaying – that he wrote a personal letter to the six craftsmen involved, stressing the importance of promoting 'the art of masonry in our country' and thanking them for their collaboration, which had resulted in 'a model example of Finnish brickwork'.[41]

The decision to use brickwork for the Town Hall was unusual at the time in Finland. Bricks were generally reserved for industrial buildings, as in the adjacent Enso-Gutzeit factory, and in his work at Sunila. Aalto handled brickwork as richly coloured and textured planes, as the surfaces of volumes rather than tectonically-expressed bearing walls. Malcolm Quantrill has speculated that the design of Säynätsalo was influenced by the work of Willem Dudok in Hilversum, which Aalto presumably saw during his visit to the city in 1928.[42] Although it should be said that Dudok's best known buildings, such as the Hilversum Town Hall and Vondel School, were not finished by then. Quantrill points to the cantilevering of the council chamber, the slit window running just beneath the eaves, and the relationship of the lower wall to the chamber above as evidence of influence, and describes these 'references' as one of the 'predominant impressions' made by the composition. He may be right, but in the absence of clearer evidence we cannot be sure. A more distant, but pervasive, influence over Aalto's volumetric approach to composition seems to me to be Russian Constructivism, and at Säynätsalo he handles the mass of the council chamber with the freedom typical of a building like Melnikov's celebrated Rusakov Club in Moscow.

The raised courtyard is almost exactly the same size as that at the Villa Mairea, and Quantrill argues that another of the 'predominant impressions' of the building is of the 'disjointed unity that characterizes the groupings of buildings in the traditional farms of Middle Finland'.[43] In a provocative essay on Finnish vernacular farmhouses, Ranulph Glanville

40

45

suggests that, 'the very existence of such courtyards both internal and external, in virtually every Finnish building, is the key to the "Finnishness" of Finnish architecture, from the remotest past right up to the present day'.[44] While such comparisons are intriguing, I think we should be wary of trying to suggest too direct a link, either in Aalto's intentions or in the way the building is understood by its community. It may be that the courtyard was intended to evoke subliminal memories of traditional farms, but Aalto's use of the form was clearly associated in his mind both with the conventional courtyard-types cited in his report – parliament houses and courthouses – and that paradigm of public space, the piazza.

The report points out that, 'in buildings with central courts the corridors are very short compared to the floor area of rooms. Internal corridors should not and must not be used in public buildings'.[45] The justification may have been economy of circulation – although a one-sided corridor hardly meets that criterion – but its adoption was clearly involved with the essentially *public* nature of the Town Hall. Hannah Arendt has observed that, 'the term "public" signifies two closely interrelated but not altogether identical phenomena. It means, first, that everything that appears in public can be seen and heard by everybody and has the widest possible publicity . . . Second, the term "public" signifies the world itself, in so far as it is common to all of us . . . This world, however, is not identical with the earth or with nature . . . The public realm, as the common world, gathers us together and yet prevents our falling over each other, so to speak. What makes mass society so difficult to bear is not the number of people

involved, or at least not primarily, but the fact that the world between them has lost its power to gather them together, to relate and to separate them.'[46]

As we shall discuss in the next chapter, Aalto was acutely conscious of the effects of a mass, technological society and its impact on 'the little man'.[47] What he was attempting to create at Säynätsalo was an essentially public place for the community – a place which, as Arendt puts it, could 'gather them together', both physically and symbolically. The towering council chamber provides a visual and symbolic focus, and the raised courtyard is a public space literally and metaphorically lifted up above the world of commerce represented by the planned shops and bank below. Although Schildt suggests that Aalto saw the courtyard as a place for public gatherings, its treatment casts doubt on whether this was the primary intention – the court was mainly grassed rather than paved, and there is no path linking the two sets of steps – and such a space would clearly be most attractive during the summer months when politics take second place to the enjoyment of nature. It seems rather a symbolic *res publica*, an emblem of public power – should the citizens ever feel the need to take matters into their own hands – but primarily a space around which the officials can be seen going about their business in the glazed corridor. Conceptually, the corridor is as much part of the court as it is of the building, confirming the accessibility of the administration. In the raised court, the worlds of nature – civilized as a garden; culture – the library, the realm of ideas and knowledge; and administration and politics – the offices and council chamber – are harmoniously joined. Even the access routes express the conjunction, the main approach stairs clearly belonging to the world of 'culture', and the free-form grass steps to 'nature'.

The route to the council chamber is emphatically public, its brick walls and stairs continuing the external finish inside. The low passage cranks up and around the chamber, which is revealed as a lofty room, its unexpected grandeur emphasized by the dimness through which you see the roof-trusses. The council leaders sit in a row at a table, replete with the symbols of democracy – a ballot box and Aalto-designed gavel; high on the brick wall behind them is a large map of the island, intended to have been balanced by the Léger painting – nature and culture in partnership again. To the left is a small lectern placed almost uncomfortably close to the wall – a subtle invitation to keep speeches short, perhaps? Councillors and officials are provided with armchairs and desks, while citizens may observe the proceedings from wooden benches around the perimeter of the room

46

48

– smooth and inviting to the touch, their profile seems to echo memories of the seating in Greek amphitheatres or the benches along Florentine *palazzi*. When required, additional benches are available, behind sliding wooden screens to the rear of the room. The council chamber – and the Town Hall as a whole – not only accommodate the functions of democratic government, but also give them powerful symbolic expression: the movement, actions and relationships of people are intensified and given meaning in a place articulated in response to the patterns and significance of the activities it accommodates. There is no hint of contrivance, no straining for effect, but a seemingly 'natural', organic connection to life – hence, as Susanne Langer observed in *Feeling and Form*, the reason for architects' frequent recourse to biological analogies.[48] Aalto's celebrated ability to 'do what comes naturally' is, it goes without saying, a matter of supreme artistry, this embodied vision of an ideal setting for the democratic process, a supreme artifice.

Despite its surprisingly small scale – it is even more intimate than it appears in photographs – the Town Hall is both a building of monumental presence and a marvellously successful everyday place. In *Space and Place*, Yi-Fu Tuan writes that the 'feel' of a place, 'is made up of experiences, mostly fleeting and undramatic, repeated day after day and over the span of years. It is a unique blend of sights, sounds, and smells, a unique harmony of natural and artificial rhythms such as times of sunrise and sunset, of work and play. The feel of a place is registered in one's muscles and bones'.[49] Understood in this way, 'sense of place' is a quality arising from the interaction between people and an environment over time, but it can be enhanced, 'speeded up' so to speak, as Tuan goes on to note, by the intensity of experience a setting affords. For the occasional visitor – or the architectural pilgrim on a once in a lifetime visit – Säynätsalo is an intense and unforgettable experience: the incomparable visual *gestalt*; the enclosure of the courtyard – no mere 'space' but a constructed 'place' (an effect now slightly diminished by the lost paving, which bound the ground plane to the enclosing walls); the domestic scale of the sunny corridor contrasting with the unexpected grandeur and shade of the council chamber, reached via an ascending cavern of brickwork lit by slices of sun. All these qualities are memorable even after a brief visit.

For everyday users it is an intimate, eminently habitable place, which infiltrates their memories at the level of 'muscles and bones' – the ascent to the courtyard, the feel of the purpose-made door-handles, the faint scent of timber in the council chamber, the incidental places to sit, the passage of sun around the corridor – all become integral parts of day-to-day use of the building. It is at one with its setting: the mullions and slatted timber doors rhyming with the surrounding trees, while the varied roof angles, formal articulation, and engulfing plants all contribute to a feeling that this is not so much a single building as a complex which has grown over time. Perhaps Aalto's love of ruins had something to do with minimizing that 'shock of the new' which is so often antithetical to fostering a sense of place – or perhaps it was a sign of nostalgia for the traditional culture of place which he knew was everywhere melting into air.

Göran Schildt tells us that Aalto often remarked, in his old age, that 'you can't save the world, but you can set it an example'.[50] Säynätsalo was one such example, of architecture as the making of 'place', the humanizing of abstract space. Goethe captured this in two wonderful lines of poetry: 'Field, wood and garden were to me only a space/Until you, my beloved, transformed them to a place'.[51] Aldo van Eyck echoed the same thought when he described a door as 'a place made for an occasion'.[52] Aalto would surely have agreed. His advice to a student designing a window was to try 'to think of it occupied by the girl he loved'.[53] Fine advice, certainly, but words are easy – whereas imbuing a building so completely with the imprint of human life, as Aalto did at Säynätsalo, demands prodigious, imaginative resources, marking it out as one of the finest architectural achievements of the century.

Individual,
Institution,
City

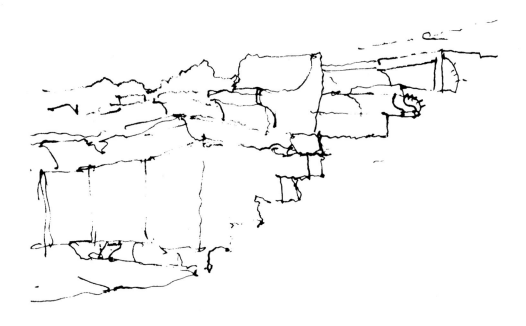

On a higher level scepticism is transformed into its apparent opposite, to love with a critical sensibility . . . It can result in such a love for the little man that it functions as a kind of guardian when our era's mechanized life style threatens to strangle the individual and the organically harmonious life. **ALVAR AALTO** [1]

IN 1921, the student Aalto wrote about a festival in Alajärvi Church: 'I sat next to the precentor in the gallery and enjoyed the festive spirit and devotions and Engel's beautiful dome. It was a joy to the eye to see the old women march up to the altar rail in their Sunday frocks in all the world's finest colours: dark green and ochre and caput mortuum and raw umber (genuine Winsor and Newton). The finishing touch is provided by a sweet little old lady in deep ultramarine. I send up an ardent prayer that she will go to the right place among the colours in front of the altar-cloth. And she does in fact kneel next to black and raw umber. My prayer has been heard. "Now tolls the great bell in God's tower." And later, when I am leaving the church, I feel what a complete human being I am, chemically free from sin and well-meaning. For a moment one has received the gift of seeing the beautiful in everything.'[2] The tone is light-hearted, but the passage says as much about Aalto's attitude to architecture and life as anything he ever wrote. The beauty of Engel's church and of the women's clothes are all of a piece – an example of the kind of 'cultural harmony' he believed architects had an ethical duty to create in an increasingly brutal world. The conflict between 'the little man' and technological civilization is a recurring, indeed frequently the dominant, theme of most of his later articles and lectures. Implicit in the 'biological' critique of Functionalism, it came to the fore as a result of his experiences of a fully industrialized society in the USA, where he was invited to spend time during the War following the success of the New York pavilion.

'American literature is radical', he wrote in 1947, 'it is striving to show us the reign of terror of industrial production over the little man'.[3] For the cinema-loving Aalto, the 'little man' was epitomized by Charlie Chaplin's hero in *Modern Times*, which depicted 'an era of continual struggle against mechanization and machines'.[4] He believed that 'far-reaching mechanization leads directly to dictatorship', regardless of the political system, because 'a well-organized industrial system must be managed hierarchically ... This is the punishment for Western man's self-righteousness'.[5] In his initial enthusiasm for Functionalism he accepted, with apparent equanimity, that craftsmen would inevitably turn into an 'assembly brigade'.[6] However, he later lamented that 'the building site will become a railroad yard'.[7] He clung on to the belief that 'it must be possible to humanize technology', and post-war buildings, such as Säynätsalo Town Hall, were intended to demonstrate that traditional craftsmanship could be combined with industrially produced building components, fixtures and

3   4

fittings.[8] For Aalto, architecture was always a form of mediation: between man and nature, in the struggle for existence, and between 'the little man' and the bureaucratic institutions and technologies of a mass society.

Finland seems an unlikely setting in which to focus on such problems, but because economic modernization came late to the country its effects were all the more sudden. Industry was completely restructured after the Second World War; the resulting 'Great Move' of population from north to south, and from farms to factories, was completed in fifteen years; and the traditional patriarchal family rapidly broke down as women went into the factories or took charge of the farms. Karelia was lost to the USSR in the Winter War of 1939–40, and some 400,000 evacuees had to be resettled; the rapprochement with the Soviet Union involved extensive war reparations, finally completed in 1952; and growing economic dependence on the USSR was manipulated so that Finland drifted politically away from the West. Against this background, the image of 'creative Finland' was actively promoted by a few leading industrialists, and the second 'Golden Age' in architecture and design presented a glowing picture to the outside world. Finnish designers won *Grand Prix* at all the Milan Triennales between 1951–64;[9] their work 'blossoming', as Benedict Zilliacus has written, 'out of the grey poverty of the post-war years like a magnificent tulip'.[10] The massive influx of population to the towns and cities

1 (Previous page) sketch of the Theatre of Dionysus, Athens, 1953. 2 (Previous page) interview booths in the National Pensions Institute, Helsinki, 1956. 3, 5, 6 Balustrades in the main building of Jyväskylä University, 1952–7.

4 Leather-wrapped handrail in Finlandia Hall, Helsinki, 1967–71: the tactile qualities of Aalto's buildings are nowhere more apparent than in his design of handrails. 7 Foyer of the main building, Technical University of Helsinki.

5   6   7

necessitated new public buildings – libraries, churches, town halls, colleges, schools – and the provision of 'more beautiful everyday goods' remained the ideal of industrial design. In a lecture marking his installation as a member of the Finnish Academy in 1955, Aalto argued that: 'it should be possible to make of a small country a laboratory for people's intimate environment', to demonstrate how industrialization could be turned to more human ends.[11]

Commitment to the cause of 'the little man' was grounded in Aalto's individualistic view of life, reflecting his love of ancient Greece and the romance of Jacob Burckhardt's *The Civilization of the Renaissance*. Schildt remarks that Aalto genuinely believed that 'ordinary donkey-drivers and wool carders could . . . live a rich and free life on the piazzas of the Italian towns'.[12] One of his favourite books was Kropotkin's *Memoirs of a Revolutionist*, and while he had as little interest in the ideology of anarchism as in any other theoretical system, Kropotkin's concept of 'mutual aid' which 'claims its rights to be, as it always has been, the chief leader towards further progress', was clearly something with which he instinctively identified.[13] Writing about the challenge of reconstruction, Aalto lamented the end of work by 'mutually-minded groups' and its replacement by 'wage-controlled labour from the factory bench'.[14]

Aalto's 'anarchism' directly influenced his attitude to architecture – most obviously in his distrust of what he saw as the authoritarian rules of all stylistic systems – and was complemented by a belief in the accessibility of cultural values rooted in the socialist ideals of William Morris and the Arts and Crafts movement. He thought of planning as 'a guardian of ethics and human freedom'.[15] Moreover, he was convinced that 'socially responsible planning of buildings' would, in time, 'replace speculative building projects across the board'.[16] Aalto had little faith in political action – he never voted – and was as happy to work for large corporations as for the Communist Party, for whom he designed the House of Culture in 1955 – just as in the 1920s, in Jyväskylä, he built a Workers' Club and a headquarters for the right-wing White Guard. His instinctive blend of anarchism and socialism, and patrician belief in the role of the creative individual, were politically and theoretically inconsistent, but provided the basis for a life-long effort to 'take the little man's frame of reference and what benefits him as a positive yardstick for everything we do'.[17]

In *Minima Moralia*, Theodor Adorno writes that: 'technology is making gestures precise and brutal, and with them men. It expels from movements all hesitation, deliberation, civility. It subjects them to the implacable, as it were ahistorical demands of objects. Thus the ability is lost, for example, to close a door quietly and discreetly, yet firmly. Those of cars and refrigerators have to be slammed, others have the tendency to snap shut by

8 Perspective of the entrance foyer
for the competition entry for Tallinn
Museum of Art, 1937. **9**, Perspective
for the competition entry for the
National Pensions Institute, 1948.
10–15 Competition entry for the

National Pensions Institute, 1948, alternative plans, elevation, models and
perspective: Aalto submitted two
variant designs both with the motto
'Forum Redivivum'; the alternative, suf-
fixed B, **13**, was awarded the first prize.

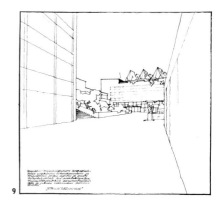

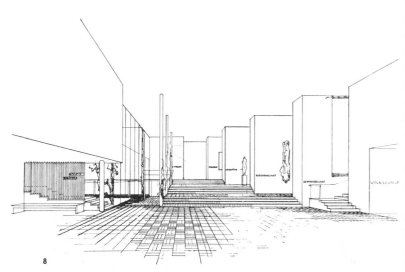

themselves, imposing on those entering the bad manners of not looking
behind them, not shielding the interior of the house which receives them.
The new human type cannot be properly understood without awareness of
what he is continuously exposed to from the world of things about him,
even in his most secret innervations.'[18] Aalto's intense concern with such
apparently minor issues as the coldness of tubular steel furniture and the
inadequacies of 'rational' lighting, reflect a similar understanding of the
potentially brutalizing effects of technology and badly designed buildings.
He once recalled a discussion on the proportions of stairs in a lecture at
the University of Gothenburg, to which the Rector responded by recalling
a passage in Dante, 'where it says that the worst thing in the Inferno is that
the stairs had the wrong proportions'.[19]

Aalto could no more design a staircase with the wrong proportions than
he could provide it with a balustrade unresponsive to human presence and
touch, and his handling of staircases provides an ideal illustration of how
the concern for 'the little man' was manifested in his architecture.
Consider, for example, the staircase to the council chamber in Säynätsalo
Town Hall. The handrail is made of wood, and its profile shaped so as to
be not only comfortable, but positively inviting to the touch. It leads continuously up from the entrance and runs across the top-most landing to
the public gallery at the rear of the room; although not needed there 'func-

tionally', its presence serves as an invitation to enter. Aalto's railings frequently extend beyond the stairs they serve to suggest the extent of public
access, and in the main building of the University of Technology at
Otaniemi, they wrap around the screens at the bases of the stairs and seem
to be as much a part of the wall as a feature of the stair – inviting you to
lean against them, just as the bench at the base of an Italian palazzo allows
casual appropriation. Aalto's handrails were always designed with the
human hand in mind: many are of straight sections of wood combined
with brass at changes of direction; where they are of metal, they are normally wrapped with leather to provide a warm, tactile surface. His acute
sensitivity to such seemingly minor details is symptomatic of Aalto's pro-
foundly humanistic understanding of architecture.

In the main building at Jyväskylä University, the staircase provides the
archetypal example of what George Baird has described as, the 'basic
human image of Aaltoesque space' – the 'space of the balustrade'.[20] It rises
in an indoor 'street' between the wall of the adjacent 'building' and a solid
balustrade, which reveals the slope of the stairs and level sections of the
landings. The steps themselves are wholly contained behind the massive
balustrade wall – unlike, as Baird points out, the more typical treatment of
major public stairs, such as those of Michelangelo's Laurentian Library or
Garnier's Paris *Opéra*, which thrust boldly into the space and project their
lower steps out beyond the balustrades. For all his love of the extrovert life
of Italy, Aalto's staircases respond sensitively to the needs of the more
introvert Finnish temperament, providing well-contained landings which
act as both prospect and refuge. Similar arrangements occur throughout
his work: where stairs descend into a public space, such as a foyer, they are
generally shielded by a combination of solid wall and a screen of vertical
timber sections. The 'space of the balustrade' is even implied by the
various claddings Aalto applies to his walls and columns – tile 'flutings',
timber fins, rattan wrappings, or slabs of stone – which, like the mouldings
and proportions of classical design, respond to human scale.

Aalto's responsiveness to the human subject in the design of details is
matched, as we saw in the design of the Paimio Sanatorium, by consideration of perceptual factors in the planning and massing of volumes. Andres
Duany has analysed at length how Aalto consistently manipulates the
building silhouette as a means of binding together disparate elements or
generating monumental presence.[21] As the diagrams above indicate, the sil-
houettes of building groups, individual buildings and elements within

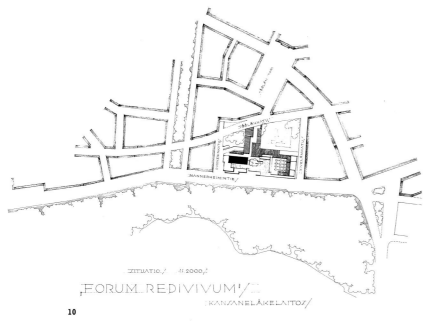

'FORUM REDIVIVUM' A

/KANSANELÄKELAITOS/

10

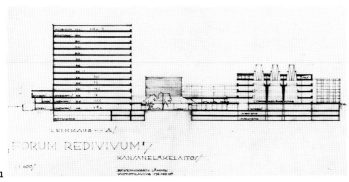

'FORUM REDIVIVUM'

/KANSANELÄKELAITOS/

11

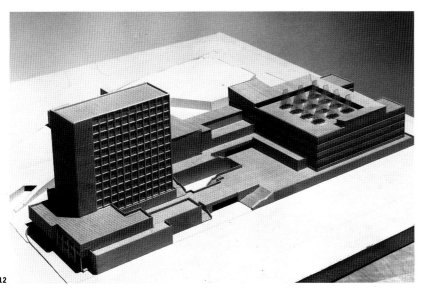

12

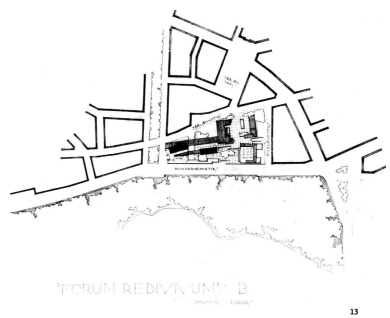

'FORUM REDIVIVUM' B

13

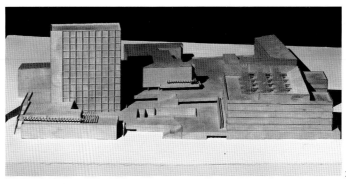

14

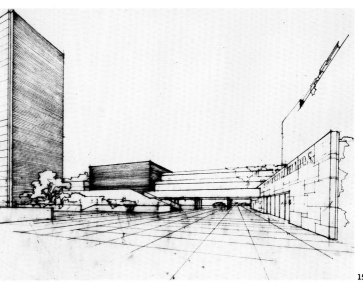

15

them are typically controlled by an echelon profile, which frequently rises to a culminating form or point – a strategy reflecting, as we shall see in the next chapter, the tradition of the 'city crown'. Similarly, Aalto never forgot the lessons learnt in the 1920s about the use of perspective as a spatial device: many of his plans and sections open out, as Duany observes, 'to make more space available to the eye . . . dematerialize the boundaries and create an ethereal space free of focus'.[22] This is a key tactic in rendering architectural space landscape-like. The earliest sectional example is the Viipuri Library, and one of the most subtle, the Rautatalo, we consider later in this chapter; in plan, the arrangement is characteristic of his housing layouts, whose blocks fan open to engage the landscape.

The plans of many of Aalto's public buildings, however, are organized to do precisely the opposite, closing down the visual field to reinforce the sense of enclosure and 'place' – as for example at Jyväskylä University – or as a means of presenting to the visitor the potential routes through, and entrances within, a building. This is a familiar strategy in projects for museums, such as the classic early instance in the competition design for Tallinn of 1937, or in public foyers like those of Finlandia Hall and the House of Culture. Aalto, as Duany points out, was alone amongst the masters of Modern architecture 'in bringing perceptual determinants to bear on the abstract idiom of the twentieth century'.[23] This was one of the most enduring legacies of his study of the classical Greek sites, and a key to understanding the sense one has in Aalto's buildings that they are designed both for and around the human subject as a means of helping 'the little man' feel at home in the modern world, where technical demands generally dominate sensual needs, let alone delight. For Aalto, avoiding the chill of cold steel or manipulating a site plan in response to the geometry of human perception were equally important to the humanistic project of his architecture.

The competition in 1948 for one of the major institutions of the welfare state – the National Pensions Institute – provided an ideal opportunity to develop ideas about how architecture could mediate between the individual, the institution and the city. The Institute functions as a semi-independent public bank and remains the hub of Finland's highly regarded welfare insurance system, which visitors came from all over the world to study during the 1950s. The site for the competition was a large, sloping triangle of land facing Töölö Bay, on a prime location along Mannerheimintie, the busy main road running north-west out of the centre of Helsinki, along

17

18

16

19

20

which were located the Parliament House and National Museum – and later Finlandia Hall and the Opera House. Aalto typically hedged his bets and submitted two entries, both entitled 'Forum Redivivum', the alternate designated by the suffix 'B'. The required accommodation included the Pension Bank itself; extensive office space, some for rent; a 500 seat multi-purpose concert hall and exhibition space; and a large restaurant.

The main idea of his scheme, Aalto explained, 'was to create open squares making available spacious pedestrian zones at different heights depending on the given terrain, completely sheltered from motor traffic'.[24] The offices were accommodated in a twelve-storey tower aligned parallel to Mannerheimintie and rising from a two-storey podium which defined one end of a raised piazza built over two decks of parking; the top floor was occupied by social spaces. The piazza had a sunken, tree-filled well at its centre – an open-air version of the Viipuri Library spatial configuration – and looked out over Töölö Bay; it was contained by the Pension Bank to the north and the concert hall to the west. In version 'B', which won the competition, Aalto proposed expanding the site to the south to address Hesperiankatu, the main boulevard of the Töölö district, and introduced shops and flats facing the concert hall and restaurant across an open market-square – a traffic-free precinct for the open-air market still held in an adjacent square. Both schemes recall the planning of projects from the 1920s, such as the entry for the Finnish Parliament House or the Italian hill-town churches (one of which was designed for a nearby site in Töölö) and the linked piazzas in the 'B' project are, of course, precisely the kinds of urban spatial composition admired and analysed by Camillo Sitte.

The mix of activities Aalto proposed on the site and within the buildings challenged the functional zoning of modern planning and was intended to promote the vitality of a real urban place, the range of institutional, commercial, leisure and residential uses ensuring activity during the evenings as well as the day. The idea of raising the public open spaces above the road made obvious sense in terms of enhanced views, but was also vital in Aalto's mind to protect them from the noise and fumes of cars. Speaking at the RIBA in 1957, he explained the raised courtyard at Säynätsalo on these grounds, much to the bemusement of some present![25] But while traffic was hardly a problem in a tiny island community, it mattered for Aalto that his buildings offered examples relevant beyond the particular case. Modern urban squares needed to be at an appropriate physical and psychological distance from the deleterious effects of traffic to create a

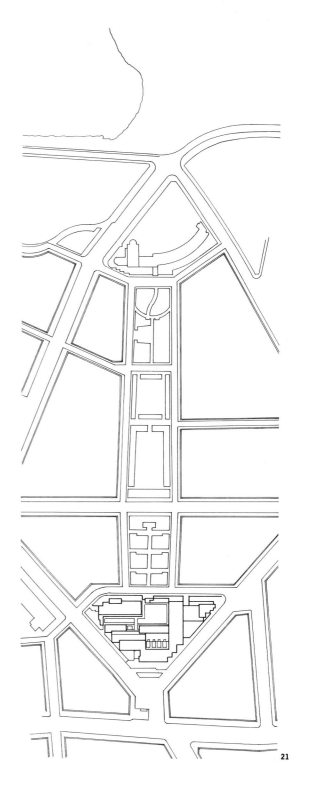

21

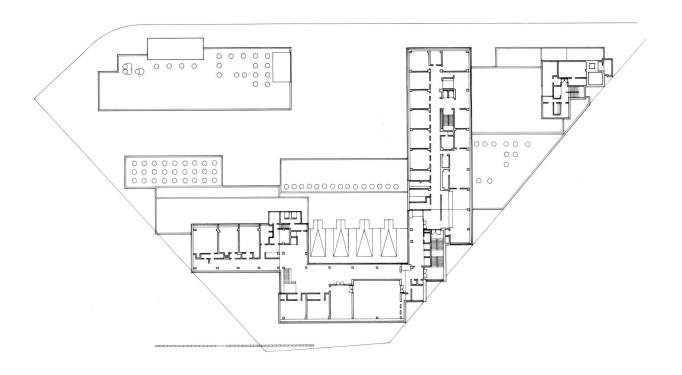

22

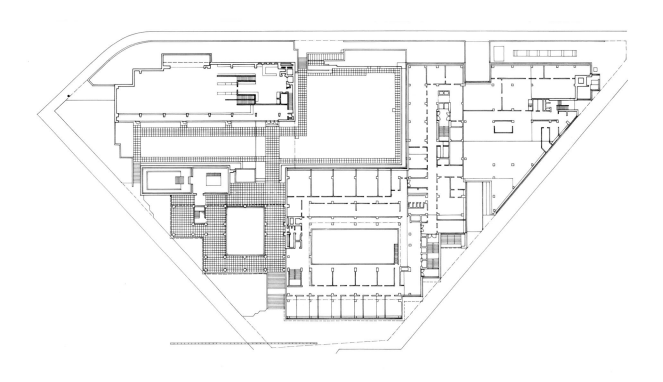

23

24 Main hall, National Pensions Institute, Helsinki, 1956: lit by dramatic, 12-metre-high roof-lights, it was originally filled with interview booths (p 147). **25** National Pensions Institute, long section through main hall and raised garden: though in his final design Aalto was forced to compromise many of the institute's original features, he retained the idea of a group of buildings on a raised podium. **26** Traditional lamp, cottage from Kuortane, Seurasaari Open Air Museum. **27–29** Lamps from throughout the National Pensions Institute, 1956: Aalto's purpose-made lights recall traditional Finnish models.

24

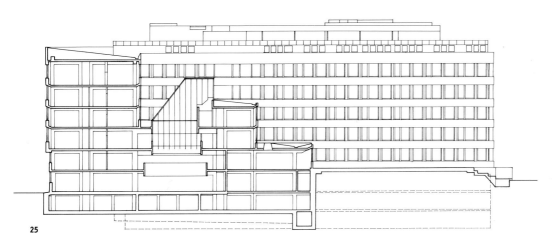

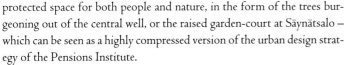

protected space for both people and nature, in the form of the trees burgeoning out of the central well, or the raised garden-court at Säynätsalo – which can be seen as a highly compressed version of the urban design strategy of the Pensions Institute.

Aalto was concerned that cities were becoming 'amorphous masses where town halls, libraries and other communal institutions, yes, even such a venerable institution as the Bank of Finland, are mere corner buildings on leased lots without the traditional imprint of government and the social contract'.[26] A major task of architecture, therefore, was the creation of buildings, 'which are symbols of the social life, symbols of what may be called democracy – the building owned by everybody'.[27] The Pensions Bank clearly provided such an opportunity and was envisaged as a large square volume, with alternating bands of brick and glass distinguishing it from the curtain-walled office building. A free-standing screen wall, clad in squared ashlar over which plants could grow from a roof-planter, formed a dignified entrance facade addressing the piazza. For the internal organization, Aalto returned to another theme first explored in the 1920s – the central, top-lit hall: a piazza within the building.

This grand, four-storey space was ringed with open access galleries for the offices; the floors stepped in slightly as they rose and the balcony fronts also sloped, creating a subtle taper to emphasize the height as the space rose to twelve enormous rooflights fully twelve-metres high. Their three layers of glazing – needed to insulate and avoid condensation – both rose from, and plunged into the great hall below, a storey-height coffer preventing direct sunlight from entering the space. Aalto referred to the faceted forms as 'crystal skylights'.[28] In the perspective view across the piazza, it is difficult not to interpret them metaphorically as abstract ice-

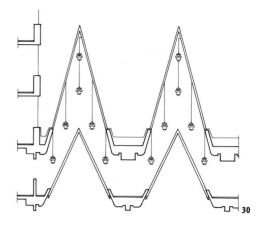

formations – although their steeply sloping sides are clearly eminently functional in shedding snow. His intention was to create a year-round public space appropriate to the Finnish climate, and the skylights both filter light into the heart of the building and act as an emblem of the Nordic landscape in the city.

The Pensions Institute fell foul of political problems and Aalto only received instructions to proceed in 1952, but on a different site and with a significantly changed programme. More offices for the Institute itself were required, and it was also decided to eliminate the concert hall and exhibition space; nor was there room for the shops and flats Aalto had added to the mix. The site is further out of the centre, an awkward triangular plot visible from, but set some thirty metres behind, Mannerheimintie; to what is effectively its rear, it closes a long axis to the sea down a linear open space. Aalto retained the idea of a group of buildings on a raised podium, and the top-lit space is also present: positioned directly off the main entrance, it became a large hall accommodating small booths where case-workers could interview clients. The rooflights are almost as tall as originally intended, but reduced to four in number, and, due to the greatly reduced scale of the hall, glazed as upward extensions of the space rather than as dramatic crystals of light plunging into it – the result is impressive, but inevitably lacks something of the drama of the original scheme.

The building presents a six-storey frontage towards Mannerheimintie, and to either side the accommodation steps back forming an echelon that can be read as a series of layered facades, the alternating bands of brick and windows emphasizing the changes of plane. The lower two floors are recessed and contain the main entrance, positioned asymmetrically in the block, but centrally in the gap between the buildings leading down to Mannerheimintie. The entrance sits in the podium, breaking the line of a stone plinth that runs around the complex, forms a bench either side of the doors, and appears at various points to be hewn from a granite outcrop on the site – the pink and russet colours in the rock are echoed in the strata of brickwork above. The massive bronze doors suggest the security of a bank vault, but are set in a continuous glazed screen, confirming that this is an accessible, public institution. To the left, a broad flight of stairs leads up to the podium beneath the continuous slab of offices supported on tile-clad circular columns, and to the rear the accommodation steps down to form a more intimate scale around the raised garden.

The employees' restaurant is accommodated in a separate single-storey building, positioned in the southern corner to minimize overshadowing of the garden, and reached either via a short walk in the open air or, in inclement weather, entered from the podium below. The restaurant presents a blank wall to the street and continuous full-height glazing to the garden, across which it looks to the plant-covered, slate-clad wall of the library from which small spouts of water descend into a long channel. The parts furthest from the glazed wall are lit by rooflights and the walls are clad in the dark blue glazed ceramic tiles that later migrate to the outsides of Aalto's buildings. The staircase up from the podium is lined with off-white tiles, which give way to ochre-coloured ones around the servery; overhead the ceiling is formed of a grid of small curved aluminium plates radiating heat from concealed steam-filled pipes. A row of rectangular piers mark the change of level, up two steps, to a narrow eating area adjacent to the garden – the main space of the cafeteria thus resembles a slightly sunken court, the basic principle for the planning of the entire complex which unfolds both inside and out as a succession of actual or implied courts.

An internal court reappears, not surprisingly, in the library. This is a perfect miniature of Viipuri, totally introverted – despite its similarly secluded location and potential for views of the raised garden – and complete with circular lens rooflights and sunken well surrounded by a narrow 'space of the balustrade'. The stacks of books are lit by lamps in brass reflectors cantilevered out on thin brass rods: formed of two intersecting cylinders, the reflectors' ends are sliced by the familiar serpentine line. Aalto designed several other lamps specially for the building, as well as furniture and fittings, and the result is a set of interiors of rare consistency. The boardroom is calm and elegant, but it makes no ostentatious display of luxury or privilege and received no more attention than the interview booths in the main hall. These – sadly no longer in use – were made of brass, black leather and fine wood panelling, calm and dignified settings symbolizing the state's care for its citizens, regardless of their status or means.

The waiting hall outside the directors' offices is typical of Aalto's attention to every part of the building. Its ceiling is of square white panels laid between strips of timber whose rhythm above the corridor part of the space suggests a human gait. To the side, seating is provided between the columns and here the ceiling changes to continuous timber strips, and the angles of the columns are lined with timber to just above the head of a

32, 33 National Pensions Institute, Helsinki, 1956, main hall and staff dining room: the employees' restaurant is accommodated in a separate single-storey building. **34** National Pensions Institute: although the raised garden is publicly accessible, it forms a tranquil retreat for the staff; it is a very different space from the raised piazza that Aalto originally envisaged.

32

33

34

seated person, creating an implied space of 'refuge'. In handling such ordinary needs with extraordinary attention to the psychological as well as visual quality of every decision, Aalto confirms the feeling throughout the building that the needs of the individual – of 'the little man' – are preeminent in this 'symbol of what may be called democracy – the building owned by everybody'.

However, for all its manifest democratic credentials as an urban and political statement, the building remains slightly problematic. The genuinely public places of the early proposal gave way to quasi-public, but effectively private, spaces: the raised garden is a tranquil retreat from the city, not an integral part of it; and the central hall does not create the grand internal forum envisaged in its first incarnation. To a great extent such changes were programmatic and out of Aalto's control, but his belief in the architect as a disinterested professional who could be relied upon to represent the public interest was not without its dangers of paternalism. Allied, as here, to a benevolent bureaucratic institution, it continually ran the risk of producing a static, essentially de-politicized social utopia as a substitute for an authentic public realm: the employees can happily spend the whole day in a wonderfully varied environment complete with a subsidized restaurant sited to give them the feeling of 'going out to lunch'. Since Aalto's time, needless to say, precisely such *ersatz* public spaces have become ubiquitous features of the commercial utopias of shopping malls and corporate headquarters – I have in mind complexes such as the spectacular SAS building outside Stockholm designed by Nils Torp – while the public realm proper becomes increasingly inhospitable.[29]

It is apparent from the design of the Rautatalo (1952–5), or 'Iron House', which owes its name to the Association of Iron Dealers for whom it acts as a headquarters that Aalto was aware of such problems. This occupies a prime site in Keskuskatu just off Esplanadi, the principal boulevard of central Helsinki (in effect, a linear park), and opposite a side entrance to the massive Stockmann's department store, designed by Sigurd Frosterus in 1916 and finally completed in 1930. The plan is simplicity itself, making full use of the available land: shops occupy the basement and ground levels and part of the first floor, which Aalto conceived as a *piano nobile*.[30] Although of standard height, it reads as more significant on the elevation due to the omission of alternate mullions, and at its heart is an exquisite top-lit *piazzetta* and café. The Italian vocabulary comes naturally to describe the space, for not only is it intended to function as an internal

35

38

36

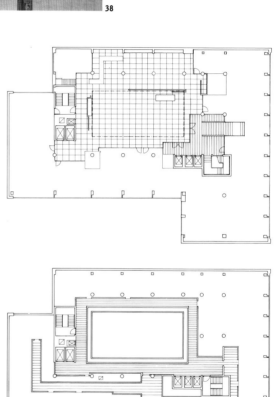

37

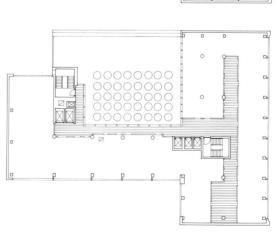
39

36 Café Colombia, Rautatalo, Helsinki, 1952–5: the café opens up on to the first-floor internal piazza. 37 Administration Building of the PYP Bank, Helsinki, 1964. 38 Stacked bronze handles of the Rautatalo, designed by Aalto 39 Plans for Rautatalo, showing the internal court. 40 Exterior view along Keskuskatu with Rautatalo on left. 41 Section of Rautatalo.

42 Interior view of the top-lit court of Rautatalo: paved and lined with travertine, the court is one of the most successful of Aalto's internal piazzas.

40

41

42

public space, it is also finished in stone – white Carrara marble on the floor, and grainy travertine for the balcony balustrades – and has a small fountain, also of Carrara marble. The pale umber streaks in the creamy travertine run vertically, creating a subtle counterpoint with the dominant horizontal stratification so that even in the city centre, the grain of the Finnish landscape is subliminally evoked.

For the glass entrance doors, Aalto designed the 'stacking' bronze handles, which appear on many of his later buildings: here they are used in pairs, and their complex double-curves suggest the forms of both human musculature and classical mouldings. The entrance makes a decisive break in the run of shop-fronts and is deeply recessed, implying that the public space of the street continues into the building and up the broad stairs to the *piazzetta* within. The upper tier of balconies is stepped back, creating the impression that the space extends indefinitely on both sides, while above hovers the now familiar grid of circular lens rooflights, dispensing their diffuse Nordic light. As in the Paris pavilion, they are provided with external lamps to prolong the day – and, in Helsinki, melt any snow. To one side, receding into the shadows created by the balconies above, is a café – the Cafeteria Colombia – lined with dark blue tiles, partially screened by the fountain and adjacent planter, and artificially lit with ceiling and pendant lamps to create a warm, intimate ambience. Animated by the almost Byzantine glitter of the shiny tiles, the space is conducive to conversation and a marvellous setting for the Finnish social ritual of drinking coffee, which flourishes in the open air during the brief summer, but for most of the year has to retreat indoors. The popular café now overflows into the *piazzetta* itself, which never became quite the bustling public space Aalto intended: the shops and offices did not generate sufficient numbers of people, and the introverted Finns were reluctant to cross the space, preferring to take the long route to the café around its perimeter, under the psychological as well as physical protection of the balconies.[31]

The street facade is a curtain-wall hung from a steel sub-structure and framed by narrow pilasters of brickwork to either end which mediate the transition to the adjacent buildings – most importantly the bank designed by Eliel Saarinen, whose height determined that of the Rautatalo. The mullions and transoms are clad in copper over cork insulation and form a deeply modelled rectilinear frame – a form of construction first proposed for the office tower in the National Pensions Institute competition. Later, in the design of the Scandinavian Bank (1962–4), Aalto used bronze to

43

43 Academic Bookshop, Helsinki, 1966–9. **44–46** Exterior view, and ground- and first-floor plans: the bookshop occupies the corner of Keskuskatu and the Esplanade (note the marble surrounds to the windows on the principal elevation, facing the Esplanade); like the Rautatalo, the bookshop is organized around a top-lit space.

44

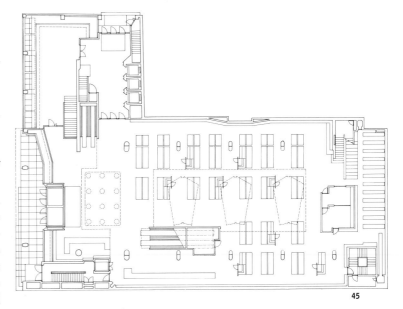

45

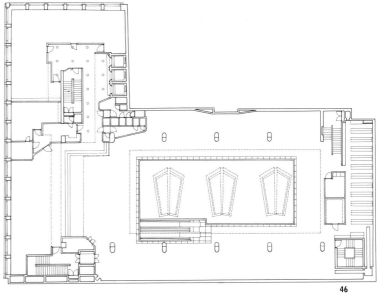

46

create a delicate facade – more 'curtain' than wall – which responds to the proportions and scale of the adjacent buildings and whose complex subdivisions delineate the lines of structure behind and suggest the layering of Renaissance facades. For the Academic Bookshop, which occupies the corner site on Esplanadi beyond the Saarinen bank and was won in competition in 1962 but not constructed until 1966-9, he returned to copper and combined the sub-divisions of the Scandinavian Bank facade with the bolder grid of the Rautatalo. Aalto responded to the corner site by introducing narrow strips of white marble around the glazing in recognition of the greater significance of the entrance frontage to the Esplanade.

The first Academic Bookshop was opened in 1893 and, in keeping with the idealistic efforts of the time to establish a Finnish national culture, it was always intended to be more than a money-making business. It continues to fulfil this role, acting as a focus for intellectual life, promoting the national literature and giving access to foreign books.[32] Like the Rautatalo – and Frosterus's Stockmann store opposite, by whom it is owned and to which it is linked by an underground passage – the Bookshop is organized around a large top-lit space. The sales floors occupy the ground and first floors, linked by an escalator, and the second-floor administrative offices are on an open gallery overlooking the shop, again slightly set back from that below. The rooflights are smaller versions of the 'crystal' type invented for the Pensions Institute: pentagonal in plan, they occupy deep, light-filled voids whose faceted sides suggest they may have been cracked open by ice; the angled glazing plunges into the atrium to form natural chandeliers which seem to radiate, as much as transmit, the natural light.

The interior is finished in white throughout – ceilings and walls plastered and painted, floors and balcony parapets surfaced with white marble – and brightly lit by day and night. Thanks to the profusion of shoppers – despite the high prices, Finns are among the world's most avid buyers of books – the Bookshop is the bustling piazza that never quite materialized in the Rautatalo. To the rear it is overlooked by the Café Aalto, a calm retreat and popular meeting place: a survey conducted by the *Helsingin Sanomat* (Finland's leading newspaper) for the shop's hundredth anniversary confirmed that for 'the capital's scholars, writers, and journalists . . . the high point of the working day was a visit to the Academic Bookstore'.[33] Although spaces of comparable – indeed, much greater – scale are now familiar in shopping centres around the world, Aalto's Bookshop possesses a calm dignity which lifts it above the norms of commercial design and

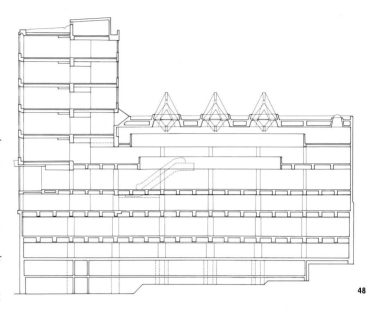

48

expresses its important role in Finnish cultural life.

Aalto's other major building in central Helsinki, the headquarters of Enso-Gutzeit – one of the largest paper and cellulose companies (partly government-owned) – was designed and built in 1959–61. The site, which Aalto proposed for the Parliament House in his competition entry of 1923, is on Katajanokka island and occupies a strategic place in the urban structure. Located below the distinctive profile of the Russian Orthodox Church, which looms on a granite outcrop above, it forms the visual termination of the linear parkway of the Esplanade and overlooks an inlet of the Baltic and the Market Place, whose urban role Aalto likened to the Riva degli Schiavoni in Venice.[34] He envisaged the building as mediating between the Neo-classical centre of Helsinki, dominated by Engel's Cathedral in nearby Senate Square, and the sea: its palazzo-like form – complete with a flat-roofed loggia for meeting and eating – and brilliant marble surfaces, were clearly inspired by memories of Venice, but the simple image seen from the Esplanade, which also greets visitors arriving by ferry, belies a design of surprising complexity.

The facade is formed of square windows set in coffered marble surrounds, the module supposedly generated from a frankly specious proportional 'analysis' of the Neo-classical centre.[35] Three bays on the left-hand end of the harbour elevation are omitted at ground level to form a linear arcade/*porte-cochère* to the urban frontage, and the regular facades give no hint of the fact that the block is dramatically carved away to let light into the inevitable top-lit, interior court – the seemingly violent, *ad hoc* treatment of the volume is decidedly shocking after the calm regularity of the principal elevations. Porphyrios interprets it as a classically-derived 'inflection' towards the Byzantine cathedral, but also suggests that it 'conjures up images of a quarry or of cleavages occasioned by inclement weather and land tremors'.[36] The effect is reminiscent of the disparity between the approach and rear of Paimio, while the grid of fenestration takes us even further back to the insistent regularity of the Agricultural Co-operative building in Turku; the coffered windows – like the floating balconies of the Rautatalo – can be traced to sketches for the League of Nations Building competition in 1926–7.[37] Aalto re-used the marble coffers as the elevational motif for a series of *palazzi* along the west shore of Töölö Bay, proposed as part of his grandest urban project – the plan for the new centre of Helsinki, commissioned in 1959.[38]

The plan embraced the area between the main railway station,

47

49

50 Plan for Helsinki centre, 1961.
51 Project for Helsinki city centre, 1964: greeted initially with great acclaim, Aalto's plan for the city centre gradually fell foul of partisan interests.

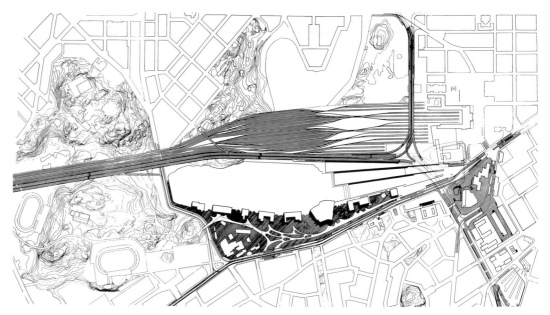

50

51

52   53

Parliament House and Töölö Bay and was intended to create both a functioning centre for an increasingly metropolitan city, and an emblematic focus for the independent, democratic country. Both the need for a new centre, and the problem of the chaotic railway yard, which presented views of railway cars and decrepit warehouses to the elevated Parliament House, had long been the subject of debate, and of several abortive plans. As part of his second Greater Helsinki Master Plan, produced in 1918, Eliel Saarinen proposed filling in Töölö Bay – originally an inlet from the sea, but cut off by the railway embankment – and driving a vast 90-metre-wide Royal Avenue (also known as the Avenue of Freedom) through to the square in front of the railway station, which he suggested be converted into a post and telegraph office.[39] In a plan prepared in 1927, Oiva Kallio likewise advocated filling in the bay.[40] However, a 1932 scheme by the City Planning Office favoured its partial retention, and in Yrjö Lindegren and Erik Kråkström's competition-winning plan of 1948 it was kept in its entirety.[41] Aalto, not surprisingly, followed suit.

Along the bay's eastern shore he proposed an elevated highway – the new Avenue of Freedom, placed above the railway tracks – affording dramatic views of the whole city, including the range of cultural *palazzi* sited along the opposite shore and shielded from Mannerheimintie by an existing park. These included an academy, congress hall, concert hall, opera house, art and architecture museums, a municipal library, and sites for several other unspecified activities. The buildings were cantilevered out above the water combining, as Nils Erik Wickberg has suggested, 'an element of the palaces of the *Canal Grande*, but also of the Finnish shore-side sauna cottage'.[42] As they approached the city centre, the highway and line of new buildings framed a vast triangular piazza. Designed on three levels, it covered a parking garage for 4,000 cars thereby, Aalto argued, enabling the compact old city to be pedestrianized. Ever faithful to his beloved Italy, Aalto christened it 'Forum Triangulum'. However, it later became known as Terrace Square: just as the wings of the Paimio Sanatorium opened to welcome visitors, the three triangular wedges of Terrace Square fanned out to receive Töölö Bay – emblem of nature in the city – in a symbolic embrace of the whole country.

The plan was greeted with great acclaim when Aalto presented it to President Kekkonen, the Speaker, Prime Minister and other distinguished guests on 22nd March 1961, and none of the parties represented on the city council had any objections to the scheme. But, like the earlier proposals, it gradually fell foul of partisan interests. For the nature lovers, the buildings and the traffic they would generate were an unacceptable intrusion into the idyllic park; the Terrace Square was thought dreary and lacked the enclosing buildings expected of an urban space; the city traffic planners attempted to discredit it as unworkable; and in 1970 a modified scheme became the focus of criticism by left-wing activists for pandering to 'wealthy car owners' rather than siting the cultural facilities out in the suburbs where the working classes lived. To their credit, the city council stuck by Aalto through all the criticism – not least from some of their own officials – and in 1973 he submitted a revised plan.[43] By this time the first of the proposed cultural buildings – the Finlandia Concert Hall (which we will examine in the final chapter) – had already been built to his designs; he also reserved a site for the Opera House at the north end of the bay, which was later adopted. The building, finally completed in 1993, sadly fails to rise to the challenge of its programme and splendid site, although internally it is rapidly establishing a good reputation as a performance space.

The remainder of the 'élitist' cultural facilities were eliminated as a concession to public criticism, but this time the plan foundered under the newly mobilized environmentalists' opposition to the proposed highway and the increased traffic they argued would result. In 1976, the year of Aalto's death, they managed to get the council to pass a resolution that the main traffic artery should not be built, thereby seriously undermining the plan's credibility. Many of the problems it addressed remain – notably the unsightly railway yard – and the inner end of what would have become Terrace Square is now assigned to a Museum of Modern Art, to be built to a controversial competition-winning design by the American architect Steven Holl.[44] The possibility of realizing an overall plan of comparable vision seems to have been lost – as Osmo Lappo suggested in an interview in *Helsingin Sanomat* in 1981, 'Aalto was the last man who could have achieved something similar [to Engel's Senate Square], but there was no longer any Czar. Democratic control diminishes the risk of mistakes, but also prevents good overall solutions. Today we can only make jigsaw puzzles.'[45] The failure of his ambitious plans for the nation's capital was the greatest disappointment of Aalto's professional life, but he had considerable success in applying similar thinking to the planning and design of more modestly-scaled town centres and of two large academic campuses, to consideration of which we may now turn.

The Town Centre and the Academic Campus

Exactly as the Medieval cities once upon a time lost their fortification walls and the modern city grew out beyond them, the concept of the city today is in the process of shedding its constraints. But this time it is happening, not to lead once again to the creation of a larger unit, but rather so that the city will become a part of the countryside. ALVAR AALTO [1]

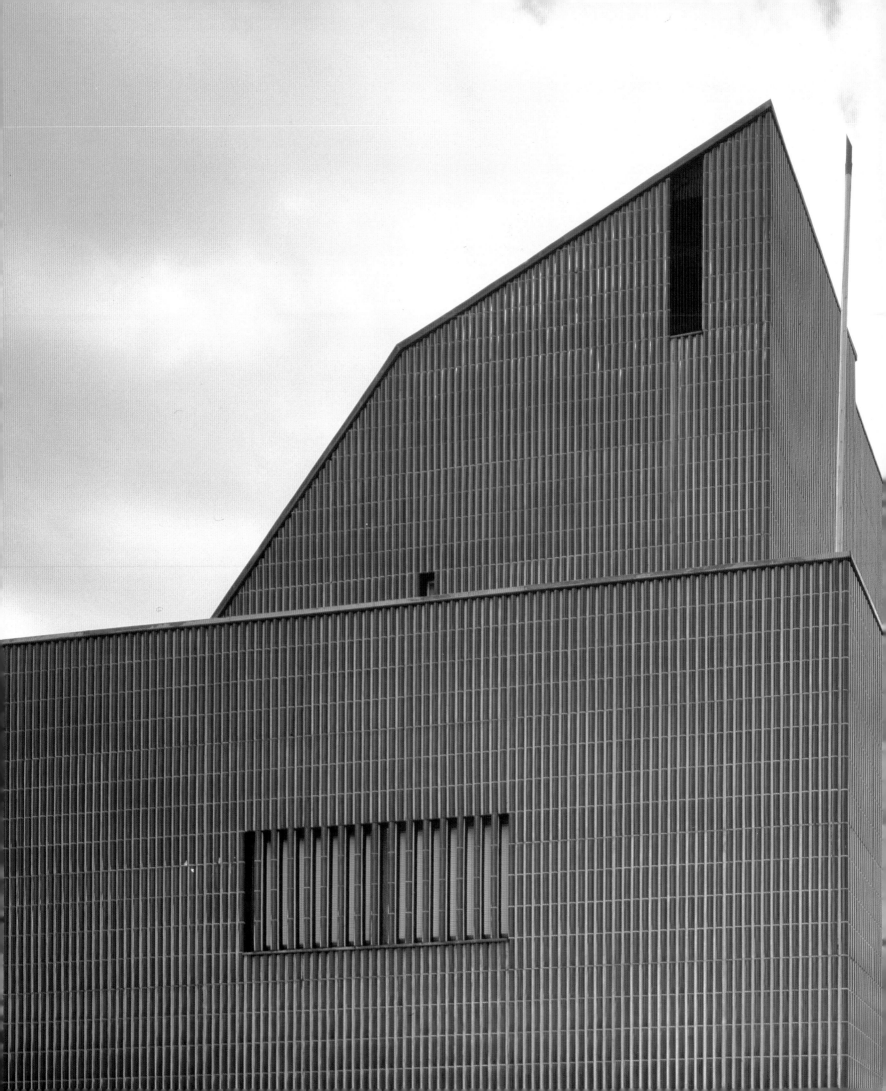

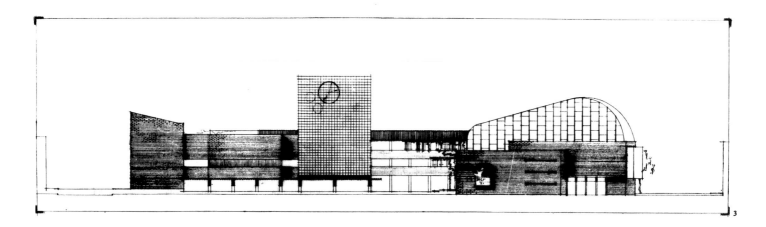

AALTO'S attitude to the town was grounded in his love of Italian urban culture, but it was only in the youthful enthusiasm of the 1920s that he attempted to transplant Italian models directly to Finnish soil. In 1932, in a remarkably prescient article entitled 'The Geography of the Housing Question', he speculated on the impact of the telephone on settlement patterns and argued that 'it allows for geographic decentralization based on local groupings', and demonstrated with 'a funny, almost graphic, clarity . . . what the ideal conditions for settlements are when the need for contact between people is set as the criterion'.[2] Written at the height of his enthusiasm for mainstream European Modernism, the article is clearly in line with the thinking behind the Athens Charter, and Aalto remained committed to such an approach to housing throughout his career. But unlike Le Corbusier, who at the time of drafting the Charter apparently discounted the need for a monumental urban centre, Aalto, when faced with the challenge of designing town centres, drew directly upon older European traditions exemplified by Camillo Sitte's analysis of urban space and the tradition of the 'city crown'.[3] (*Die Stadtkrone*, the city crown, was the title of a book by Bruno Taut, published in 1919, which became widely known as a counter-argument to the garden city.)

The traditions represented by Sitte and Taut were both present in the book *Staden som lonstverk* ('The City as a Work of Art'), written by Aalto's friend Gustav Strengell in 1922. Strengell, like Sitte before him, delighted in the 'organic' order that emerged from the seemingly adventitious historical processes of urban development; and while Aalto shared this enthusiasm, he was also influenced by the seemingly antithetical garden city tradition, which Lars Sonck, amongst others, had advocated as particularly appropriate to the layout of small Finnish towns.[4] Aalto believed that, 'as a norm one may clearly hold to the desirability of as high a percentage as possible of single-family dwellings in immediate contact with nature'.[5] He argued that, 'in Finland nature itself suggests, in a remarkable manner, a spread-out mode of settlement'.[6] These ideas on the interweaving of town and countryside are demonstrated in plans such as those for Imatra (1947–53) where, even close to the centre, large tracts of farmland and forest are preserved.[7] They are also evident in so-called 'Reindeer Horn Plan' prepared for Rovaniemi in 1945.[8] However, as with his great plan for Helsinki, Aalto had little success in realizing his larger scale visions, politics invariably intervening to thwart his holistic approach.

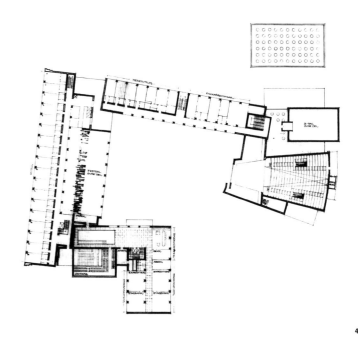

The first opportunity to propose a complete town centre came in 1944, in Sweden rather than Finland, for the small, relatively new mining community of Avesta.[9] Aalto's plan combined a range of functions – offices, cafés, shops, workers' club, theatre and library – to create a picturesquely varied group of buildings around an informal pedestrian square. The composition was dominated by the cubic form of the city hall – complete with clock – and by the raking roof of the theatre, which was placed at an angle to the surrounding city grid as a mark of its civic status. The project contains the seeds of all Aalto's later town-centre plans but was rejected by the community, who disliked the relationship to the surroundings and particularly objected to Aalto's determination to combine different functions in the same buildings; the town hall wing, for example, had boutiques on the arcaded ground floor, and the library stood above shops. Aalto argued that such combinations of activities were healthy in promoting day- and night-time use of the civic centre – a principle he later applied, as we have seen, to the National Pensions Institute – and hoped that by grouping them he could create a complex of sufficient scale, variety and presence to with-

1 (Previous page) sketch of tower, San Gimignano, Italy, 1948. 2 (Previous page) Seinäjoki Town Hall, Seinäjoki, 1961–5: it is clad in Aalto's favourite dark blue tiles, which suggest masonry coursing and the verticals of the forest. 3, 4 Elevation and plan for unrealized project for Avesta town centre, Sweden, 1944. 5 Plan for Jyvaskyla centre, 1965. 6 Project for Rovaniemi city centre, 1965: impressive on paper, the urban centre lacks the master's touch in its posthumous realization. 7, 8 Otaniemi campus plan, 1949, sketch and plan.

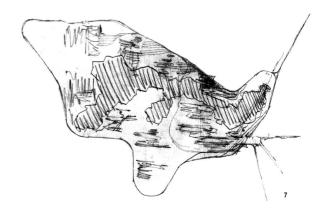

7

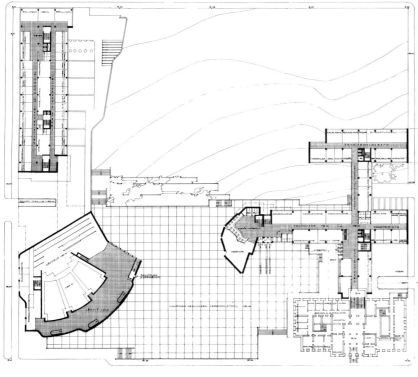

5

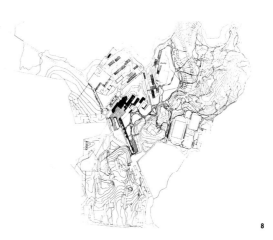

8

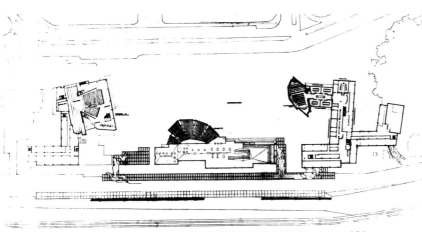

6

10

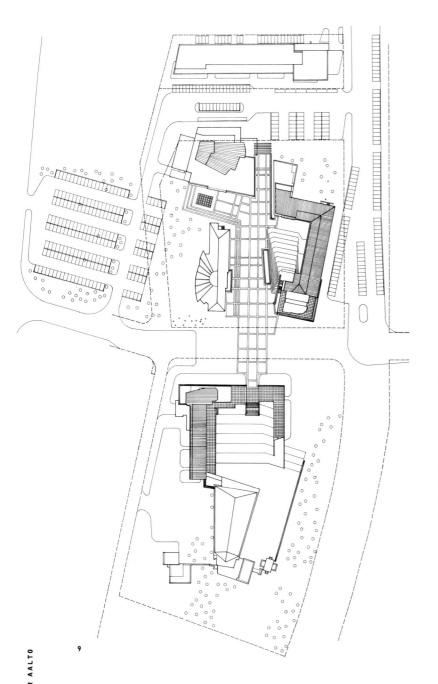

9

stand the onslaught of commercial buildings, which, in many cities, had already wiped out any possibility of establishing the civic complex as a visual and symbolic 'crown'.

In 1949, as part of his comprehensive plan for Imatra – the need for which arose as a result of the territorial concessions made to Russia under the 1944 peace treaty – Aalto produced a detailed, but wholly unrealized design for the town centre, whose boldly articulated silhouette of towering masses clearly shows the influence of Italian hill-towns. The plan proposed an open-sided square, framed on three sides by the town hall and administration building, a theatre, an apartment building and a fire station. The stage of the theatre could open sideways on to a balcony overlooking the square, as well as into the auditorium through a conventional proscenium arch. The town hall was designed as an L-shaped plan capturing an implied courtyard, with a butterfly roof, long external staircase (akin to that employed in the competition entry for the new Finnish Parliament building in 1923) climbing up to a cubic council chamber, which sat on an 'acropolis' of freely angled grass steps; the similarities with the smaller Säynätsalo Town Hall are obvious, and hardly surprising, as they were designed in the same year.

The ideas developed at Avesta and Imatra were later applied to the new centres for the Finnish towns of Seinäjoki, Rovaniemi and Jyväskylä. None of these was completed by the time of Aalto's death in 1976, but both Seinäjoki and Rovaniemi have subsequently been realized in line with drawings and sketches produced in the office during his lifetime. The most successful is Seinäjoki, which will be considered in detail here as representative of Aalto's approach and achievement. Rovaniemi, although impressive on paper, clearly lacks the master's touch in its posthumous realization; despite the fact that the completed buildings at Jyväskylä were finished during his lifetime (the planned town hall remains on paper), there is a slackness in both overall spatial organization and detail, and a tendency to indulge in gratuitous form-making, which cast doubts on the extent of Aalto's personal involvement with much of the design.

Aalto began work on what would become the Seinäjoki town centre when he won the competition for the church, which he called 'The Cross of the Plains', in 1952. Construction did not start until 1958, and the following year he won another competition for the design of the complete centre, comprising – in addition to the large church and parish centre – a town hall, library, civic theatre and municipal offices. Aalto conceived the

11

12 Seinäjoki town centre, 1958–, view of
town hall with church in background:
the planning of the town centre reflects
Aalto's love of Greek sites; the town hall
sits on a miniature grass 'acropolis'

with the council chamber itself
rising like a geometric hillside over
an abstracted architectural forest.
13–14 Street lamps in Seinäjoki,
designed by Aalto.

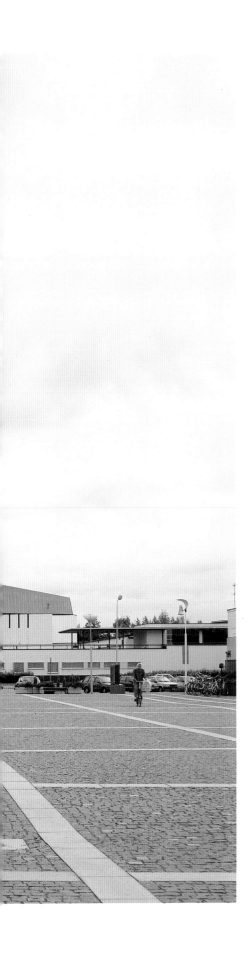

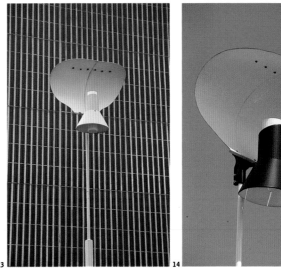

13   14

town centre as a traffic-free precinct of three interlinked squares. The first,
in front of the church, is framed by the extensive accommodation required
for the parish centre – offices, meeting rooms, facilities for children – and
approached up a broad flight of steps from Koulukatu, a wide street which
cuts across the centre. Designed to form an extension of the nave, the
grassed 'square' can accommodate up to 15,000 people for services when
the church's west wall, consisting of large sliding doors, is opened:
Seinäjoki acts as the religious centre for the Lutheran church in central and
northern Finland, hence the need to cater for such large numbers `on
special occasions.

The second square, defined by the town hall (1961–5), library (1963–5),
and theatre (1968–87), is more like a broad street, paved with a tartan grid,
which runs across Koulukatu up to the entrance to the church precinct,
while the third is essentially a space for cars, hidden to view from the
pedestrian areas. Although not obvious at first sight, the arrangement of
the town hall and library closely follows the pattern established at
Säynätsalo: the town hall is wrapped around a landscaped courtyard, all
but taken over by the grass steps, which here create an informal amphitheatre from which to view civic events in the 'forum' of the street-square
below.[10] The Säynätsalo pool has likewise been expanded here to form an
elongated basin, into which water spouts from a low stone wall, and the

15

16

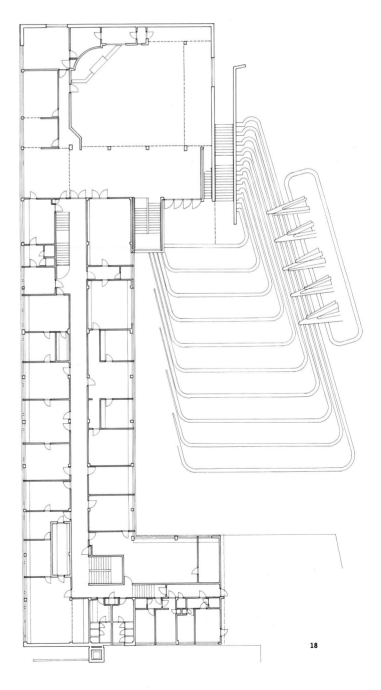

council chamber rises to loom large over the predominantly low-rise surroundings.

The main public/ceremonial spaces of the town hall are clad in Aalto's favourite dark blue tiles, which effectively suggest both the coursing of traditional masonry and the vertical texture of the forest. The tiles appear as vertical stripes or rectangular patches across the 'internal' courtyard facades of the administrative accommodation, establishing dominant vertical accents in what would otherwise be a predominantly horizontal effect. They also form a counterpoint to the structural grid behind, which is rendered almost illegible in the elevations; this is a typical example of that avoidance of 'artificial architectural rhythms' we first noted in connection with the Villa Mairea. The council chamber itself rises like a geometric hillside over this abstracted forest. Seen from the pedestrian side, it is a sectional 'slice', which one might expect simply to be extruded, but it steps back in plan and curves around at the opposite corner in response to the plan below, in which the seating is laid out diagonally in the rectangular room, and focused on a quasi-classical circular alcove behind the raised table.

To avoid a visual clash with the richly coloured and highly articulated form of the town hall, the library presents a surprisingly reticent entrance elevation to the main public space. The long, white-rendered facade is set above a dark stone base, establishing the familiar 'geological' stratification of the overall mass, while the windows to the offices are covered by a protective screen of closely spaced, vertical, white-painted metal bars, which rhyme with the birch trees planted in the small park behind. Once inside, one of Aalto's most arresting and felicitous spaces unfolds, with bookshelves fanning out beneath an undulating ceiling designed – as at Viipuri – to distribute reflected light evenly throughout the interior. The organization similarly follows the spatial type developed at Viipuri: the central control desk looking out over a sunken reading area; the volumetric articulation of the programme into a figural library hall, which reads externally as an undulating *Aalto* wall facing the lawn, spattered with silver birches; and a low, linear block of support spaces.

The theme of the richly modelled ceiling is one to which Aalto returned throughout his later work – in the Villa Carré in France, as well as in numerous churches and auditoria to be considered in the next chapter – but nowhere is it more gracefully or appropriately deployed than here. In Jørn Utzon's later development of the theme, as for example in the Sydney

19

20

19–22 Seinäjoki Library, Seinäjoki, 1963–5, views from above and ground level, section and plan. **23** Interior of Seinäjoki Library: the fan-shaped plan organized around a central control desk, the sunken reading room, and the complex section, which distributes natural light throughout the interior, are characteristic features of Aalto's libraries – and nowhere more convincingly combined than here.

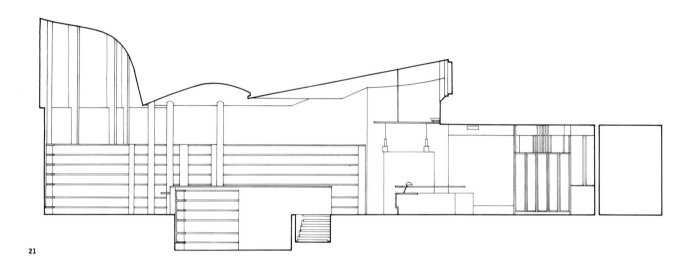

21

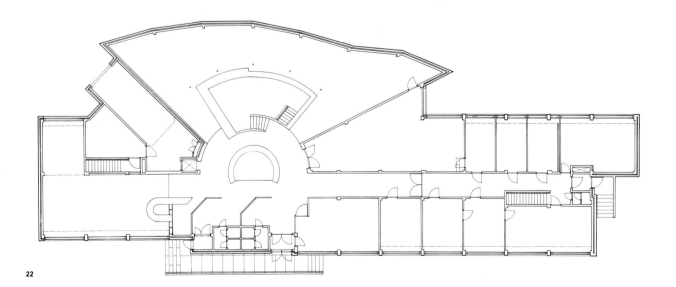

22

23

Opera House or Bagsvaerd Church, the designs are presented as explicit references to clouds, and with the landscape metaphors, which we have seen run throughout Aalto's work in mind, it is difficult not to read this ceiling as a highly abstracted sky. It does not recall the unbroken vault of southern Europe nor the misty veil evoked in Viipuri, but a typical northern sky of shifting clouds and broken sun. This is a reading reinforced by the main photograph Aalto chose to illustrate the interior in his *oeuvre complète*, in which the space is animated by dappled sunlight admitted through the horizontal louvres which run along the clerestory above the book-cases.[11]

The theatre, which also acts as a convention centre for the region, and was designed with simple stage arrangements to encourage amateur use, was completed in 1987, eleven years after Aalto's death, and lacks the detailed refinement evident in both the town hall and library. However, the organization and form were worked out as early as 1968–9, and are carefully contrived in response to the overall town-centre plan. The main entrance is marked by a substantial trellis that effectively closes the civic space – beyond lie the administration building and car park – and once inside, the spacious foyer leads round to a restaurant and coffee-shop, which offer a superb view back along the length of the pedestrian space towards the church. The wedge-shaped auditorium and fly towers rise above the main horizontal mass of the building, joining the council chamber, library reading-room, and church hall and bell-tower to form a series of civic 'monuments'.

For all the undoubted virtuosity of its component parts, the overall composition of the Seinäjoki centre is not easy to come to terms with. Quantrill, for example, dismisses it as 'suburban', 'a loose collection of buildings that simply do not connect either spatially or visually' and fail to give the expanding town the needed 'sense of urbanity'.[12] But to judge it in terms of conventional urban space – the kind Aalto sought to create in his National Pensions Institute competition projects, for example – is surely to misread his intentions. Seinäjoki is not Helsinki, but a provincial town lying well to the north where snow is a feature of the environment for several months in winter; in such a climate, streets and pavements are traditionally wide and the 'urban space', such as it is, defined – or perhaps more accurately *implied* – as much by fences as buildings. While the town centre has been read by Demetri Porphyrios as an attempt to stretch the fabric of the various buildings' secondary spaces to create an urban realm,

from which the figurally articulated major volumes within rise as monumental 'crowns', its organization clearly suggests the influence of Greek site planning.[13] (This, as we noted in examining his classicist church projects, was a key early influence, almost certainly mediated by Le Corbusier's eulogies of the Acropolis in *Vers une Architecture*.)

By the time he came to design Seinäjoki, Aalto had first-hand experience of Greek sites, and his sketchbooks attest to the value he placed upon them.[14] While the buildings seem only to engage in a half-hearted struggle to define and contain space, they succeed magnificently as a composition of interrelated masses. This they do in a manner admirably suited, as Andres Duany points out, to offer a prototype for many architects today 'working in irrevocably suburban places, for whom the conventions of the European city are too precise, and those of the Anglo-American suburb too weak. To these Aalto can show the way.'[15] That 'way' is not easily followed, for in the design of the Seinäjoki centre, as in almost everything he undertook, Aalto had total control of details down to the street furniture. One notices, for example, how critical the lamps are in reinforcing the definition of the sacred precinct in front of the church and establishing the pedestrian space between the library and town hall. (The street-lamp, a development of the type first set out at Paimio, is amongst the most elegant of such designs of Aalto's career.)

As he made clear in an essay entitled 'The Decline of Public Buildings', Aalto's main concern in the design of town centres was to establish a civic precinct in which the public buildings could bear 'the traditional imprint of the government and the social contract'.[16] He likened them to 'the vital organs in the human body' and when he asserted the need for 'a proper urban fabric', he had in mind the need 'to create anew the differentiation necessary for an organized community' – a differentiation which demanded the creation of 'open public places – squares, parks and arcades – where citizens … [can] gather'. At a time of increasing fragmentation and privatization of 'public' space, we could do well to note this differentiation today. The town centre at Seinäjoki offers just such a sequence of spaces, tuned to the Finnish climate and temperament – the two, of course, intimately related. Aalto's civic space is a built landscape, in which the enclosure of that quintessential Finnish space, the courtyard formed in a forest clearing, is allied to an heroic disposition of 'volumes brought together in light'.[17] The view along the pedestrian street, with the grass steps of the town hall rising to the left and the bell-tower and nave of the church

25, 26 Technical University of Helsinki, Otaniemi, 1953–66, view of main building alone and from distance with accommodation blocks in foreground: the amphitheatre-like form of the main building is the visual and symbolic centre of the campus, placing the lecture theatre – the pre-eminent 'machine' of a classical education – at the heart of the university; the accommodation blocks form a defensive wall for the pedestrian campus beyond.

25

26

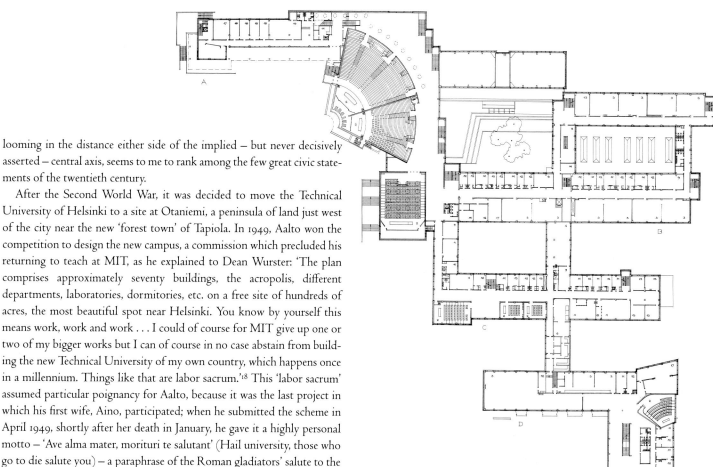

looming in the distance either side of the implied – but never decisively asserted – central axis, seems to me to rank among the few great civic statements of the twentieth century.

After the Second World War, it was decided to move the Technical University of Helsinki to a site at Otaniemi, a peninsula of land just west of the city near the new 'forest town' of Tapiola. In 1949, Aalto won the competition to design the new campus, a commission which precluded his returning to teach at MIT, as he explained to Dean Wurster: 'The plan comprises approximately seventy buildings, the acropolis, different departments, laboratories, dormitories, etc. on a free site of hundreds of acres, the most beautiful spot near Helsinki. You know by yourself this means work, work and work . . . I could of course for MIT give up one or two of my bigger works but I can of course in no case abstain from building the new Technical University of my own country, which happens once in a millennium. Things like that are labor sacrum.'[18] This 'labor sacrum' assumed particular poignancy for Aalto, because it was the last project in which his first wife, Aino, participated; when he submitted the scheme in April 1949, shortly after her death in January, he gave it a highly personal motto – 'Ave alma mater, morituri te salutant' (Hail university, those who go to die salute you) – a paraphrase of the Roman gladiators' salute to the emperor.[19]

The competition layout of the Otaniemi site reflects similar ideas to the Imatra and Säynätsalo town-centre plans, with an echelon of buildings defining a series of courtyards, leading up to the 'acropolis' placed at the high point of the site on which a large paved square was presided over by a massive butterfly-roofed main auditorium. The allusion to classical antiquity was made explicit, here, by the inclusion of a colonnade of ruined columns – not copies, naturally, but originals, which Aalto believed his friends in Italy would be able to procure for the student architects as examples of the highest cultural achievement. In practice, the budding architects have had to make do with a revetment of white Carrara marble around the inner walls of their courtyard, and a series of marble walls, free-standing or detached by strips of glazing. The only other building to get even a hint of such lavish materials is the library, and nowhere but in Finland, surely, could an architect, even of Aalto's stature, get away with such blatant partiality!

In the final scheme, realized in stages from 1952, the central piazza and acropolis-like effect are diminished in importance, but the allusion to Greece is reinforced by the adoption of an amphitheatrical form (designed

in 1955) to house the main lecture theatres. Even the detailing of the ventilation openings in the copper roof suggests tiny Greek temples – deliberate or not, we may never know – but Aalto must surely have delighted in the fact that technical necessities gave rise to such an overtly, and appropriately, allusive form. The external amphitheatre comes complete with a small 'stage' sunk into the paving, but the form is perhaps too self-contained and self-conscious to encourage the kind of informal occupation Aalto presumably hoped to encourage.

The Otaniemi campus amounts to a catalogue of building types that Aalto developed throughout his career. The main lecture theatres represent the culmination of a line of thinking about auditoria, which began

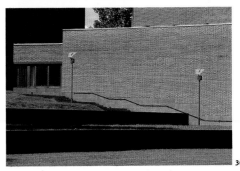

with the similarly circular forms and complex section of the theatre proposed in a 1930 competition project for Zagreb hospital; the library and student residence are entered from a tapering *cour d'honneur* like that first employed at Paimio;[20] and the departmental buildings are organized around courtyards. The final result is less urban than implied in the original competition entry, and although the central amphitheatre looks a little stiff and contrived to my eye, the complex presents an outstanding example of Aalto's ability to marshal levels and building masses to create a feeling of monumentality without the slightest hint of pomposity or oppressiveness.

The year after he secured the Otaniemi commission, Aalto had similar success with the competition for the new Pedagogical Institute in his original home town of Jyväskylä. The Institute – now the University – owed its origins to the strong educational traditions of the town, which, as we noted in the opening chapter, was the first to have a Finnish-language school – and to which Aalto liked to refer as the potential 'Athens of Finland'.[21] Aalto's competition motto left no doubt about his approach to the problem, he called it simply 'Urbs', and envisaged the main building with its large 'Festival Hall' as belonging as much to the city as to the University. This is a role it admirably fulfils as a meeting and concert hall for the citizens as well as students.[22] The University buildings were originally laid out in the form of a 'U' around a traffic-free campus centred on the sports field – a literal 'campus'. The buildings converged slightly, a perspectival device to reinforce the sense of enclosure. However, this effect is now less apparent due to the substantial expansion of the University, which has necessitated closing the open end of the 'U'.

As at Otaniemi and the town-centre plans, the influence of Greek site planning can be detected in the subtle adjustments of the buildings to the topography and each other – none is subservient to the rest, each gently asserting its identity in the ensemble. Likewise, in the overtly temple-like form Aalto gave to the staff dining room, with its colonnade of five square, the marble-clad piers distinguish it from the timber mullions of the glazed clerestory of the adjacent student refectory: both read as self-contained pavilions surmounting largely unrelieved brick walls, architectural counterparts for the cliffs of a natural acropolis. Internally, the student refectory is a marvellously welcoming space in which to eat, its L-shaped plan offering the choice between a large, main dining area and a more intimate secondary space to which you are naturally drawn when few people are present.

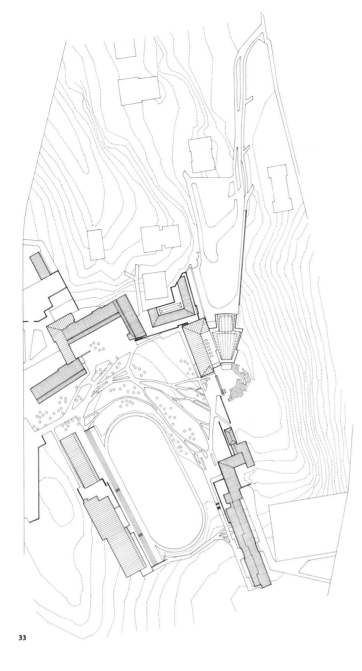

33

34

In the design of the classroom blocks, which constitute a working primary school integral to the teacher-training college, Aalto stressed the importance of avoiding an institutional atmosphere by breaking the large complex down into several apparently smaller schools, with six classrooms grouped around each staircase.[23] The classrooms themselves are articulated internally into two teaching areas, the angled re-entrant space forming a cloakroom off the main corridor. As Frederick Gutheim points out, throughout the design of the University, the rooms are thought of individually, rather than uniformly 'to serve average purposes'.[24]

Although they were designed as part of a single master-plan, Aalto's handling of the various buildings is predictably heterogeneous. Visually, the campus is bound together by the vertically-striated clerestories, which cap many of the buildings and serve to integrate them visually with the surrounding forest. Though Aalto sustains the fiction of a settlement grown over time by varying his treatment of the different parts of his buildings. The roofs are expressed alternately as copper 'hats'; the intention was perhaps to recall traditional dormers, or, as Porphyrios suggests, 'National Romantic survivals'.[25] Other roofs are flat, or suppressed as monopitches behind the glazed clerestories. The walls are generally of brick, but occasionally rendered or treated as partial glazed curtain walls. Columns range from tiled and tree-like, to overtly Corbusian white 'pilotis', while the windows are variously designed as rectangular openings, continuous screens, or, in one instance, as a Corbusian *fenêtre en longueur*. In plan the circumstantial distortions and adjustments to the topography create a series of small courts and narrow passages, reminiscent of Medieval urban fabric as much as of a 'planned' complex.

Although the site plan and subsidiary buildings are of considerable interest, Jyväskylä's importance in the Aalto corpus lies in the design of the main building – of which, surprisingly, no adequate drawings have hitherto appeared in print. The building is organized into two sections either side of an internal 'street': to the north, overlooking the campus, is a rectilinear block of teaching rooms – small lecture theatres, seminar rooms and laboratories – while to the south is the main lecture theatre, its raked seating stepping up above a shared cloakroom and a large foyer, which opens to the town and adjacent woodland through a continuous screen of full-height glazing. In this combination of a landscape-like space, foyer to the auditorium and covered piazza for the town, and a tall 'street' with its grand *scala regia* rising behind a sheer cliff of brickwork, Aalto's metaphor-

33, 34 Jyväskylä University (originally the Pedagogical Institute), Jyväskyla, 1952–7, site plan and view of the main building or Festival Hall: a literal campus, the university is organized around a central playing field. **35** The main building of Jyväskylä University acts as an interface with the town.

35

36–39 Jyväskylä University, Jyväskylä, 1952–7, view of the main building, of one of the intimate courtyards around the campus, of the rear of the teaching block adjacent to the Festival Hall, and of the campus at the rear of the main building with the student cafeteria and staff dining room on the right.

36

37

38

39

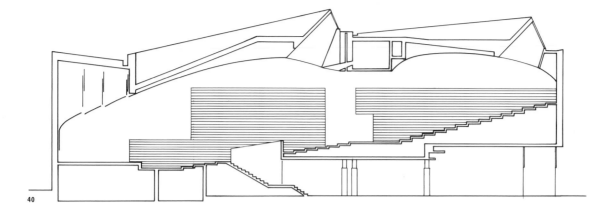

40

41

42

ic approach to design and responsiveness to human needs can be seen in all their richness: what he creates here is a small internalized urban realm, the public spaces of a 'forest town' adapted to the severe climate of central Finland.

The raked underside of the auditorium is mediated by a stepped series of acoustic panels, whose banded ribbing echoes the effect of the half-round tiles used to clad the columns and sections of wall around the café; these curves are repeated as a pattern on the specially designed curtains, which can still be bought from Artek. This form of ceiling is found again in many of Aalto's theatre and concert hall foyers, but in later designs – as, for example, in the nearby city theatre completed after his death – the effect is frequently marred by the use of synthetic materials and a tacky metal-edge trim. Here, the edges of the planes are simply formed by a forty-five degree angled cut, behind which is fixed a small circular section of timber, leaving the edge to read as a slightly irregular serration. This is a small matter, on the face of it, but when you see the more conventional detailing elsewhere, its deadening effect is immediately apparent.

The staircases into the auditorium plunge down into the foyer behind the now familiar screens of vertical poles, and the chunky 'Doric' columns are clad in tiles to suggest by turns classical fluting and the barks of trees – as at the Villa Mairea, the columns and their reflections seem to become an integral part of the surrounding forest. The auditorium itself is fan-shaped and designed in two spatially articulated sections, the upper part of which can be screened to operate as an independent theatre. The ceiling is formed of two broad curves; the one above the main, lower section sweeps down in a continuous arc behind the stage in a manner, which, like the articulation of the two sections of the interior and the rooflighting arrangement, clearly anticipates the design of the Vuoksenniska Church at Imatra, as well as later auditoria. To its rear, the auditorium block is articulated as faceted planes enclosing a shallow series of steps, which form an informal open-air amphitheatre adjacent to the main route through the building and campus.

The design of the 'street' and main stair to the teaching block are equally interesting. The staircase, as we noted in the previous chapter, provides a prime example of what George Baird has christened 'the space of the balustrade'. In the design of the balustrades and handrails themselves, Aalto again reveals his supreme sensitivity to the human presence. Where the staircase feeds sideways on to the different floor levels, the handrails are doubled and wrapped around the ends of the balusters; on one landing the

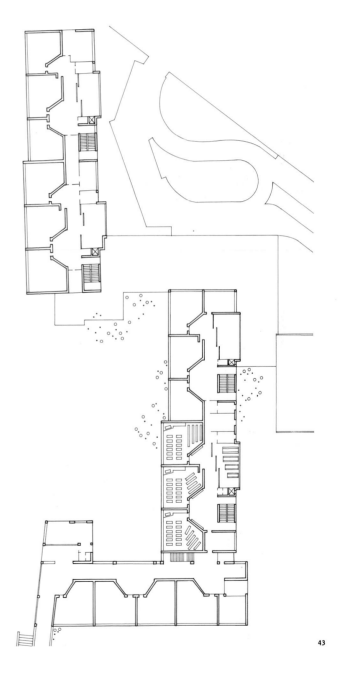

43

44

44 Main building Jyväskylä University, Jyväskylä, 1952–7, view of the internal 'street', which forms a main route through the campus. **45** Foyer of the raked theatre at Jyväskylä University:
the forest appears to flow right into the foyer, creating a landscape-like counterpoint to the adjacent 'street'. **46, 47** Plans for the main building of Jyväskylä University.

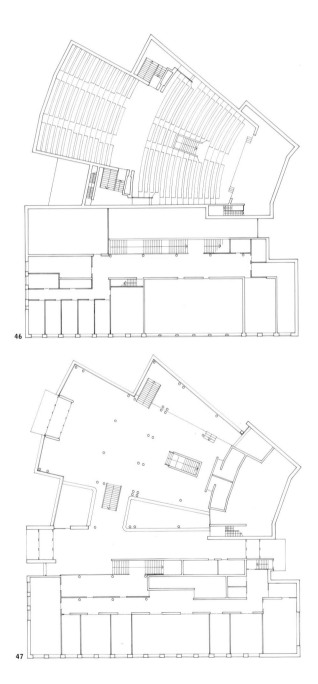

section is rectangular, with a rounded top, while on another it is circular – a subtle variation which particularizes each floor. Along the circulation spaces, which serve the small lecture halls and laboratories, the balustrades – made of simply framed rectangular panels of steel uprights – fit between the columns, but the wooden handrail runs continuously past them, deviating both inwards *and* upwards. A beautiful visual 'event', it is precisely tuned to the comfort of the arm, as the visitor can confirm by running a hand along the rail and imagining the effect if Aalto had opted for the more obvious solution of simply bending the rail in the horizontal plane. This deeply humanistic architecture is composed of many such subtleties.

The circulation arrangement created by the long main stair is remarkably elegant, but does have one major drawback in that it necessitates the planning of lecture rooms wider than they are deep. These Aalto arranges as 'squared-up' stepped amphitheatres of the kind he originally proposed for the library of the Finnish Parliament House in 1923. The proportions would be acceptable if the rooms were primarily for listening to a lecturer; Aalto, a gifted orator and ever a classicist at heart, doubtlessly believed lectures to be the basis of true education.[26] However, the lecture rooms are less than satisfactory for teaching, which is increasingly dependent upon visual aids; the projection screen is effectively unreadable from the edges of the rooms. Despite these minor shortcomings, the main building at Jyväskylä remains one of the major achievements of Aalto's middle years and has become a much-loved part of the town, amply fulfilling his hopes that it would become a civic as much as an academic place.

The urban fragments Aalto was able to realize in both Otaniemi and Jyväskylä hint at the qualities he might have achieved had his large-scale town plans for Imatra and Rovaniemi, amongst others, been realized. Unlike so many ensembles of buildings from a single hand, Aalto's town centres and academic campuses never become oppressive or boringly 'consistent'; sustained by his love of the variation of 'organic' form – whether of nature or traditional settlements – he finds reasons to vary the form and handling of the component buildings in ways, which rarely, if ever, seem gratuitous or contrived. For Aalto, it was impossible to separate the act of planning from that of designing: the building from its context; furniture from the building; and he could work effectively at every scale, from overall urban structure down to the details of chairs and glassware, to instil harmony into everyday surroundings.

Places of Assembly

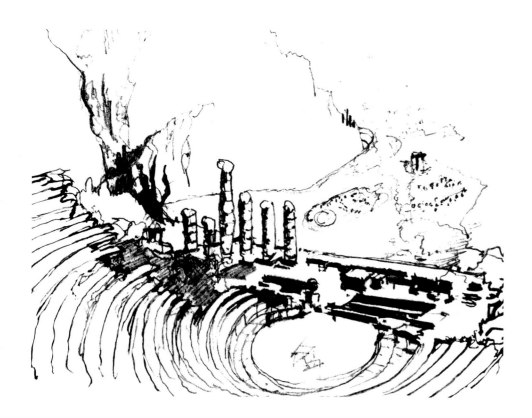

A church . . . needs pure and devout forms, whatever these forms may
be. Purity of form can only arise from careful and highly developed
artistic work, which calls for a dedicated and highly developed artist.
ALVAR AALTO [1]

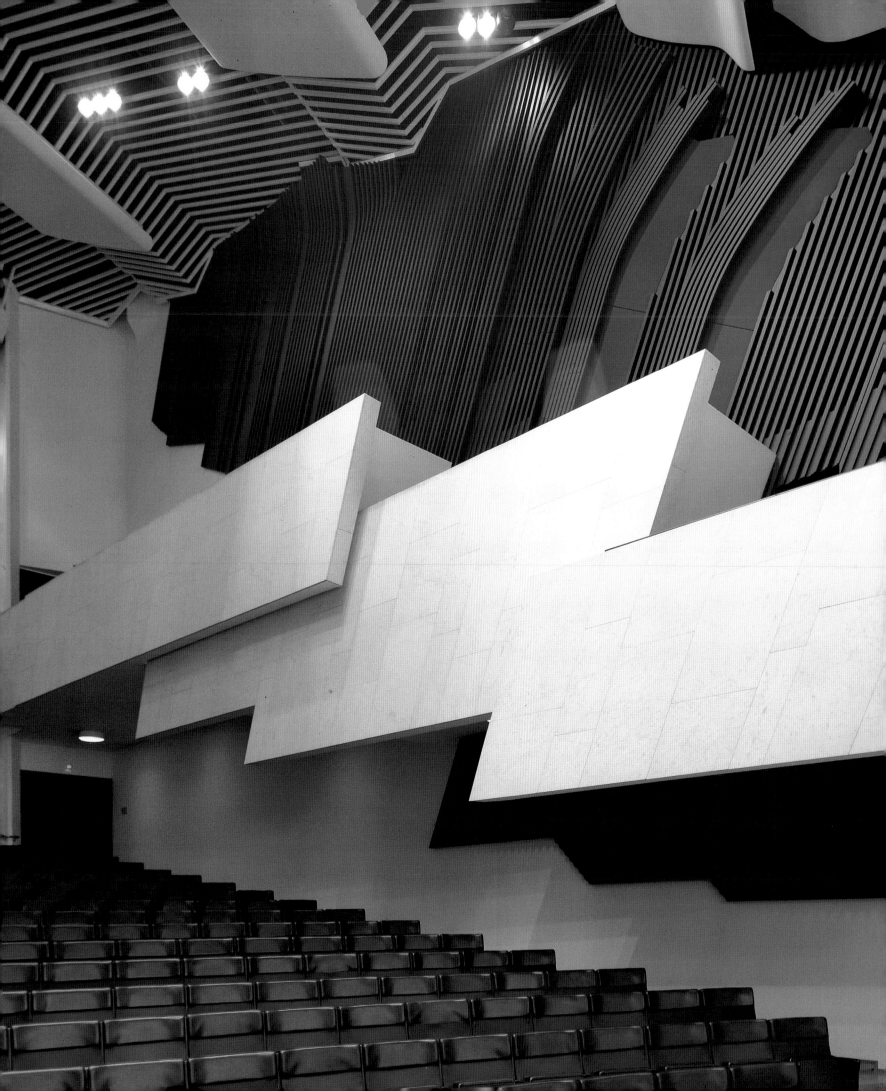

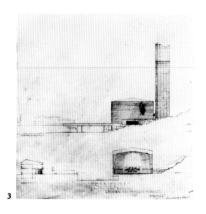

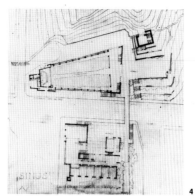

THE Lutheran Church plays a vital role in the culture of the Nordic countries, and although it is more independent of state control than elsewhere in Scandinavia, the church in Finland is closely tied to the government: the Parliament passes church laws, the President appoints bishops, and the church has the right to levy taxes from its members. The substantial tax income is used, among other things, to help sustain an extensive church-building programme; commissions generally being offered through the competition system. Membership of the church is still considered by many to be integral to their national identity, and almost ninety per cent of the population elect to be members and pay their taxes. Regular church attenders, however, amount to no more than four per cent of the population, but a further ten per cent are regularly involved in other church activities, such as nurseries, youth groups, work with the elderly and so forth. The role of the church is as much social as religious, and the majority of churches support a wide range of facilities in their parish centres. Aalto himself, Schildt tells us, was sceptical about religion but respected the church as a social institution.[2] This is an attitude typical of the majority of Finns, for whom the celebrations of key phases of life – birth, initiation to adulthood, marriage and death – still properly take place in church and carry an importance now rare elsewhere in predominantly Protestant countries.

Because of the competition system, the design of churches continues to offer Finnish architects the opportunity for architectural experimentation, although it also confronts them with a major dilemma. As an institution, the Church has generally been perceived as inherently conservative, and innovation has been more at the level of formal variations on familiar type-forms than on a fundamental re-evaluation of the nature of the type itself. In an article published in 1928, written in late 1927 as he first came under the influence of Functionalist ideas, Aalto observed that, 'we cannot create new form where there is no new content. We cannot make a church building as a whole the perfect representation of civilization in 1927; we cannot create modern church architecture in the true sense of the word since the content (the divine service) for which the form was created is an old tradition with no connection with the pressing problems of our time.'[3] This difficulty was compounded by ambiguities at the heart of the Lutheran liturgy, which made it problematic even for the clergy to define clearly the requirements of a modern church. Gustaf Strengell, in a perceptive analysis of the competition for the Tehtanpuisto parish in Helsinki, published in *Arkkitehti* in 1932, drew attention to the contradiction between the resplendent, quasi-Catholic communion service and the sermon preached by someone in formal black attire, questioning whether it would ever be possible to give the Lutheran Church a rational, modern form in keeping with its functions.[4]

The 1906 Dresden Congress of the Lutheran Church sanctioned the 'form language and expression of the day' as acceptable in church design.[5] However, designs remained conservative and it comes as no surprise that, during Aalto's classical phase, the entries for church competitions – including the one built example at Muurame – were, of all his projects, the most overtly derived from Italian stylistic precedents. With the onset of Functionalism, the tension between a would-be radical, innovative architecture and an inherently conservative institution was inevitably heightened. Lutheran services demand good acoustic qualities, not only for the sermon, but also for the spoken or chanted responses of the congregation and music. (The choral works of J. S. Bach, to name only the most distinguished example, were, of course, written for the Lutheran Church.) Consequently, acoustic requirements provided a 'functional' starting point for Modernist architects.

Aalto's entry for the Tehtanpuisto competition was presented with sections intended to demonstrate how the vaulted ceiling was calculated to ensure an even distribution of sound waves throughout the interior, but spatially the aisled, basilican-like form remained thoroughly traditional. Although ill-conceived in acoustic terms – the cusps of the vaults would have created serious problems – the vault-like forms reappear some twenty years later in the competition-winning design for the large church at Seinäjoki, where the allusion to Gothic form is heightened by the tapering fins on the columns, which are clearly intended to recall Gothic piers. However, the Seinäjoki design, which was produced in 1952, but not completed until 1960, is disappointing, surprisingly lumpen externally and unadventurous internally.

Aalto's basic approach to church design, to which he remained loyal throughout the following twenty years, was established two years earlier with the competition-winning design for the Lahti church (which had to wait even longer, until 1970, to start construction, and by then on a different site). The design is unusual in combining the body of the church and bell-tower. There is a long-standing tradition of free-standing belfries in Finland that Aalto generally followed. In plan the arrangement is

1 (Previous page) sketch of the
amphitheatre at Delphi, Greece, 1953:
fascinated with the amphitheatre form,
he took every opportunity to introduce
it into his designs. **2** (Previous page)
auditorium of the Finlandia Hall,
Helsinki, 1967–71, with its floating
balconies. **3, 4** Competition entries
for the Church of the Cross, Lahti,
1950. **5** Plan of Lahti, as built. **6** Sketch
for the Church of the Three Crosses,
Vuokkseniska, Imatra, 1957–9.

6

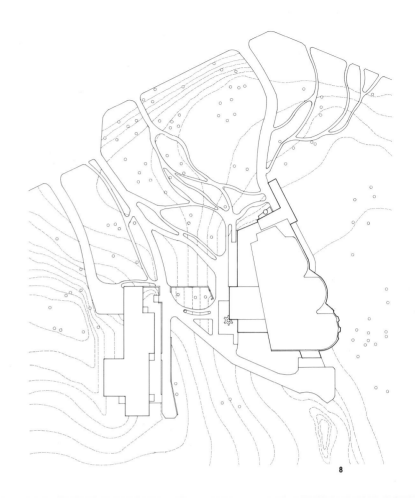

Church of the Three Crosses,
Vuokkseniska, Imatra, 1957–9, view
from the south, site plan, and church
seen through trees: the massive bell-
tower was designed to compete with
the large chimneys of the surrounding
industrial district.

typologically conventional, with a central aisle and tapering ranks of
seating focused on the altar. The elevated pulpit, presided over by an
acoustic reflector evocative of a *baldacchino*, is placed to the left, and the
organ ranged to the right. This is precisely the arrangement we find in the
one masterpiece amongst Aalto's church designs, that of the Church of the
Three Crosses which serves the Vuoksenniska district of Imatra.

The town of Imatra spreads over many miles and the skyline is peppered
by factory chimneys, some as high as 140 metres. In describing his design,
Aalto notes that in a large industrial area such as this the social functions
of the church are especially important.[6] This is clearly reflected in the
spatial sub-division of the interior and the formal articulation of the exterior. The church consists of three volumes, which can be combined to
form a single hall for 800 people, or subdivided by massive (30 tonne, 400
mm thick) reinforced concrete sliding partitions, mechanically operated
and run in oil tracks in the floor. Thus divided it creates a 'church' to seat
290 worshippers, the focus of which is the three crosses from which it
takes its name, and two independent parish halls, accessible via separate
entrances with their own lobbies. The church likewise has its own
entrances, located in the 'front', east facade, and, more conventionally, to
the west at the end of the central aisle. Both are primarily for use on ceremonial occasions: the former typically for funerals when only the church
proper is required, and the latter for processional entries on festival days
and weddings.

Externally, this tripartite organization is suppressed beneath a continuous copper roof, but clearly reflected on the northern side of the building.
Built close to the surrounding forest, this elevation consists of three
swelling, copper-clad forms, each subtly different to its neighbour: the
central bay is a continuous convex arc; to its left, the church bay begins as
a shallow arc and turns into a straight tangent behind the organ, while to
its right the overall convex curve is sub-divided into a series of small
concave arcs, like over-sized classical flutings – an arrangement which
anticipates the articulation of the congress wing of the Finlandia Hall.

The bulging curves to the north are counterpointed by a long straight
wall to the south, which in turn runs at an angle to the orthogonally organized entrance areas. The gently tapering plan, which follows the pattern
adopted in the second project for the Tehtanpuisto competition and subsequently exaggerated at Lahti, has been aptly described by Reima Pietilä
as the 'straights of the twisting fan overlaid with smoothly pulsating

10–12 Church of the Three Crosses, Vuokkseniska, Imatra, 1957–9, view of north-east entrance, detail of windows in roof, and the church as seen from the east: a complex array of copper-clad 'light-guns' is used to bring indirect natural light into the interior.

13 View of the Church of the Three Crosses from the north-west: the tripartite internal organization is clearly reflected in the east elevation facing the forest, but is not so readily apparent from the northern approach.

10

11

12

spherical lines'.[7] Aalto explained the asymmetry as a response to the Lutheran liturgy, with its duality between altar and pulpit, and indicated that the curves were adopted for acoustic reasons; the acoustics of the interior were the subject of detailed investigation using light models with adjustable mirrors to trace rays through the space. Equally significant, surely, is the fact that the curved forms – indicative, as we have seen, throughout Aalto's work of the free forms (and 'freedom') of nature – are ranged against the forest, while the straight wall creates a 'front' to address the city and relates to the tall vertical form of the bell-tower. This dialogue, between curved and straight, natural and man-made, is fundamental to the articulation of the whole design and is made explicit by the published site plan. In it the outlines of the church and adjacent pastor's house, lines of paths and steps, and site contours are drawn with equal weight to suggest that reciprocity between building and landscape, which lies at the heart of Aalto's conception of architecture.[8]

This highly articulated plan is combined with a section based on three asymmetrically curved vaults to generate the most complex and sophisticated spatial form in Aalto's entire *oeuvre*, and ideas explored throughout his career are brought together in a masterly synthesis. The idea of an undulating vault goes back to the lecture room in the Viipuri Library, where it ranged across a simple rectangular volume, and, as we noted in the previous chapter, is clearly anticipated in the design of the lecture theatre at Jyväskylä University.[9] The swelling forms of the plan are likewise found in earlier designs from the 1950s, such as the House of Culture, which we will examine later in this chapter.

Just as impressive as the spatial configuration is the extraordinary inventiveness with which Aalto handles both the natural and artificial illumination of the interior. Guides are fond of telling visitors that their church has more than a hundred windows, no two of which are the same.[10] This great variety of openings is by no means a gratuitous display of architectural invention, but a symphonic orchestration of light to create a series of different moods in both space and time. Beginning at the altar, one notes how the rear 'wall' is lit by two hidden slots of glazing, tucked behind projecting concrete fins. (I place 'wall' in inverted commas, because both the form, which is spatially continuous with the ceiling, and lighting are calculated to dissolve the sense of containment.) This produces an effect in which the space that can be read as being in continuous motion towards the altar, seems to disappear precipitously behind the three crosses. It leaves

13

14

them standing, metaphorically, in an open, indeterminate space – an architectural abstraction of Golgotha. The glazed slots admit early morning sun, but during the morning service sunlight animates the altar through the tripartite rooflight overhead, the brightly illuminated crosses casting indistinct shadows on the wall behind and advancing perceptually into the space. By evening, sunlight is filtered through a small blood-red stained-glass crown of thorns, placed in a stepped sequence of five rectangular openings along the west elevation. The artificial lighting is equally carefully conceived, with lamps specially designed for the church. These are suspended at different heights from the ceiling, but in a pattern which reinforces the axis to the altar, and the fittings themselves consist of a cluster of four curved metal reflectors, one segment of each formed by vertical brass rods; the overall effect is reminiscent of candlelight, and the light filtered through the brass rods suggests a miniature forest.

The central hall is naturally lit by three 'light guns', down which light descends mysteriously from above. The effect is similar to that which Le Corbusier exploited in the chapel at Ronchamp, created here not by an actual thick wall, but by a simulated one formed by copper-covered projections. The western-most space features a single opening baffled by one of Aalto's familiar timber screens, formed of closely spaced, white-painted slats of timber. The three large windows along the north elevation are both stepped and canted inwards – for acoustic reasons, according to Aalto – to create a substantial void into which the moveable partitions can slide. This detachment of the inner and outer skins of the wall is a familiar Baroque device, but, as Robert Venturi noted in 1966, was 'unique in recent architecture'.[11] It enabled Aalto to manipulate both space and light to magical effect, the interplay of irregularly spaced mullions, vertical outside and sloping inside, capturing a luminous volume of space and creating, through parallax effects as you move past, one of his most alluring evocations of the light and space of the forest. This suggestion of organic life is echoed in the ribbed apertures in the ceiling through which filtered and pre-heated air is admitted and waste air extracted. Their form inevitably recalls fish gills, and animates the whole building. Reyner Banham aptly describes them as 'humping its copper roofs defensively against the sky and lifting cautious windows, like watchful alligator eyes, above the white substructure in which it seems to burrow'.[12]

Spatially, the interior is a magisterial piece of three-dimensional composition in which Aalto's ability to create spaces, which are both formally rigorous and responsive to the nuances of human action, is shown at its height. One notes, for example, how the balcony for the choir is subtly

14–16 Church of the Three Crosses, Vuokkseniska, Imatra, 1957–9, view from south-east, section and plan: the ceremonial entrance for processional entries on festival days is located at the end of the central aisle.

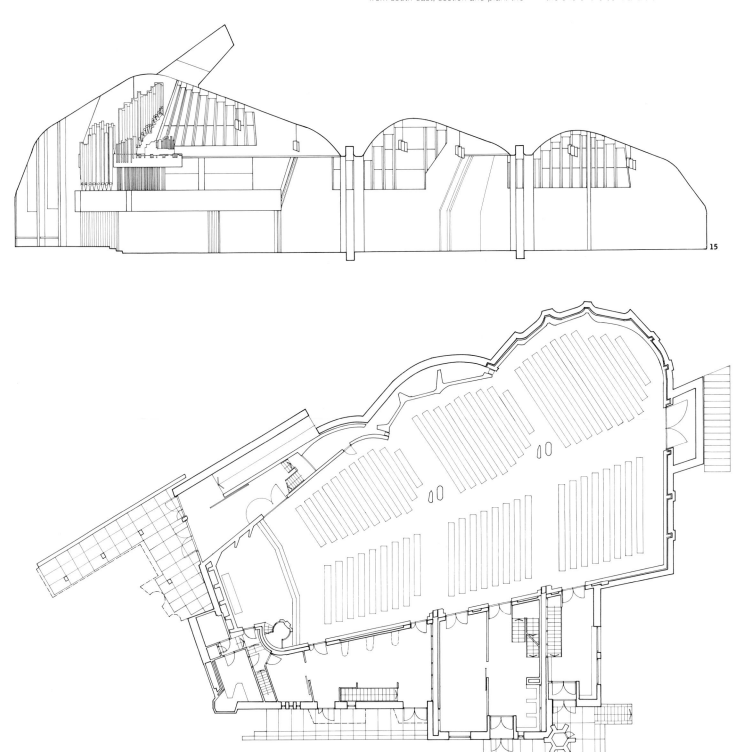

15

16

17 Interior of the Church of the Three
Crosses, Vuokkseniska, Imatra, 1957–9.

17

18–21 Church of the Three Crosses, Vuokkseniska, Imatra, 1957–9; views of altar, east windows and aisle: the church takes its name from the three crosses, which are postioned to the right, behind the side-lit altar. The double-layered windows in the east elevation are designed to accommodate the sliding partition that divides the interior into three, creating a complex spatial inter-play between inside and out.

19

20

angled to address the congregation, and how the long straight southern wall wraps around the pulpit and then meets the 'vanishing' end wall in a profile of exquisite tension, bulging outwards slightly above the pulpit to frame a space-within-a-space for the preacher.

But for all its undoubted brilliance as a design, the church does not quite convince as a piece of religious architecture. In part this is due to the bulky contrivance of the sliding partitions, which for all Aalto's skill in integrating them into the form, still introduce both an alien 'mechanical' element and a disturbing but perceptible smell of oil. In fact they have proved in practice far from convenient to use, and prone to breakdown. Where Aalto attempts to engage with church tradition directly, for example, in the altar area, which is paved with strips of marble, or the crown-of-thorns stained glass window, the effect is uneasily 'ecclesiastical'. It is by no means as successful, for example, as Le Corbusier's re-casting of stained glass as hand-painted windows at Ronchamp. And even where his skill and originality are most apparent, for example in the double-skin 'forest' windows, the result is not totally convincing; the windows are beautiful set-pieces, but do not really read as fully part of the space they illuminate.

That Aalto was acutely aware of the difficulties of creating an authentic modern church art, as early as 1925, is apparent from an article he wrote 'On Our Church Architecture'. In it he lamented the lack of 'religious feeling' in contemporary churches, and criticized 'art for churches', arguing instead that, 'a simple, unpretentious room' in which 'one single detail . . . a crucifix on a grey limestone wall, heightens the atmosphere of devotion, is a hundred times more beautiful than columns and ornamental flourishes framing an altarpiece many metres high'.[13] Spatially, the Imatra interior is far from simple, but the overall effect is surprisingly restrained, as befits the austere Lutheran tradition. However, compared with, what remains for me, the outstanding religious building in modern Finnish architecture – Erik Bryggman's Resurrection Chapel at Turku cemetery – there is something missing. Bryggman's design is easy to criticize as an unresolved admixture of themes and motifs drawn from National Romanticism, Nordic Classicism and Functionalism, but immediately captures the heart as a devotional space. As a formal composition, Imatra is in a different class, but still fails to create that 'religious feeling' to which Aalto aspired, and which, in this irreligious age, is amongst the most elusive of architectural qualities.

Whatever its ultimate shortcomings as a religious space – and many will

21

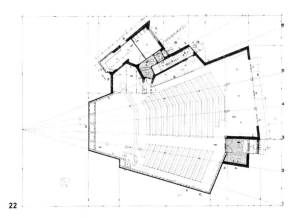

22

22, 23 Wolfsburg Church, Wolfsburg Germany, 1960–2, plan and interior: a later design in which Aalto was able only able to realize the plasticity of the Imatra interior in section. **24, 25** Church and parish centre, Riola di Vergato, Italy, 1966–7, plan and interior: executed after Aalto's death, the detailing owes little to his hand. **26** Seinäjoki Church, Seinäjoki, 1966. **27** Competition entry for the Lyngby Chapel and cemetery, Denmark, 1953: the *cavea*-like forms reflect Aalto's passion for Greek amphitheatres, they are proposed here on a scale akin to that of amphitheatrical villages built around natural harbours.

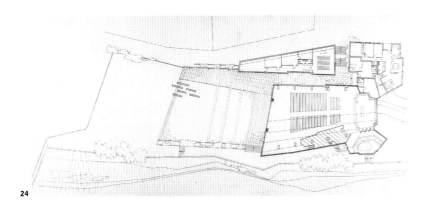

24

25

26

doubtless disagree with my assessment – the Imatra design is much the most successful of Aalto's churches.[14] Following its completion, he realized the delayed projects in Seinäjoki and Lahti, and two others in Wolfsburg in Germany, and Riola, near Bologna in Italy. Both are disappointing: the Wolfsburg design is in the same line as Imatra, but the plasticity of the space is realized only in section, and at Riola, unusually for Aalto, the structural system dominates the interior. This is a clumsy affair of reinforced concrete frames, like over-sized bent-wood chair legs (Aalto's development of the chair-leg as 'the little sister of the column' was as felicitous as its reverse here is disastrous). Executed posthumously, the detailing of the Riola design also owed little to Aalto's own hand and the result is sadly diagrammatic.

Of Aalto's later church designs, the most promising was the competition-winning scheme of 1967 for the Parish Centre of the Altstetten district of Zürich. This took up the theme of the concrete rib structure earlier proposed for Riola, but here the asymmetrical ribs are continuous with the ceiling and tightly integrated into the space. The asymmetrical, staggered arrangement of the seating neatly responds to the twin-centres of the Lutheran liturgy – altar and pulpit – as well as to the sacramental font, and the section, which is a kind of half-basilica.[15] As an urban composition, the building is also admirably conceived and it is a pity that it remained on the drawing-board. It promised a worthy successor to Imatra, with a comparable internal fluidity of space allied to a tight urban form, which also relates it to the line of the National Pensions Institute and Säynätsalo Town Hall. If churches presented Aalto with a slightly ambiguous challenge, the design of auditoria, theatres and concert halls held no such difficulties. Indeed,

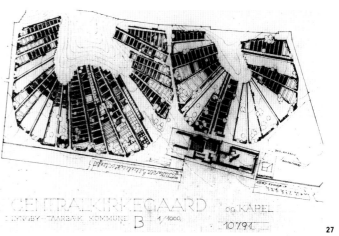

27

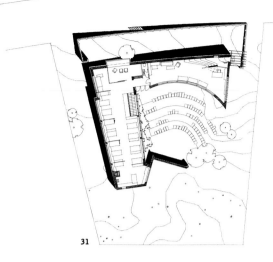

28

31

29

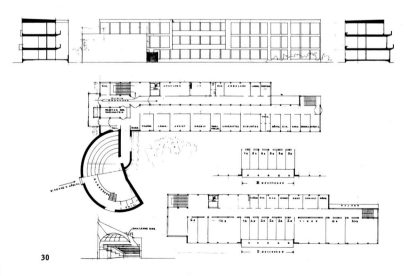

30

such was his fascination for the auditorium as a type that, throughout his career, he took every opportunity to introduce auditorium-like forms into his designs at every scale. They varied from lampshades stepped like circular staircases to the external amphitheatres at the Otaniemi campus and Aalborg Museum, right up to the vast *cavea*-like forms proposed for the cemetery at Lyngby. The studio wall and garden of his own office in Munkkiniemi are structured by an amphitheatrical arrangement of stone steps, the Greek-fluting of the base of the studio wall providing yet another reminder of Greece. Auditoria also enabled Aalto to explore the potential of freely curving forms, and the undulating walls of the New York Pavilion clearly lie behind many of his later designs. Surprisingly, given his love of the theatre as a form and institution, Schildt tells us that Aalto rarely attended performances; it nonetheless represented for him an ideal form of human association, 'an open and voluntary encounter of independent individuals'.[16]

Aalto's first opportunity to realize a large-scale auditorium, intended for concerts as well as lectures and congresses, came in 1955 with the commission from the Communist Party to design their House of Culture in Helsinki. Aalto responded to the twin components of the brief – administrative headquarters and auditorium – by juxtaposing a linear block of offices, organized along a central corridor, with a swelling mass of masonry, which appears freer in form than is actually the case, the plan being only a slightly asymmetrical variation on his favourite Greek amphitheatre form. In presenting the project, Aalto emphasized the importance of acoustics in the design of the space, which features various adjustable surfaces capable of acting as absorbers or reflectors in turn.[17] Spatially the interior is compelling, but although it performs adequately in acoustic terms, it has to be said that the amphitheatrical form is a less than ideal starting point, allowing little use to be made of first reflections from the side walls, now recognized as one of the keys to satisfactory acoustic design, especially for music.

The House of Culture was completed in 1958, and the following year Aalto won the competition for the opera house in Essen with one of the finest designs of his career. This sadly had to wait over thirty years to be completed. While the result is undeniably impressive, and follows the drawings Aalto left to the letter, it lacks the refinement which he would undoubtedly have brought to its detailing. The project itself was ideally suited to Aalto's approach, presenting, in urban terms, the challenge of

28, 31 Aalto's office, Munkkiniemi, Helsinki, 1955–6, exterior and plan: the amphitheatre type appeared here in its most intimate form. **29** Sketch of mountain, Delphi, 1953. **30** Competition entry for Zagreb Hospital, Zagreb, 1930–1: this was Aalto's first use of the amphitheatre form. **32–34** House of Culture, Helsinki, 1958, built for the Communist Party, exterior, and interior views of auditorium: this was Aalto's first opportunity to realize a large-scale auditorium, intended for concerts as well as lectures and congresses.

33

32

34

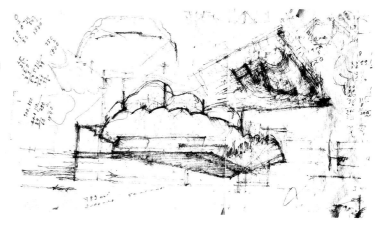

won the competition to design the building in 1959, and although he continued to develop the design throughout his life, it was not realized until over thirty years later.

39

relating both to the city fabric on one side and to parkland on the other. Aalto responded with a succession of cranked walls addressing the city and a vast undulating surface facing the park. The auditorium interior is clearly derived from the New York Pavilion and gives palpable form to the natural – and here specifically geological – metaphors that pervade his work, the multiple layers of balconies appearing in the model as great undulating strata of rock floating above the stalls below. This arrangement enabled Aalto to create an intimate relationship between audience and stage, appropriate to operatic performances, and to ensure that the auditorium appeared relatively full even when half empty: the balconies, clad in brilliant white Carrara marble, fulfil their architectural function regardless of the presence of people. The flank walls are lined with indigo-coloured acoustic surfaces formed with closely spaced timber slats, which lean towards the stage and are interleaved with curved pieces that recall the early wood experiments – or giant skis. Aalto first realized a large-scale version of such forms in the interior created for the Institute of International Education on a site adjoining the United Nations Building in New York, where they were adopted as a much watered-down version of a sculptural 'forest' originally proposed for the space.[18]

After having won the competition, Aalto worked on the design of Essen at intervals right through until his death in 1976, responding to the city's desire to make economies. Some of the ideas developed at Essen were incorporated in the design for Finlandia House in Helsinki, on which he began work in 1962. The concert hall was eventually built between 1967 and 1971, with the congress wing following in 1973–5. Finlandia Hall formed part of Aalto's grand plan for Helsinki, examined earlier, and was the only one of his 'Venetian palazzi' to be realized. It contains a concert hall to seat 1,750 people, a chamber music hall for 350, and a sub-divisible restaurant capable of accommodating up to 300 people. The irregular wedge-shaped auditoria rise from the predominantly horizontal mass and are entered from a grand public concourse at first-floor level, reached via broad and wonderfully inviting stairs. As you rise, the greatest and most fluid of all Aalto's interior landscapes unfolds against the armature of the long straight wall addressing Töölö Bay beyond. Faced with a space of such surpassing quality, it is difficult to comprehend how a critic as intellectually acute as Demetri Porphyrios could read it as an 'empty buffer that neutralize[s] the tension between dissimilar geometries of shifted grids,' and as a 'collection of loose fragments . . . fenced around to be safe from dispersal.'[19]

37

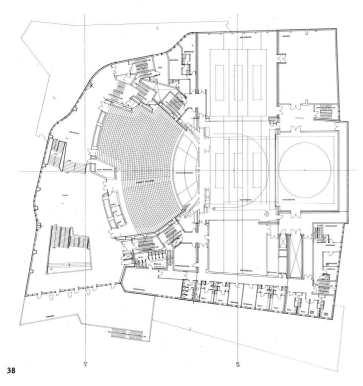

38

40–41 Finlandia Hall and Congress Centre, Helsinki, 1962–75, ground and foyer level plans. **42** View of Finlandia Hall, looking along the congress wing to the main entrance: set in a linear urban park along the shore of Töölo Bay, it houses the congress centre conference accommodation, the chamber music hall, and the main concert hall.

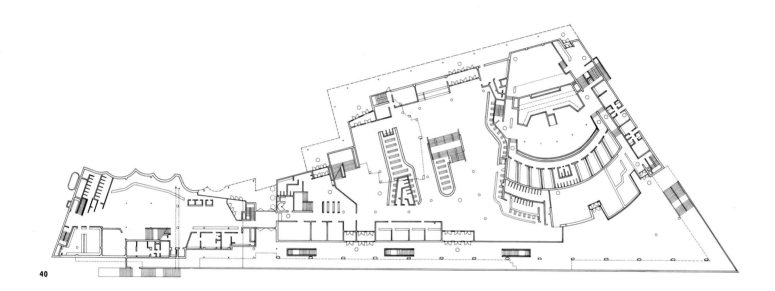

40

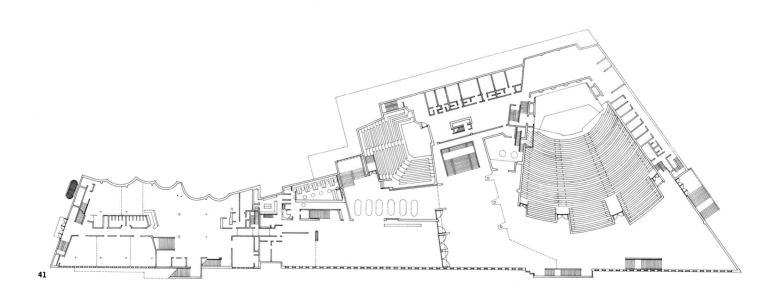

41

42

44

Aalto's spaces are difficult to read in plan, and their quality depends critically, as we noted in the discussion of the Festival Hall in Jyväskylä, on the quality of the detailing. Similarly shaped spaces in the later Jyväskylä city theatre feel flaccid compared with the fluid, but always tautly controlled foyers of Finlandia Hall, where, in the visual dialogue between the two rock-like masses of the auditoria, Aalto reveals yet again his total mastery of visual form. Spaces such as these defy normal kinds of formal analysis and can only be understood by moving through them: in plan, for example, the projections of the three columns, which support the circulation gallery, appear slightly contrived, the balconies wrapped around them too small to be of use. But in practice they are crucial to the modulation of the whole space, slowing, as it were, the flow of the foyer across to the glazed screen and creating a succession of angled forms, which, from below, rhyme with the corners beyond; at gallery level, they create tiny promontories from which to survey the space below, which expands far into the distance along the length of the foyer to the chamber music hall. Finally, and how typical of Aalto, despite being placed in a line and evenly spaced, they appear to be 'special' events in the space, asserting their individuality and refusing to be subject to the servitude of mere geometry.

As befits a national monument, characteristic features of the Finnish landscape are abstracted and evoked throughout Finlandia Hall, from the bold horizontal stratification of the overall massing, especially clear on the Töölö elevations, to the insistent forest-like vertical divisions of the glazed screen facing the bay. Similarly the hovering horizontals of the circulation galleries are counterpointed by closely spaced vertical slats, which seem to float weightlessly, pure textures hanging in space. With Asplund's Skandia cinema in mind, it is difficult not to read the interior of the auditorium itself as a highly abstracted landscape: the indigo blue acoustic screens suggests the night sky against which the white balconies hover like banks of cubist clouds, while the ceiling suggests a more literal cloudscape – an idea especially apparent in Aalto's sketches for the section.[20]

Visually the concert hall is a triumph, the most successful auditorium of his career, albeit slightly compromised by less than satisfactory sight-lines for some of the seats to the rear – and for most on the elegant balconies. But acoustically it proved to be a disaster due to an ill-conceived 'invention', which Aalto had been nurturing since the 1930s as a means of creating variable acoustics. His idea was to design an optically closed, but acoustically 'transparent' ceiling through which sound could enter a large void and be variably reflected back down. This he tried to achieve using large, conspicuous, solid 'louvres' (the 'clouds' in the metaphoric landscape). In practice the sound waves disappeared, never to return, and the space intended to be tuneable to resemble anything from a small lecture theatre to a vast cathedral, was less than ideal for any form of performance. To save the space, the ceiling was completely sealed and subsequent acoustic treatment has helped to enliven what remains an acoustically rather dry space. Although ill-conceived at the time, Aalto's idea of a 'transparent ceiling' was not without its possibilities, and with the advent of lighter, more permeable materials, a technically successful solution somewhat along the lines he envisaged was successfully adopted at Essen by the German executive architects.

The exterior of Finlandia Hall has found fewer admirers than its magisterial interiors, Quantrill describes it as a 'collection of monumental fragments'[21]. However, its over-sized main auditorium mass (the would-be acoustic cathedral) remains to my eyes a compelling composition, especially when seen from a distance across Töölö Bay. The entrance elevation facing the park, which runs along Mannerheimintie, is surprisingly mute, certainly less successful than the later congress wing that undulates in re-entrant curves around a succession of rock outcrops, architecture deferring to precious fragments of nature in the heart of the city. Quantrill, ever eager to assert the claims of Reima Pietilä, suggests that the plan of these bays leaves no doubt that their source of inspiration was Pietilä's Dipoli building at Otaniemi (the competition for which, incidentally, Aalto acted as judge).[22] However, as I suggested earlier in this chapter, they are clearly anticipated by the western-most bay of the Imatra church. Whatever their source, the result is a delightful wall, which ripples gracefully through the

45, 46 Finlandia Hall, Helsinki, 1967–71,
views of main foyer, looking down
and up the stairs, and of the cloakroom: designed to cope with the
Finns' bulky winter clothing,
the cloakroom is extensive.

45

46

47, 48 Main auditorium of Finlandia
Hall, Helsinki, 1967. **49** Cross section
of Finlandia Hall. **50** External view
of Finlandia Hall: the exterior of the
hall has found fewer admirers than
its magisterial interiors.

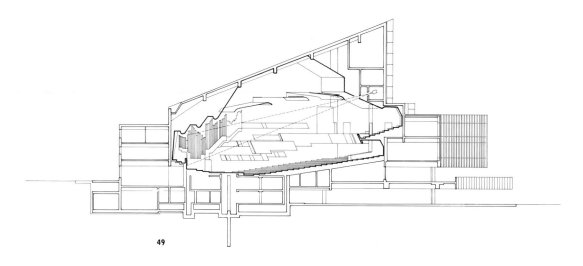

49

47

48

park and makes a wonderfully felicitous transition from ground to sky through layers of black granite, glass, vertically striated metal screens, white marble, and vertical sheets of glazing divided by prominent mullions and slender, staggered transoms. Internally, the ceiling meets the undulating wall by breaking into a series of shallow arcs, which then rise in a gentle curve to meet the glass in a manner reminiscent of the Seinäjoki library: in plan, the curves follow precisely the profile of the external walls, but seen in perspective they create a syncopated rhythm between the vertical and horizontal planes which, is a sheer delight – and pure Aalto.

While the visual qualities of the exterior of Finlandia Hall are open to debate, sadly, like the concert hall, it has suffered from major technical failings. Aalto's desire to transplant Italian culture to Finnish soil found expression here, as in several later prestigious cultural and commercial buildings, in the use of thin slabs of white Carrara marble as a cladding. In practice, the material has proved unsuitable for the Finnish climate and the panels have bent like bananas, to the point at which they now threaten to break loose from their fixings. The precise reasons are the subject of ongoing debate, but the combination of wide temperature variations, lack of ventilation behind the cladding, and too thin sheets has proved fatal, and the re-cladding of the building remains the subject of both financial and technical agonizing; meanwhile the exterior is increasingly being disfigured by cramps and safety nets.

Despite its undoubted technical shortcomings the Finlandia complex constitutes the major achievement of Aalto's later career during which, it has to be said, a slackening of control is apparent in many projects. Aalto ran a large and successful practice (the forthcoming *oeuvre complète* edited by Göran Schildt will catalogue over a thousand projects), so it is hardly surprising, especially as he advanced into his seventies, that by no means all received his close personal attention. Aalto's style is elusive and difficult to emulate, and even at the level of detail, where his repertoire might appear to be more amenable to codification, its qualities seem to elude all but the most gifted assistants. In the foyers and main auditorium of Finlandia Hall, however, we still see him at the height of his powers and the result is one of the great spatial sequences in modern architecture, in which, for all its grandeur, the individual never for a moment feels overwhelmed. Untainted by any hint of superficial opulence, Finlandia Hall stands as a powerful testimony to Aalto's vision of building for 'the little man', of an architecture in which the individual is always at the centre and in which we seem to walk and breathe more easily.

50

Conclusion

George Kubler, in his wonderful book *The Shape of Time*, remarks of artistic achievement that 'times and opportunities differ more than the degree of talent'. Aalto chose his time and place well. Born in a country where architecture was valued as a means of promoting national identity, he came to maturity as it finally achieved independence after 900 years of foreign rule. From the time of Engel in the early eighteenth century, fine public architecture had been accepted in Finland as a hallmark of civilized life, and the infrastructure to support an architectural culture was actively fostered. By Aalto's lifetime the polytechnical institute at which he studied was on a par with comparative institutions in Europe; an impeccably administered competition system had become the primary means of procuring public buildings to meet the needs of a rapidly modernizing nation; and Finnish industry had retained a base of craft skills and ability to respond flexibly to short-run production requirements.[1] (Although Aalto made more telling use than most of the opportunity to design purpose-made fittings, he was following an accepted pattern of professional practice rather than going against the grain).

Artistically, Aalto's timing was also perfect. National Romanticism, that glorious after-glow of nineteenth-century culture, was a spent force by the time he began his studies, but its ideal of the building as a 'total work of art' remained as a paradigm of the potential of architectural design to inform every aspect of an environment. The Nordic Classical style in which he began his career was an outward- and forward-looking movement, firmly rooted in the disciplines of the mainstream of Western architectural tradition, with the plan as the generator, clarity of form and refinement of proportion providing the bed-rock upon which Le Corbusier and others forged the formal language of Modernism. Although Aalto enthusiastically embraced the new movement when it reached the Nordic countries, it was clear to him from the outset that the 'International Style' must not become a stylistic formula, but a way of thinking and working to be adapted to specific cultures and landscapes. (The severe northern climate remains an inescapable imperative for the Finns, and one of the main sources of that 'wholesome Nordic sanity' greatly admired abroad.)[2] Few countries offered more fertile ground for the second phase of the Modernist adventure than Finland, and, despite the conservative culture against which Aalto and his fellow Modernists struggled in the 1930s, nowhere has innovative modern design been more widely accepted as the basis for public culture.

Like all great art, Aalto's architectural achievement is inseparable from this national context, but not bound by it. Writing in 1976, Manfredo Tafuri and Francesco Dal Co suggested that his 'historical significance has perhaps been rather exaggerated; with Aalto we are outside of the great themes that have made the course of contemporary architecture so dramatic. The qualities of his works have a meaning only as masterful distractions, not subject to reproduction outside the remote reality in which they have their roots.'[3] Seen from the perspective of the 1990s, however, the relevance of his work has never been more apparent. The resurgence of regressive, and increasingly violent, nationalism in Eastern Europe and elsewhere provides an urgent reminder of people's continuing desire for local identity within an expanding global culture. Similarly, as the devastating impact of the developed world's industrial economies on the planet's ecology are becoming all too apparent, the need to reconnect ourselves to nature, both physically and psychologically, is urgent – a thing the Finns have never lost sight of as regular and frequently protracted retreats to their beloved forests, lakes and saunas remain an indispensable part of life for most. Through their adaptation to the particularities of place – of people and landscape, culture and climate – Aalto's buildings offer themselves as precedents for a truly 'ecological' architecture. His achievement confirms that such an architecture can only emerge from a profound meditation upon architectural culture, engagement with appropriate materials and technologies, and a social contract which gives meaning and value to the architect's professional role.

It is not the least of the virtues of many of Aalto's buildings that they now appear ordinary, even unremarkable at first glance. Their appeal is to the whole human being, not merely to the eye – still less cameras or magazines with their insatiable appetite for the latest look. Believing that 'great ideas arise from the small details of life',[4] and in 'the commonplace as a crucial architectural factor',[5] Aalto always designed with the day-to-day needs of people in mind: unlike so much modern architecture whose icy, designerly perfection is soon violated, his buildings are enriched rather than diminished with use. When the occasion demanded it, he designed monuments that have stood comparison with the greatest architectural achievements of our time. However, it was his rare ability to create poetic places out of the everyday, which was born out of an intense concern for the needs of 'the little man' and love of his native landscape, that marks him out as one of the twentieth century's great architects.

Notes

Aalto and Finland

1 Sigfried Giedion, *Space Time and Architecture: The Growth of a New Tradition*, 3rd edition (Cambridge, Harvard University Press, 1959), p. 567.

2 Quoted in Göran Schildt, *Alvar Aalto: The Decisive Years* (New York, Rizzoli, 1986) p. 135. This is the second of Schildt's informative three-volume biography of Aalto. The first volume, *Alvar Aalto: The Early Years* was published in 1984, and the third, *Alvar Aalto: The Mature Years*, appeared in 1989. A fourth volume, comprising a *catalogue raisonnée*, is planned. Future references to the volumes will be given as Schildt, *Early Years*, *Decisive Years*, or *Mature Years*.

3 Giedion, op. cit., p. 565.

4 The phrase appears in Malcolm Quantrill, *Alvar Aalto: A Critical Study* (Helsinki, Otava, 1983), p. 7.

5 Göran Schildt (ed.), *Alvar Aalto: Sketches*, tr. Stuart Wrede (Cambridge, MIT Press, 1985). Future references to this key source of Aalto's writings will be given as *Sketches*.

6 Schildt, *The Decisive Years*; 1920s classicism has been the subject of widespread interest – see, for example, the exhibition catalogue *Nordic Classicism 1910–1930* (Helsinki, Museum of Finnish Architecture, 1982), the proceedings of The Second International Alvar Aalto Symposium, (*Classical Tradition and the Modern Movement*, Helsinki, 1985), and features in the recent studies of Aalto cited below. For Aalto's links with the Modern Movement see, in particular, Paul David Pearson, *Alvar Aalto and the International Style* (New York, 1978, reprinted London, Mitchell, 1989). The most comprehensive study to date remains Malcolm Quantrill, op. cit., and the most searching, provocative and contentious is Demetri Porphyrios, *Sources of Modern Eclecticism* (London, Academy Editions, 1982). The most stimulating formal analysis is Andres Duany, 'Principles in the architecture of Alvar Aalto', (*Harvard Architecture Review 3: Precedent and Invention*, New York, Rizzoli, 1986, pp. 104–19.)

7 Schildt, *Early Years*, p. 82. The biographical details are from the same source.

8 Albert Christ-Janer, *Eliel Saarinen* (University of Chicago Press, 1948), p. 1.

9 Elias Lönnrot, *The Kalevala*, tr. Keith Bosley, (Oxford, Oxford University Press, 1989), p. xiii.

10 Ibid., p. 204.

11 Aalto's speech is published in Schildt, *Sketches*, pp. 162–4.

12 The best general sources on the period are: John Boulton Smith, *The Golden Age of Finnish Art* (Helsinki, Otava, 1985); the exhibition catalogue *Finlande 1900* (Palais des Beaux Arts, Brussels,

1974); J. M. Richards, *800 Years of Finnish Architecture* (Newton Abbot, David and Charles, 1978); and Nils Erik Wickberg, *Finnish Architecture* (Helsinki, Otava, 1959). For a detailed discussion of the period see also Ritva Tuomi, 'On the search for a national style', *Abacus: Museum of Finnish Architecture Yearbook 1* (Helsinki, 1979), pp. 57–96.

13 As, for example, in Sixten Ringbom, *Stone, Style and Truth* (Helsinki, Finnish Antiquarian Society, 1987).

14 Quoted by Neil Kent, *The Triumph of Light and Nature: Nordic Art 1740–1940* (London, Thames and Hudson, 1987), p. 140.

15 Tuomi, op. cit., p. 61.

16 Alvar Aalto, 'Architecture in Karelia'. In Schildt, *Sketches*, pp. 80–3.

17 Marc Treib, 'Gallen-Kallela: a portrait of the artist as an architect', *Architectural Association Quarterly* (July–September 1975), pp. 3–13.

18 Aivi Gallen-Kallela, *Kalela* (guidebook, 1970), p. 19.

19 Sonck was arguably the most inventive of the National Romantic architects. The best source on his life and work is the exhibition catalogue, *Lars Sonck 1870–1956: Architect* (Helsinki, Museum of Finnish Architecture, 1982), in which his early work is examined by Paula Kivinen. See also Tuomi, op. cit.

20 Quoted by Marika Hausen in Marika Hausen, Kirmo Mikkola, Anna-Lisa Amberg and Tytti Valto, *Eliel Saarinen: Projects 1896–1923* (Cambridge, MIT Press, 1990), p. 33.

21 Ibid., p. 84.

22 Boulton Smith, op. cit., p. 133.

23 Ibid., p. 127.

24 Ringbom, op. cit., p. 172.

25 Ringbom, op. cit., p. 171.

26 Christ-Janer, op. cit., p. 9.

27 Vilhelm Helander and Simo Rista, *Modern Architecture in Finland* (Helsinki, Kirjayhtymä, 1987), p. 17.

28 Schildt, *Early Years*, p. 160.

29 For a detailed account of the building, see Marika Hausen, Anna-Lisa Amberg, Tytti Valto, *Hvitträsk: the Home as a Work of Art* (Helsinki, Museum of Finnish Architecture, 1987).

30 Richards, op. cit., p. 119.

31 Porphyrios, op. cit., p. 20.

32 The competition was for many years attributed to the Gesellius Lindgren Saarinen office, but research has confirmed that it was the work of Saarinen alone – and his solo effort was one of the factors in the break-up of the practice in 1905. See Hausen et al., *Eliel Saarinen*, op. cit., pp. 160–9.

33 Quantrill, op. cit., p. 11.

34 Riitta Nikula, *Armas Lindgren 1874–1929* (Helsinki, Museum of Finnish Architecture, 1988), p. 149. The article originally appeared in *Ateneum*, 9–11 (1901). Riitta Nikula described these opening sentences as 'classics of our architectural literature'.

35 Camillo Sitte's ideas were widely influential in the Nordic countries. The first edition of *Der Städtebau nach seinen künstlerischen Grundsätzen* was published in 1889. The first English translation appeared in America in 1949, with an introduction by Eliel Saarinen (whose own book *The City*, 1944, drew heavily on Sitte).

36 Quoted by Asko Salokorpi in 'Lars Sonck's town plans' (*Lars Sonck*, op. cit., p. 127).

37 Lars Sonck, 'Modern vandalism. Helsingfors Stadplan' was published in *Finsk Tidskrift* (1898, pp. 262–87), and *Teknikern*, (1898, no. 179, pp. 109–25).

38 Quoted by Salokorpi, op. cit., p. 129.

39 Lars Sonck, 'The arrangement of our small towns' (re-printed in English in *Abacus: Museum of Finnish Architecture Yearbook 3*; Helsinki, 1982; pp. 37–44).

40 See Jonathan Moorhouse, Michael Carapetian, Leena Ahtola-Moorhouse, *Helsinki Jugendstil Architecture 1895–1915* (Helsinki, Otava, 1987), for comprehensive documentation.

41 The article originally appeared in two newspapers and the journal *Arkitekten* (later re-named *Arkkitehti*). It was re-published in English in *Abacus: Yearbook 3*, op. cit., pp. 49–79.

42 Roger Connah, *Writing Architecture* (Cambridge, MIT Press, 1989), p. 106.

43 Hilding Ekelund, 'Modern Architecture and Tradition', *Abacus: Yearbook 3*, op. cit., p. 176.

44 Elizabeth Gaynor, *Finland: Living Design* (New York, Rizzoli, 1984), p. 9.

45 Ibid., p. 209.

46 Ibid., p. 11.

47 Johanna Jääsaari,. 'Urbanization, identity and the environment', *LEIF* (Life and Education in Finland), 2/1992, pp. 40–4.

48 See David Nicholson-Lord, *The Greening of the Cities* (London, Routledge, 1992).

49 Helander and Rista, op. cit., p. 17.

50 Juhani Pallasmaa, 'Architecture of the forest', *The Language of Wood* (Helsinki, Museum of Finnish Architecture), pp. 16–22.

51 See for example Scott Poole, 'The construction of silence', *The New Finnish Architecture* (New York, Rizzoli, 1992), pp. 28–45.

52 From various aphorisms on architecture by Blomstedt in the exhibition catalogue *Aulis Blomstedt, Architect. Thought and Form: Studies in Harmony* (Helsinki, Museum of Finnish Architecture, 1980).

Classical Foundations

1 Alvar Aalto, 'Motifs from Times Past', *Sketches*, pp. 1–2. Originally published in *Arkkitehti* in 1922.

2 In the newspaper *Iltalehti*, quoted in Schildt, *Early Years*, p. 113.

3 From an article published in *Ateneum* in 1901. Quoted in Boulton Smith, *The Golden Age of Finnish Art* (Helsinki, Otava, 1985), pp. 11–12.

4 Ibid., p. 117.

5 'Romantic Classicism' is used, for example, by Asko Salokorpi, *Modern Architecture in Finland* (London, 1970), p. 14; 'Swedish Grace' was a popular term used to describe the Swedish exhibits at the Paris Exhibition of Decorative Arts of 1925 – for a critical evaluation see Gillian Naylor, 'Swedish Grace . . . or the acceptable face of Modernism', ed. Paul Greenhalgh, *Modernism and Design* (London, Reaktion Books, 1990); 'Modern Classicism' was used by Henrik Andersson in 'Modern Classicism in Norden', *Nordic Classicism 1910–1930*, (Helsinki, Museum of Finnish Architecture, 1982) pp. 11–28; 'Light Classicism' has been proposed by Igor Herler, viz, 'Early Furniture and Interior Designs' in *Alvar Aalto Furniture*, ed. Juhani Pallasmaa (Helsinki, Museum of Finnish Architecture, 1984) pp. 14–59; for 'Doricism' see Demetri Porphyrios, 'Scandinavian Doricism: Danish and Swedish architecture: 1905–1930', *Classicism is Not a Style* (London, Architectural Design and Academy Editions, 1982), pp. 22–35; 'Nordic Classicism' was adopted as the title of a major touring exhibition organized by the Museum of Finnish Architecture in conjunction with colleagues in Denmark, Norway and Sweden, and its excellent catalogue (*Nordic Classicism 1910–1930*) remains the most comprehensive document on the period.

6 Karl Fleig (ed.), *Alvar Aalto, vol 1*, (Zürich, Artemis, 1963), p. 17. (The 3 volumes of this book were published in 1963, 1971 and 1978, respectively, by Artemis. Any future references to the works will be given as Fleig (ed.), *Alvar Aalto*, vol. I, II or III.) The Modernist style of architecture is always referred to as 'Functionalism' in the Nordic countries.

7 Schildt, *Early Years*, p. 68.

8 From an article in *Casabella*, no. 200, (1954), quoted in Schildt, *Mature Years*, p. 214.

9 Henrik Andersson, art. cit.

10 Schildt, *Decisive Years*, p. 11.

11 Quoted by Kirmo Mikkola in 'The transition from classicism to functionalism in Scandinavia', from the proceedings of The Second International Alvar Aalto Symposium (*Classical Tradition and the Modern Movement*, Helsinki, 1985), pp. 42–73. For a

discussion of new materials see also Henrik Andersson, 'Swedish architecture around 1920', in *Nordic Classicism*, op. cit., pp. 123–35.

12 Quoted by Karl-Erik Michelsen in 'On the borderline of the Modern: architects vs. masterbuilders' (ed. Pekka Korvenmaa, *The Work of Architects: the Finnish Association of Architects 1892–1922*; tr. Jüri Kokkonen; Helsinki, The Finnish Building Centre, 1992; pp. 91–110).

13 Quoted from Paulsson's book *Den nya arkitekturen* (Stockholm, 1916) p. 110, by Kirmo Mikkola, op. cit., p. 64.

14 See Björn Linn, 'The transition from classicism to functionalism in Scandinavia', in *Classical Tradition and the Modern Movement*, op. cit., pp. 74–105.

15 Herler, art. cit., p. 16.

16 See Simo Paavilainen, 'Martti Välikangas and the classicism of the 1920's in Käpylä', *Arkkitehti*, no. 1 (1981), pp. 27–31, and English text on p. 51. The district plan was by Birger Brunila and Otto-Iivari Meurman.

17 Asko Salokorpi, op. cit., p. 15.

18 J. S. Sirén, 'As ideals of form change: opaque and transparent reality', a lecture given in 1950 and reprinted in *J. S. Sirén: Architect 1889-1961*, exhibition catalogue, tr. The English Centre (Helsinki, Museum of Finnish Architecture, 1989). Sirén was the leading academic classicist, and Professor of Architecture at the Helsinki Institute of Technology from 1931–57. He designed the major monument of the 1920s, the Finnish Parliament House.

19 Henrik Andersson, art. cit., pp. 13–15, and Lucius Burckhardt (ed.), *The Werkbund* (London, The Design Council), pp. 105–6.

20 Heinrich Tessenow, *Hausbau und dergleichen* (Berlin, 1916); for first English translation see 'House-building and such Things' (tr. Wilfried Wang, *9H*, no.8, 1989), pp. 9–33.

21 Simo Paavilainen, 'Classicism of the 1920's and the classical tradition in Finland', tr. Edward Grew, *Abacus: Museum of Finnish Architecture Yearbook* (Helsinki, 1979), pp. 98–129. Paavilainen notes that Hilding Ekelund, one of the leading classicists in Finland, obtained a copy of Tessenow's book in the year of its publication.

22 For developments in Denmark see Lisbet Balsler Jørgensen, 'Classicism and the functional tradition in Denmark' in *Nordic Classicism 1910–30*, op. cit., pp. 50–6. Petersen's articles on 'Textures' and 'Contrasts' are published in the same catalogue, pp. 35–8 and 45–8; 'Colours' appeared posthumously.

23 See Janne Ahlin, *Sigurd Lewerentz, Architect 1885–1975* (Cambridge and London, MIT Press,

1987), pp. 35–7.

24 See Henri Schildt, 'Erik Bryggman in Italy', *Erik Bryggman 1891-1955* (exhibition catalogue; tr. Jüri Kokkonen; Helsinki, Museum of Finnish Architecture, 1991), pp. 80–107.

25 Quoted in ibid., p. 107, note 37.

26 See Schildt, *Early Years*, pp. 131–7 for details. Aalto's wife, Aino Marsio, graduated two years before him and had already been to Italy in 1921. Her contribution to their work is the matter of much debate. Schildt's view, for which he cites the evidence of assistants in the office, is that she was primarily the best critic of his ideas whose judgment Aalto trusted implicitly: the drawings in the Aalto Archive await thorough research, but Aino's hand is apparent as 'editor' of Aalto's endless flow of invention. She organized the office and kept Aalto's mercurial talent under control; and contributed significantly to interior and furniture design, glassware etc. – during the 1930s she was integral to the development of Artek, which was established to produce Aalto furniture.

27 Ibid, p. 103.

28 Quoted from Hilding Ekelund, 'Italia la bella', *Arkkitehti 2* (1923) in Simo Paavilainen, 'Classicism of the 1920's and the classical tradition in Finland', *Nordic Classicism 1910–30*, op. cit., p. 103.

29 The passage was inspired by a landscape in one of Mantegna's frescos in the Chapel of the Eremitani in Padua and is taken from a fragment of text, intended as an introduction to an unwritten book, and published in Schildt, *Decisive Years*, pp. 11–12.

30 A Spanish architect, Fernando Chueca, who helped host Aalto on a visit to Madrid in 1952 oberved that: 'In Italy he did not deign to look at the monuments of the Renaissance and Baroque so that he could seek out what was essential to the Mediterranean tradition. He is only interested in the spontaneous design of towns and villages, especially in mountain areas. Many times, over the following days, he asked us to show him "towns rooted in the earth"; that was how he put it.' Quoted in Göran Schildt, 'The travels of Alvar Aalto: notebook sketches', *Lotus 68* (1991), pp. 34–47.

31 The article is quoted in full in Schildt, *Early Years*, pp. 206–10.

32 Ibid., pp. 252–5.

33 Alan Colquhoun, *Modernity and the Classical Tradition: Architectural Essays 1980–87* (Cambridge and London, MIT Press), p. 30.

34 Porphyrios, 'Scandinavian Doricism', *Classicism is Not a Style*, op. cit., p. 23.

35 Ibid., p. 31.

36 Quoted by Kirmo Mikkola, art. cit., p.55.

37 See Stuart Wrede, *The Architecture of Erik Gunnar Asplund* (Cambridge and London, MIT Press, 1980), p. 33.

38 Schildt, *Early Years*, p. 280.

39 Ibid., p. 141. The quotation is from a newspaper interview published following a visit in 1926 to Sweden and Denmark, during which Aalto saw the Woodland Chapel – with which he would surely already have been familiar from publications, and from his earlier contact with Asplund in 1923 following the Gothenburg exhibition.

40 From a collection of essays in Swedish entitled 'Efforts in architecture' (1963). Quoted by Wrede, op. cit., p. 126.

41 *Arkitektur* was the main Swedish architectural review; somewhat confusingly it first appeared as *Tekniski Tidskrift*, then as *Arkitektur* from 1918 to 1921, and thereafter as *Byggmästeren*.

42 First published in Paul David Pearson, *Alvar Aalto and the International Style* (New York, Mitchell, 1978), p. 20.

43 See Lars Pettersson (ed.), *Finnish Wooden Church* (exhibition catalogue; tr. Jüri Kokkonen; Helsinki, Museum of Finnish Architecture, 1989).

44 E.g. Malcolm Quantrill, *Alvar Aalto: A Critical Study* (Helsinki, Otava, 1983), p. 35.

45 See Nils C. Finn, 'The Workers' Club of 1924 by Alvar Aalto: The Importance of Beginnings', *Perspecta 27* (New York, Rizzoli, 1992), pp. 52–75.

46 From the original specification re-published in English in Satu Mattila (ed.), *Työväentalo*, tr. Jonathon Moorhouse, 2nd enlarged edition, (Jyväskylä, Alvar Aalto Museum), 1984.

47 Surprisingly, none of the accounts of the Lister Courthouse with which I am familiar refer to the treatment of the entrance foyer as an 'outside' space, but the intention seems clear enough.

48 Schildt draws attention to this ambiguity in a lucid discussion of Aalto's treatment of space: *Early Years*, p. 223.

49 Elina Standertskjöld notes that the decoration is 'a detailed copy of the Holy Sepulchre of the Rucellai San Pancrazzio chapel in Florence', in *The Line: Original Drawings from the Alvar Aalto Archive* (exhibition catalogue; ed. Kristiina Paatero and tr. Hildi Hawkins; Helsinki, Museum of Finnish Architecture, 1993), p. 23.

50 The felicitous analogy of an apse was first suggested, to my knowledge, by Göran Schildt: *Early Years*, p. 226.

51 Alvar Aalto, 'E. G. Asplund in Memoriam', *Sketches*, pp. 66–7. Originally published in *Arkkitehti*.

52 Wrede, op. cit., p. 85.

53 Beautifully described by Simo Paavilainen as

follows: 'The grey asphalt of the pavement extends into the portico, linking the lobby to the street. In the middle of the lobby there stands a rectangular colonnade. First one comes from an exterior to an interior, but still as to an exterior. Then one descends a flight of stairs to the foyer, whose walls and ceiling were originally dark green. In the middle of the greenness stands a brightly-lit, white-walled building with cornices and red velvet doorways – a white building in a deep green space. The visitor believes that he is entering a building, but inside he finds a moon and a deep blue arch of sky. The visitor is surprised three times with variation of the same theme on his way from the sooty facade to a seat in front of the glimmering silver screen.' Quoted by Colin St John Wilson in 'Gunnar Asplund and the dilemma of classicism' (*Gunnar Asplund 1885–1940: The Dilemma of Classicism*, ed. Vicky Wilson; exhibition catalogue; London, Architectural Association, 1988).

54 Elias Cornell, 'The sky as a vault . . . Gunnar Asplund and the articulation of space', in Claes Caldenby and Olof Hultin, *Asplund* (Stockholm, Arkitektur Förlag/Gingko Press, 1985), pp. 23–33. (First published in Swedish in 1961.)

55 Written for the pilot issue of the magazine *Aitta* (which means 'shed' or 'storehouse', and refers to the most important building in a traditional farm in which the family's belongings were stored – equivalent of the better known Norwegian 'lofts'), and re-printed in full in Schildt, *Early Years*, pp. 214–18.

56 The version painted c. 1432–4 for San Domenico at Cortona, now in the city's Museo Diocesano.

57 Schildt, *Early Years*, p. 226.

58 Ibid., p. 218.

59 Simo Paavilainen, 'Classicism of the 1920s and the classical tradition in Finland', *Nordic Classicism 1910–30*, op. cit., p. 117.

60 Le Corbusier, *Towards a New Architecture*, tr. F. Etchells (London, Architectural Press, 1970), p. 174. Originally published as *Vers Une Architecture*, in Paris, in 1923.

61 Quoted in Reyner Banham, *Theory and Design in the First Machine Age* (London, Architectural Press, 1960), p. 33.

62 Designed by Hack Hampmann, Aage Rafn, Holger Jacobsen and Arne Jacobsen.

63 Schildt, *Early Years*, p. 141.

64 'PH' after the name of the designer, Poul Henningsen, founder-editor of the short-lived radical Danish magazine *Kritisk Revy* (1926–8), and a friend of Aalto.

65 Schildt, *Decisive Years*, p. 28.

66 Fleig (ed.), *Alvar Aalto*, vol 1, pp. 18–19.

67 Quantrill, op. cit., p. 42. He also reads the main stair as a 'ship's gangplank'.

68 As pointed out by Pearson (op. cit., p. 66), who also describes the original design for the auditorium as having a 'restrained Wagnerschule elegance' (p. 67).

69 In a brilliant interpretation of the Viipuri project, to which I am indebted, Simo Paavilainen suggests that Aalto may well also have been inspired by his friend Sven Markelius's first 1926 project for the Helsingborg Concert Hall, which featured a huge portal decorated with frescos and a Skandia-like foyer. See 'Viipuri Library – the 1927 Competition Entry', *Acanthus*, tr. Michael Wynne-Ellis (Helsinki, Museum of Finnish Architecture, 1990), pp. 8–17. The yearbook also includes valuable essays on the building by Kristiina Nivari and Sergei Kravchenko.

70 Ibid., pp. 15–16.

71 Kirmo Mikkola, art. cit., p. 60.

72 Simo Paavilainen, 'Viipuri Library – the 1927 Competition Entry', op. cit., p. 17.

Functionalism and Beyond

1 Alvar Aalto, 'The dwelling as a problem', *Sketches*, pp. 29–33. Originally published in *Domus* (a Finnish design magazine) in 1930.

2 Schildt, *Decisive Years*, p. 31.

3 Raija-Liisa Heinonen, 'Some aspects of 1920s classicism and the emergence of Functionalism in Finland', *Alvar Aalto: Architectural Monographs 4* (London, Academy Editions, 1978), pp. 20–7. Heinonen's study is based on her Ph. D. thesis, which is not available in English. For the relevant passage in Le Corbusier, see *Towards a New Architecture*, (tr. F. Etchells; London, Architectural Press, 1970), pp. 165–72

4 Schildt tells us that Markelius's telephone number appears much the most frequently in Aalto's bills for trunk calls made from his Turku office (*Decisive Years*, p. 47). Markelius was more ideologically and theoretically inclined than Aalto, and their contacts became infrequent after the mid 1930s, when the friendship with Asplund again came to the fore, until his premature death in 1940.

5 Ibid., p. 48. Heinonen gives the title as 'The tendencies of rationalism in modern architecture'.

6 Heinonen writes that '[Hilding] Ekelund later claimed that this lecture marked the breakthrough of Functionalism into Finland' (op. cit., p. 24), but Ekelund clearly felt she misinterpreted the interview he gave her, referring dismissively to this claim as being by 'an obscure writer' (*Arkkitehti*, 7–8, 1976), p. 28.

7 See Karl-Erik Michelsen, 'On the borderline of the Modern: architects vs. master-builders' (*The Work of Architects: the Finnish Association of Architects 1892–1922*; tr. Jüri Kokkonen; Helsinki, The Finnish Building Centre, 1992), p. 92.

8 It was published in *Arkkitehti*, no.2 (1928) and is reprinted in full in *Nordic Classicism 1910-1930*, (Helsinki, Museum of Finnish Architecture, 1982), pp. 85–8.

9 Erik Bryggman, 'Functionalism', originally published in the Turku newspaper *Åbo Underrättelser* on 30 October 1928, re-printed in *Erik Bryggman 1891–1955* (tr. Jüri Kokkonen; exhibition catalogue; Helsinki, Museum of Finnish Architecture, 1991), pp. 12–104.

10 See Kerstin Smeds, 'The Image of Finland at the World Exhibitions 1900–1992', in Peter B. MacKeith and Kerstin Smeds, *The Finland Pavilions: Finland at the Universal Expositions 1900-1992*, tr. John Arnold (Kustannus Oy City, 1993), pp. 12–104.

11 Alvar Aalto, 'Letter from Finland', *Sketches*, pp. 34–5. Originally published *Bauwelt*, 25 (1931).

12 CIRPAC: French acronym for 'International Committee for the Recognition of Contemporary Problems of Architecture'. For a summary of the activities of CIAM, see Le Corbusier, *The Athens Charter*, tr. Anthony Eardley (New York: Grossman, 1973). Originally published anonymously in French in 1943, and again, under Le Corbusier's name, in 1957.

13 In Kirmo Mikkola, 'From the technological to the humane: Alvar Aalto versus Functionalism', from the proceedings of the Second International Alvar Aalto Symposium (*Classical Tradition and the Modern Movement*; Helsinki, 1985), p. 139. Anonymity and uniformity were intended, as Le Corbusier noted without a hint of self-mockery, to encourage team work by 'dimming the occasionally embarrassing aura of certain masters who were too well known' (op. cit., p. 15).

14 Schildt, *Decisive Years*, p. 196.

15 Walter Gropius, 'Programme of the Staatliches Bauhaus in Weimar' in Ulrich Conrads (ed.), *Programmes and Manifestoes on 20th-Century Architecture*, tr. Michael Bullock (London, Lund Humphries, 1970), pp. 49–53.

16 Alvar Aalto, 'Housing construction in existing cities', *Sketches*, pp. 3–6. Originally published *Byggmästeren* (1930).

17 Quoted in Raija-Liisa Heinonen, 'Some aspects of 1920s classicism and the emergence of Functionalism in Finland', op. cit., p. 24, from an article published in the *Turun Sanomat* (7 October 1928).

18 Alvar Aalto, 'Letter from Finland', *Sketches*, pp.

34–5. Originally published in *Bauwelt*, 25 (1931).

19 Alvar Aalto, 'The dwelling as a roblem', *Sketches*, pp. 29–33. Originally pubished in the Finnish design magazine *Domus* (1930).

20 Re-printed in Ulrich Conrads, op. cit., pp. 117–20

21 Alvar Aalto, 'Speech for the Hundred-Year Jubilee of the Jyväskylä Lycée', *Sketches*, pp. 162–4.

22 Alvar Aalto, 'Stockholm Exhibition 1', *Sketches*, pp. 29–33. From a newspaper interview published in the *Åbo Underrättelser* (22 May 1930).

23 Alvar Aalto, 'The Stockholm Exhibition II', *Sketches*, pp. 18–20. Originally published in *Arkkitehti* (1930).

24 See p. 29 above.

25 Schildt, *Decisive Years*, p. 23.

26 See W. Boesiger and O. Stonorow (eds.), *Le Corbusier and Pierre Jeanneret: The Complete Architectural Works, Volume 1, 1910–29* (Zürich, Les Editions d'Architecture, 1964), p. 128–9. The five points were: the column ('pilotis') grid; free plan; roof garden; free facade; and ribbon windows.

27 Simo Paavilainen, 'Classicism of the 1920's and the classical tradition in Finland', tr. Edward Grew, *Abacus: Museum of Finnish Architecture Yearbook* (Helsinki, 1979), p. 127.

28 See Schildt, *Decisive Years*, pp. 44–5, and Malcolm Quantrill, *Alvar Aalto: A Critical Study* (Helsinki, Otava, 1983), p. 56. Pearson gives an accurate account of the structural rationale, but suggests that Aalto may have derived the forms from Markelius's rather different columns on the Helsingborg Concert Hall.

29 Schildt, *Decisive Years*, pp. 44–5.

30 Göran Schildt (*Early Years*, pp. 134–5) prints an 'almost Futuristic text' in which the student Aalto described his first flight in 1921.

31 Nikolaus Pevsner, *A History of Building Types* (London, Thames and Hudson, 1976), p. 158.

32 Le Corbusier, op. cit., p. 55.

33 Le Corbusier, *Radiant City*, tr. Pamela Knight, Eleanor Levieux and Derek Coleman (London, Faber and Faber, 1964), p. 100. Le Corbusier presented his 'Radiant City' proposals at the 1930 Brussels congress of CIAM; the book was originally published in French in 1933.

34 Text written by Aalto in 1933, re-printed in *Paimio 1929-1933: Architecture by Alvar Aalto* (tr. Jonathan Moorhouse and Leena Ahtola-Moorhouse; Jyväskylä, Alvar Aalto Museum, 1988; no. 1).

35 Quoted in P. Morton Shand, 'A tuberculosis sanatorium in Paimio', *The Architectural Review* (August 1933), pp. 85–90.

36 A surprisingly makeshift corrugated metal roof

on a timber substructure was added shortly afterwards to provide extra protection.

37 Paul David Pearson (*Alvar Aalto and the International Style*; New York, Mitchell, 1978, pp. 84–7) elaborates the influence of Duiker at length. The influence of the Zonnestraal as the 'source' for the Paimio plan has assumed the status of fact: it is referred to as such in most recent discussions of the building. Schildt downplays Aalto's supposed 'borrowings' and disputes Pearson's assertion (op. cit., p. 229, note 2) that Aalto met Duiker at a conference on concrete construction in Paris, in May 1928, as according to the office records the Aaltos did not leave for Paris until June (Schildt, *Decisive Years*, p. 54).

38 Pearson, op. cit., p. 85.

39 Quantrill, op. cit., pp. 52–4.

40 See note 17 above.

41 Schildt, *Decisive Years*, p. 194.

42 Andres Duany, 'Principles in the architecture of Alvar Aalto', *Harvard Architecture Review 3: Precedent and Invention* (New York, Rizzoli, 1986), p. 118. Duany actually says this was the 'only' reason for the inflection, ignoring the other factors.

43 Simo Paavilainen, 'Classicism of the 1920's and the classical tradition in Finland', op. cit., p. 127. Asplund's Snellman House is the classic example of an angled wing, and its first floor also featured perspectival manipulations; the Puu-Käpylä housing area in Helsinki includes a splendid false perspective 'square'.

44 To preserve anonymity, competitors identified their projects with a 'motto' of their own choosing, normally a word or phrase which evoked the spirit of the design.

45 Schild, *Decisive Years*, p. 56.

46 Alvar Aalto, 'Between humanism and materialism', *Sketches*, pp. 130–3. Text of a lecture given in Vienna in 1955.

47 Alvar Aalto, 'The humanizing of architecture', *Sketches*, pp. 76–8. Originally published in *Technology Review* in 1940.

48 For the development of Aalto's furniture, see Göran Schildt, *The Decisive Years*, op. cit., pp. 62–87, and p. 101–4 below.

49 See Elina Standertskjöld, 'Alvar Aalto's Standard Drawings 1929-1932', *Acanthus 1992: The Art of Standards* (Helsinki, Museum of Finnish Architecture), pp. 89–111.

50 The Modernist idea of 'types' is discussed at length in Reyner Banham, *Theory and Design in the First Machine Age* (London, The Architectural Press, 1960) and differs significantly from the more recent neo-rationalist interest in 'typology': see Alan Colquhoun, 'Typology and Design Method', in

Essays in Architectural Criticism (Cambridge and London, MIT Press, 1981), pp. 43–50.

51 During the 1960s the sanatorium was gradually changed to become a general hospital, but as the newly taken colour photographs show, it has survived (sun-terraces excepted) remarkably well and – judging from what they say on visits – is still greatly admired by its staff and patients.

52 The League of Nations was designed in 1927, and the Centrosoyus building in 1928, although construction took until 1935. Pearson (op. cit., p. 229, note 12) suggests the Centrosoyus as the likely 'source'.

53 Within two years of completion it was published in leading magazines in Britain, the USA, Italy and Sweden: see the comprehensive bibliography in *Alvar Aalto Synopsis: Painting, Architecture and Sculpture* (Basle, Birkhäuser Verlag), p. 218.

54 Sigfried Giedion, *Space Time and Architecture: The Growth of a New Tradition*, 3rd edition (Cambridge, Harvard University Press, 1959), p. 575.

55 Henry-Russell Hitchcock and Philip Johnson, *The International Style: Architecture Since 1922* (New York, W. W. Norton, 1932). Originally published to accompany a major exhibition at the Museum of Modern Art in New York.

56 Alvar Aalto, 'Rationalism and Man', *Sketches*, p. 47. Lecture given in 1935.

57 For an amusing and devastating early critique of the *gesamtkunstwerk* see Adolf Loos, 'The Poor Little Rich Man', *Adolf Loos: Spoken into the Void – Collected Essays 1897–1900*, with an introduction by Aldo Rossi, tr. Jane O. Newman and John H. Smith (Cambridge and London, MIT Press, 1982), pp. 124–7.

58 Its discovery amused the archivists, as Aalto was generally reluctant to acknowledge any 'influence'. Related to the author by Riitta Nikula, former Research Director of the Museum of Finnish Architecture.

59 See Elina Standertskjöld, 'The Turku Fair of 1929 – A Manifesto of Functionalism', *Erik Bryggman 1891–1955*, op. cit., pp. 108–33.

60 Ibid., p. 130.

61 See Pearson, op. cit., pp. 112–23; Simo Paavilainen, 'Viipuri Library – The 1927 Competition Entry' and Kristiina Nivari 'Viipuri Library from Paper to Final Building', *Acanthus 1990* (Helsinki, Museum of Finnish Architecture), pp. 9–17 and pp. 19–33.

62 In the first volume of his work, Aalto (Fleig (ed.), *Alvar Aalto*, 1963) recorded that 'the building was totally destroyed in the Russo-Finnish War and stands today in ruins. Since this war Viipuri is no longer Finnish territory' (p. 44). This report of

its destruction has been perpetuated in other accounts, which took Aalto at his word, but although the building suffered serious neglect it was scarcely damaged in the war, and the nearest it came to 'destruction' was a proposal to 'renovate' it in neo-classical garb according to 'the requirements of modern Soviet architecture' – see Sergei Kravchenko, 'Viipuri Library Ruined?', *Acanthus 1990*, op. cit., pp. 35–45; also Michael Spens, 'Aalto's missing masterpiece', *The Architectural Review* (May 1993), pp. 74–9. Viipuri remains in Russia, and joint Russian-Finnish efforts are now being made to restore the building.

63 This suggestion has been made by Simo Paavilainen, 'Viipuri Library – the 1927 Competition Entry', op. cit., p. 16.

64 Pearson, ever eager to identify a specific source for Aalto's ideas, suggests that the roof-lights were derived from the conical vault we noted in the previous chapter at Hakon Ahlberg's pavilion, at the 1923 Gothenburg exhibition.

65 Alvar Aalto, 'The Trout and the Mountain Stream', *Sketches*, pp. 96–8. Originally published in *Domus* (1947).

66 George Baird, in an elegant essay of great insight, offers a similar interpretation of the long 'scala regia' staircase in the main building at Jyväskylä University. See George Baird, *Alvar Aalto* (London, Thames and Hudson, 1970), p. 16.

67 'Prospect and Refuge' theory has formed the basis for an extensive body of literature on the experience and aesthetics of landscape. See Jay Appleton, *The Experience of Landscape* (Chichester and New York, John Wiley, 1975), pp. 146–63.

68 Quoted in P. Morton Shand, 'The Viipuri Library in Detail', *The Architectural Review* (March 1936), pp. 107–14.

69 Quoted in Schildt, *Decisive Years*, p. 114, from a newspaper article published in the newspaper *Hufvudstadsbladet* (13 November 1935).

70 Ibid. This letter was written in 1941, but Aalto's interest in Japanese architecture stems from 1933 when he was designing the final version of the library. In 1933–5 Alvar and Aino maintained a close friendship with a previous Japanese ambassador and his wife.

71 The phrase is George Baird's, and used to describe a generic characteristic of Aalto's treatment of handrails. Baird, op. cit., p. 15.

72 Alvar Aalto, 'The Humanizing of Architecture', *Sketches*, pp. 76–9. Originally pubished in *Technology Review* (1940), the quotation is from a discussion of the Viipuri Library.

Dwelling in the Modern World

1 Alvar Aalto, 'The Dwelling as a Problem', *Sketches*, pp. 29–33.

2 Le Corbusier, *Towards a New Architecture*, tr. F. Etchells (London, Architectural Press, 1970), p. 247.

3 *Le Corbusier and Pierre Jeanneret: The Complete Architectural Works 1910–1929* (Zürich, Les Editions d'Architecture, 1964), pp. 98–104. 'The New Spirit' – *L'Esprit Nouveau* – was the title of a magazine Le Corbusier produced with the painter Amedée Ozenfant.

4 Walter Gropius, 'Dessau Bauhaus – principles of Bauhaus production', in Frank Whitford, *Bauhaus* (London, Thames and Hudson, 1984), p. 205.

5 Alvar Aalto, 'The Dwelling as a Problem', *Sketches*, pp. 29–33.

6 In his essay 'The Painter of Modern Life' Baudelaire defined 'modernity' as 'the ephemeral, the contingent, the half of art whose other half is eternal and immutable' and observed that the modern painter concentrated on 'the passing moment and all the suggestions of eternity that it contains'. See Marshall Berman, 'Baudelaire: Modernism in the streets', *All That is Solid Melts into Air: The Experience of Modernity* (New York, Simon and Schuster, 1982), pp. 131–71.

7 In all Finnish architectural competitions, as well as awarding prizes, other schemes of merit are 'purchased' to compensate the architects for their efforts.

8 Schildt, *Decisive Years*, p. 26.

9 Externally it looked like a traditional rural building, with a double-pitched turf roof; the plan was again open and organized around a central, square fire. See Paul David Pearson, *Alvar Aalto and the International Style* (New York, Mitchell, 1978), pp. 73–5, for illustrations and discussion.

10 Schildt, *Decisive Years*, p. 26.

11 Alvar Aalto, 'From doorstep to living room', in Schildt, *Early Years*, p. 216.

12 This was actually a self-contained section of the whole apartment, to which Pauli and Märta Blomstedt, Erik Bryggman, and Werner West also contributed.

13 The 'Haus am Horn' was designed by the painter Georg Muche and included numerous innovations, including specially designed carpets, tiles, lights, and radiators, as well as furniture – for much of which Breuer was also responsible. The kitchen was one of the first realized examples of the application of scientific work-study methods to kitchen design – it was the first kitchen in Germany with wall cupboards above lower-level and continuous work-surfaces, with the main

work area in front of the window rather than at a central table. See Frank Whitford, *Bauhaus*, op. cit., pp. 143–5, and Elina Standertskjöld, 'Alvar Aalto's Standard Drawings', *Acanthus 1992: The Art of Standards* (Helsinki, Museum of Architecture, 1992), pp. 103–5.

14 Schildt, *Decisive Years*, p. 69.

15 Alvar Aalto, 'The dwelling as a problem', op. cit., p. 33.

16 We noted above (p. 40) that the article published in *Sosialisti* (December 1927), included illustrations of Le Corbusier's *Ville Contemporaine*.

17 Described in Schildt, *Decisive Years*, pp. 266–7, and illustrated in Leonardo Mosso, *L'opera di Alvar Aalto* (Milan, Edizioni di Communità, 1965), pp. 66–7.

18 Alvar Aalto, 'European reconstruction brings to the fore the most critical problem facing architecture in our time', *Abacus: Museum of Finnish Architecture Yearbook 3* (1983), pp. 120–39. Originally published in *Arkkitehti*, 5/1941.

19 Introduction to the Villa Mairea by Aalto in *Villa Mairea*, ed. Satu Mattila, tr. Jonathan Moorhouse and Leena Ahtola-Moorhouse (Jyväskylä, Alvar Aalto Museum, 1981).

20 Fleig (ed.), *Alvar Aalto*, vol. 1, p. 65.

21 Schildt, *Decisive Years*, pp. 210–11.

22 Ibid., pp. 130–1.

23 For comprehensive documentation of the building see the author's *Villa Mairea* (London, Phaidon Press, 1992).

24 Quoted in Pearson, op. cit., p. 168.

25 Schildt, *Decisive Years*, p. 154.

26 For a comparison of Fallingwater and the Villa Mairea see Alexander Purves, '"This goodly earth"', *Perspecta 25* (1989), pp. 179–201. The author's emphasis, in a fine essay, is on the contrasting attitudes to nature and the landscape, which the houses embody, but he does not comment on the connection between them. For a recent Bachelard-inspired phenomenological interpretation see Scott Poole, 'Elemental matter in the Villa Mairea', *The New Finnish Architecture* (New York, Rizzoli, 1992), pp. 18–27.

27 Aalto's description in *Villa Mairea*, ed. Satu Mattila , op. cit.

28 Klaus Herdeg, *The Decorated Diagram* (Cambridge and London, MIT Press, 1985), pp. 29–35. Herdeg's book contains an excellent analysis of the Villa Mairea from which I have derived several insights.

29 Ibid., p. 32.

30 In Satu Mattila (ed.), *Villa Mairea*, op. cit.

31 Schildt, *Early Years*, p. 153 and pp. 214–39.

32 Ibid., pp. 220–3.

33 Alvar Aalto, 'The influence of construction and materials on modern architecture', *Sketches*, pp. 60–3. Lecture given at the Nordic Building Conference in Oslo, 1938.

34 Paul Bernoulli, the site architect, related this fact in an interview with my colleague, Darren Stewart Capel, in August 1991. The redundant piece was initially eliminated by the structural engineer and only later reinstated – in the difficult war conditions Bernoulli actually had to fetch the steel section himself.

35 Ibid.

36 See Pierre Daix, *Cubists and Cubism*, tr. R. F. M. Dexter (London, Skira/Macmillan, 1983), p. 99.

37 Juhani Pallasmaa, 'Villa Mairea – fusion of Utopia and Tradition' in Y. Futagawa (ed.), *GA: Alvar Aalto: Villa Mairea, Noormarkku, Finland, 1937–39* (Tokyo, A. D. A. Edita, 1985).

38 Kenneth Frampton, 'Modern Architecture 1920–45', GA Document, no 3 (1983), p. 411.

39 In the same interview referred to in note 28 above.

40 Schildt, *Decisive Years*, pp. 117–8.

41 'The dwelling as a problem', *Sketches*.

42 Christian Norberg-Schulz, *The Concept of Dwelling* (New York, Electa /Rizzoli, 1985), p. 89.

Nature and Culture

1 Alvar Aalto, 'National planning and the goals of culture', in Aarno Ruusuvuori, *Alvar Aalto 1898–1976*, tr. The English Centre (Helsinki, Museum of Finnish Architecture, 1985), p. 34. (The article is reproduced in full in *Sketches*, but I prefer the translation of this passage in the memorial exhibition catalogue).

2 The sauna was built after the war.

3 As Chairman of SAFA, Aalto was closely involved in a range of initiatives by architects during the war years. See Pekka Korvenmaa, 'War destroys and organizes: architects and crisis', (*The Work of Architects: the Finnish Association of Architects 1892–1922*; tr. Jüri Kokkonen; Helsinki, The Finnish Building Centre, 1992), pp. 113–27.

4 Alvar Aalto, 'European reconstruction brings to the fore the most critical problems facing architecture in our time', *Abacus: Museum of Finnish Architecture Yearbook 3* (Helsinki, 1982), pp. 121–39. Originally published in *Arkkitehti*, 5/1941.

5 Ibid.

6 In an article written for the Swedish book *Arkitektur och samhälle* (Architecture and Society) – Schildt, *Decisive Years*, pp. 216–17.

7 Alvar Aalto, 'Rationalism and man', *Sketches*, pp. 47–51.

8 One of the first writers to advance an 'ecological'

interpretation of Aalto's work and suggest the 'niche' analogy was Kirmo Mikkola in 'From the technological to the humane: Alvar Aalto versus Functionalism', from the proceedings of the Second International Alvar Aalto Symposium (*Classical Tradition and the Modern Movement*; Helsinki, 1985).

9 See the short text by Aalto, 'The white table' in Fleig (ed.), *Alvar Aalto*, vol III.

10 Ibid., 'Interview with Alvar Aalto', pp. 232–3.

11 For an excellent discussion of the topic see Mark A. Hewitt, 'The imaginary mountain: the significance of contour in Alvar Aalto's sketches', *Perspecta 25* (New York, Rizzoli, 1989), pp. 163–77.

12 Such 'biological thinking', for example, pervades the *Athens Charter* (tr. Anthony Eardley; New York, Grossman, 1973), and in it Le Corbusier drew the same analogy between the biological cell and the dwelling as a 'social cell' (p. 101).

13 Quoted in Kirmo Mikkola, 'From the technological to the humane: Alvar Aalto versus Functionalism', op cit., p. 150.

14 Alvar Aalto, 'E. G. Asplund in Memoriam', *Sketches*, p. 66. Asplund's second wife, Ingrid Hindmarsh, recalled that Aalto visited Asplund almost every month during the period 1934–40 to discuss ideas and projects (Stuart Wrede, *The Architecture of Erik Gunnar Asplund*; Cambridge and London, MIT Press, 1980; note 112, p. 237).

15 Schildt, *Decisive Years*, pp. 218–21.

16 Published in English in 1930 as *The New Vision*. See also Krisztina Passuth, *Moholy-Nagy* (London, Thames and Hudson, 1985).

17 László Moholy-Nagy, *The New Vision*, rev. edition, tr. Daphne M. Hoffmann (London, Faber and Faber, 1939), pp. 13–14 and p. 198.

18 Schildt, *Early Years*, p. 38.

19 Schildt, *Decisive Years*, p. 56. Poul Henningsen's remark appeared in his magazine *Kritisk Revy*, which was published between 1926 and 1928.

20 Alvar Aalto, 'Rationalism and man', *Sketches*, pp. 47–8.

21 Alvar Aalto, 'Wood as a building material', *Sketches*, p. 142. Originally published in *Arkkitehti* in 1956.

22 Demetri Porphyrios, *Sources of Modern Eclecticism* (London, Academy Editions, 1982), p. 81.

23 Alvar Aalto, 'Rationalism and man', *Sketches*, p. 50.

24 The details of this brief discussion are drawn from Göran Schildt's detailed study of Aalto's furniture 'The decisive years', in the comprehensively illustrated catalogue *Alvar Aalto Furniture*, (ed. Juhani Pallasmaa; Helsinki, Museum of Finnish Architecture, 1982), pp. 62–89. See also Pekka

Suhonen, *Artek* (Helsinki, Artek, 1985). (Available only in Finnish and Swedish, it contains a wealth of fascinating historical illustrations).

25 In *The Architectural Review* (December 1933), p. 220. H. de Cronin Hastings was the magazine's editor.

26 Schildt points out that Aalto rejected the later wood-forming techniques, which permitted double-curves to be formed in plywood (quickly exploited by Charles and Ray Eames) as not being as appropriate an expression of the 'language of wood fibres'. (*Mature Years*, p. 115.)

27 Alvar Aalto, 'The trout and the mountain stream', *Sketches*, pp. 96–8.

28 The 'organic' nature of Aalto's forms has obscured the essentially 'classical' qualities of his work. This has been compounded by misleading attempts to ally him to the 'organic' strand of Modernism exemplified by architects such as Hans Scharoun and Hugo Häring. See, for example, Vladimír Slapeta, 'Organic architecture in Central Europe and Alvar Aalto' (*Abacus: Helsinki, Museum of Finnish Architecture Yearbook 2*, 1980; pp. 115–39).

29 George Baird was the first to draw attention to the fact that Aalto's buildings 'give the impression of *having been aged in advance*' (his emphasis). Citing Aalto's rumoured conviction 'that his buildings will not be ready to be judged until they were fifty years old', he suggested they were 'metaphors of ruins' in response to the ruinous state into which many Modern Movement buildings rapidly descended: in fifty years' time 'the invulnerable timelessness' of Aalto's work would finally become apparent. Baird, *Alvar Aalto* (London, Thames and Hudson, 1970), pp. 11–13.

30 Such trellises were first introduced on a large scale in the 1935 competition project for the Moscow Embassy, and were proposed to run right across Baker House at MIT – an idea which was dropped, but would have been in sympathy with the Institute's membership of the 'Ivy League'.

31 See Jussi Rautsi, 'Alvar Aalto's urban plans', *Transactions 9* (1986), vol. 5, no. 1, pp. 49–61.

32 See Schildt, *Mature Years*, pp. 74–5.

33 Illustrated in Winfried Nerdinger, *Walter Gropius*, tr. Andreas Solbach and Busch-Reisinger Museum (Berlin, Bauhaus Archive, 1985), p. 160.

34 Whilst in the USA, following the success of the 1939 Pavilion at the New York World Fair, Aalto proposed the establishment of a research institute to examine such problems, and subsequently hoped to persuade the US to sponsor his experimental plan for 'An American Town in Finland'. His appointment as a Professor at MIT was based on a research proposal to look at housing and postwar reconstruction. See Schildt, *Decisive Years*,

pp. 177–9 and *Mature Years*, pp. 28–40.

35 In the manuscript of an article discovered by Schildt, *Early Years*, p. 160.

36 For example in the conversation with Göran Schildt published in *Sketches*, pp. 170–2, which originally appeared as the preface to an exhibition catalogue in 1967.

37 See the excellent article, from which I have gained several valuable insights: Kerstin Smeds, 'The image of Finland at the world exhibitions 1900–1992' (*The Finland Pavilions: Finland at the Universal Expositions 1900–1992*; tr. John Arnold; Kustannus Oy City, 1993), p. 61.

38 Ibid., p. 24. In 1932, the architect Bertel Jung – who contributed substantially to Lars Sonck's work – created a scandal following a lecture by Gunnar Asplund at the Nordic Building Conference held in Helsinki, by going up to the table at which Asplund and Aalto were seated and exclaiming 'so this is where the bolshevik architects are' – which Aalto greeted by punching him on the ear. (Schildt, *Decisive Years*, pp. 86–7.)

39 Alvar Aalto, 'Architecture in Karelia', *Sketches*, pp. 80–3. Originally published in *Uusi Suomi*, 1941: the nationalist tone of the article is in part explained by its having been written during the Continuation War with Russia.

40 Ibid.

41 Alvar Aalto, 'National planning and cultural goals', *Sketches*, pp. 99–102. Originally published in *Suomalainen Suomi*, 1949. Although these comments (and those quoted below) date from later in his life, they confirm attitudes that were clearly forming during the 1930s – as the work demonstrates. In fact, Aalto's ideas – at least as expressed in words – developed very little after this period.

42 These phrases are taken from Aalto's inaugural lecture ('Art and technology', *Sketches*, pp. 126–9) on being installed as a member of the Finnish Academy in 1955.

43 Peter B. MacKeith, 'Architecture and image in the Finland Pavilions', in MacKeith and Smeds, op. cit., p. 122. Smeds's and MacKeith's essays contain the fullest accounts to date of the Paris and New York pavilions. Smeds essay, in particular, contains much valuable new material on the content of the exhibitions and the political/cultural context.

44 Fleig (ed.), *Alvar Aalto*, vol. 231, pp. 74–81.

45 From an interview in *Hufvudstadsbladet* (24 March 1937), quoted in Smeds, art. cit., pp. 53–4.

46 His disagreements became so serious that he did not attend the opening ceremony and persuaded Le Corbusier and Fernand Léger to write letters of protest. See Smeds, art. cit., p. 48, and Schildt,

Decisive Years, pp. 134–5.

47 Schildt, ibid.

48 Smeds, art. cit., pp. 70–1.

49 Quantrill, *Alvar Aalto: A Critical Study* (Helsinki, Otava, 1983), p. 81.

50 MacKeith, op. cit., p. 134.

51 Fleig (ed.), *Alvar Aalto*, vol. 1, p. 80. The relevant paragraph in German and French is omitted in the English translation.

52 Aalto introduced large, cusped flutes around the base of the curved wall of his later studio, built in 1955.

53 Aalto developed purpose-made tiles, produced by the leading Finnish ceramics company Arabia, for the interiors and exteriors of many of his later buildings.

54 Smeds, art. cit., p. 48.

55 Quantrill confidently asserts that the motto was 'clearly inspired by Shakespeare's image of the march of Birnam Wood to Dunsinane' (Macbeth IV, i, 92), and MacKeith repeats the 'derivation' (op. cit., p. 122) without attributing it to a speculation by Quantrill – thus do conjectures pass into 'fact'.

56 Schildt, *Decisive Years*, p. 161. The competition was a limited 'run-off' between the best six entrants in an earlier open competition, also won by Ervi.

57 Fleig (ed.), *Alvar Aalto*, vol. 1, p. 124.

58 The famous 'Savoy' vase won first prize in a competition in 1936 run by Karhula-Iittala, one of the leading Finnish glass companies, to find exhibits for Paris. Its name came later – from the Savoy Restaurant for which the Aaltos designed the interior in 1937, and which still remains in its original condition. The vase has become immensely popular, almost a national emblem of the 'naturalness' of Finnish design – and life.

59 Smeds, art. cit., p. 53.

60 Aalto later designed a timber screen for Artek, which consists of narrow slats of wood with half-round ends bound together by metal cables – it naturally assumes waving shapes when stood up.

61 Drawings show the disks as a random pattern, but in fact they were finally pre-fabricated in 1.2 metre squares (MacKeith, op. cit., p. 146).

62 Fleig (ed.), *Alvar Aalto*, vol. 1, p. 130.

63 The details of the exhibition are taken from Smeds, art. cit.

64 Ibid.

65 'Finnish Pavilion, New York Fair', *The Architectural Review* (August 1939), p. 64.

66 Smeds notes that Aalto commented in his report – as if to modify his vulgar Marxism – that 'it would be narrow and mistaken to consider eco-nomic activity exclusively as a backdrop for culture, so underneath the economic display there will be brief texts and a presentation on the cultural-historical factors that, perhaps more clearly in Finland than elsewhere, are the wellspring of economic progress'. (op. cit., p. 58)

67 Ibid, p. 54.

68 Ibid.

69 Aalto refers to 'typical forms and symbols existing in the Finnish landscape' in his description (Fleig (ed.), *Alvar Aalto*, vol. 1, p. 124).

70 The phrase is Kerstin Smeds's – and a good one (art. cit., p. 56).

71 Colin St John Wilson, 'Alvar Aalto and the State of Modernism', *Architectural Reflections: Studies in the Philosophy and Practice of Architecture* (London, Butterworth Architecture, 1992), p. 91. Originally given as a lecture at the 1st International Alvar Aalto Symposium, in 1979.

72 The Finnish lakes were first suggested, so far as I can find, by Sigfried Giedion (*Space, Time and Architecture: the Growth of a New Tradition*; 3rd edition; Cambridge, Harvard University Press, 1959; p. 581); office gossip liked to attribute it to his sketching style, in which such quivering lines regularly appear as notations for natural forms and in the tentative search for form; (the 'gossip' is reported by William C. Miller, 'A thematic analysis of Alvar Aalto's architecture', *Architecture and Urbanism* (October 1977), pp. 15–38); abstract art, especially that of his friend Hans Arp, has been suggested by numerous writers – the work of Ben Nicholson, who also came under Arp's influence in the early 1930s, contains curves almost identical to those of the Savoy vase.

73 From an unpublished fragment of text printed in Schildt, *Decisive Years*, p. 12.

74 Ibid, p. 138.

75 'Nature is, of course, freedom's symbol. Sometimes it is even nature that creates and maintains the concept of freedom': Alvar Aalto, 'National planning and cultural goals', *Sketches*, p. 102.

76 Fully illustrated in Fleig (ed.), *Alvar Aalto*, vol. III, pp. 14–17.

77 Aino Marsio-Aalto died in 1949 and Aalto married Elsa Kaisa Mäkiniemi in 1952; she had been the job architect in his office for Säynätsalo Town Hall. He always referred to her as 'Elissa', a form which she duly adopted.

78 Schildt, *Mature Years*, p. 267.

79 The quotation and subsequent details are from Alvar Aalto, 'Experimental house, Muuratsalo', *Sketches*, pp 115–16. Originally published in *Arkkitehti* in 1953.

80 Ibid.

81 For a range of typical examples from the 1960s see Anna-Liisa Ahmavaara (ed.), *Asumme Lähellä Luontaa* (Helsinki, Otava, 1967), chapter 4, pp. 70–94. The title means 'Living close to nature'.

82 See Colin St John Wilson, 'Alvar Aalto and the State of Modernism', *Architectural Reflections: Studies in the Philosophy and Practice of Architecture* (London, Butterworth Architecture, 1992), p. 123 and illustration no. 53 on p. 122 from Sir William Gell's *Pompeiana*.

83 First proposed, I think, by Simo Paavilainen 'Classicism of the 1920's and the classical tradition in Finland', (*Abacus: Museum of Finnish Architecture Yearbook*, tr. Edward Grew; Helsinki, 1979), p. 129.

84 Quantrill (op. cit., p. 143) makes the connection to Blomstedt – without any suggestion of irony – and sees the building as an experiment 'with a geometrical *gestalt* that is seemingly quite alien to the main line of his development'. Blomstedt became an influential teacher and theorist and formed the core of an 'opposition' to Aalto's pragmatic, empirical line. See Juhani Pallasmaa, 'Man, Measure and Proportion: Aulis Blomstedt and the tradition of Pythagorean harmonics' (*Acanthus 1992*; Helsinki, Museum of Finnish Architecture), pp. 7–25, and Erkki Vanhakoski, 'Aulis Blomstedt – works 1926–1979', in ditto, pp. 33–73.

85 Aldo Rossi, *A Scientific Autobiography* (Cambridge and London, MIT Press, 1981), p. 2.

86 Sir Uvedale Price, 'On the Picturesque, &c.' in Sir Thomas Dick Lauder, *Sir Uvedale Price on the Picturesque: with an Essay on the Origin of Taste and Much Original Matter*, (London, Wm. S. Orr, 1862), p. 82. Uvedale Price's essay was originally published in 1792.

87 Demetri Porphyrios, *Sources of Modern Eclecticism*, op. cit., p. 63.

88 Ibid., p. 12. Whilst Aalto never fully accepted some of the tenets of the main stream of architectural Modernism, to say that he was 'never a Modernist' flies in the face of the evidence – unless, of course, all 'true' Modernists have to relinquish any contact with history and espouse a total commitment to a 'quantifiable functionalism' – which would reduce the 'movement' to an insignificant blip in history . . . I do less than justice to Porphyrios's well-researched and densely argued thesis, but I find his neo-rationalist/Marxian mugging of Aalto to be based on a highly selective use of material and a provocative, but highly selective reading of many of the buildings.

89 Alvar Aalto, 'The influence of construction and materials on modern architecture', *Sketches*, pp. 61–5.

80 Ibid.

90 Schildt, *Decisive Years*, p. 230.

91 Alvar Aalto, 'Speech for the hundred-year jubilee of the Jyväskylä Lycée', *Sketches*, p. 163.

Sense of Place

1 Alvar Aalto, 'European reconstruction brings to the fore the most critical problems facing architecture in our time', *Abacus 3: Museum of Finnish Architecture Yearbook* (Helsinki, 1982), p. 131

2 Alvar Aalto, 'Between humanism and materialism', in *Sketches*, pp 130–3.

3 Sigfried Giedion, *Space Time and Architecture: the Growth of a New Tradition*, third edition (Cambridge, Harvard University Press, 1959), p. 567.

4 Juhani Pallasmaa began writing and lecturing about 'forest space' and 'forest geometry' in the early 1980s. See his essay 'Architecture of the forest', *The Language of Wood* (Helsinki, Museum of Finnish Architecture), pp. 16–22.

5 Alvar Aalto, 'National-international', *Sketches*, p 168. Originally published in *Arkkitehti* in 1967.

6 Clement Greenberg, 'Modernist Painting', ed. Francis Frascina and Charles Harrison, *Modern Art and Modernism: A Critical Anthology* (London, Harper and Row, 1982), pp 5–10. Originally published in *Art and Literature* (no. 4, spring, 1965), pp. 193–201.

7 Hendrick P. Berlage, *Gedanken über Stil in der Baukunst* (Leipzig, 1905).

8 Quoted in Stephen Kern, *The Culture of Time and Space* (London, Weidenfeld and Nicolson, 1983), p. 182

9 Ibid., p. 318 – the last phrase in an excellent book.

10 These figures are based on official statistics: the number of lakes varies, according to published accounts, from 50,000 upwards – Aalto gave it as 80,000 in his lecture in Vienna.

11 In 'Alvar Aalto', special issue of *Architecture and Urbanism* (May 1983), p. 14.

12 It is interesting to note that in *Modern Painters* (vol. v, part vi, ch. ix, sections 4–5) John Ruskin remarks in a section on 'The Pine' that it brings 'all possible elements of order and precision'.

13 Viz. Adrian Stokes's question at the end of *The Quattro Cento*: 'Or do we all need light in place of lighting . . . must we always turn South?' (in Lawrence Gowing, *The Critical Writing of Adrian Stokes, Volume 1: 1930–37*; London, Thames and Hudson, 1978; p. 180 – originally published in 1932).

14 Finnish colleagues tell me that this is a common way of referring to the sound of a kettle drum – which would be consistent with the 'marching woods' idea of the winning scheme.

15 See sketch reproduced in Michael Spens, 'Aalto's

missing masterpiece', *The Architectural Review* (May 1993), pp. 74–9.

16 In Juhani Pallasmaa (ed.), *Aulis Blomstedt, Architect: Thought and Form. Studies in Harmony*, op. cit., p. 19.

17 See Caroline Constant, *AA Files* (to be added).

18 'Abstract representation' seems the best short-hand to describe Aalto's procedure; it was first coined, I believe, by Charles Jencks in 'The perennial architectural debate', *Abstract Representation Architectural Design Profile no 48* (7/8-1983), pp. 4–22.

19 Neil Levine, 'Abstraction and representation in modern architecture: The International Style of Frank Lloyd Wright', *AA Files* (no. II, spring 1986), pp. 3–21.

20 Ibid., p. 16.

21 Le Corbusier, *The Radiant City*, tr. Pamela Knight, Eleanor Levieux and Derek Coleman (London, Faber and Faber, 1964), pp. 55–6.

22 Schildt, *Decisive Years*, p. 131. See also *Early Years*, pp. 220–2.

23 The phrase is from Christian Norberg-Schulz, *Genius Loci: Towards a Phenomenology of Architecture* (London, Academy Editions, 1980), p. 42.

24 Schildt, *Decisive Years*, p. 131.

25 See Juan Pablo Bonta, *The Interpretation of Architecture: A Study of Expressive Systems in Architecture* (London, Lund Humphries, 1979). Bonta points out that it is frequently an 'idea about a building, rather than an actual building . . . [which] can affect the course of architectural history' (p. 217), and I would not wish to suggest that any 'seeing' was an experience of raw sense data – but Bonta gives telling examples of writers repeating not merely the interpretations, but the errors of others.

26 For the concept of 'concretization' as applied to architecture, see Christian Norberg-Schulz, *Existence, Space and Architecture*, (London, Studio Vista, 1971), and *Genius Loci*, op. cit.

27 E.g. by Stephen Groak, 'Notes on Responding to Aalto's Buildings', in *Alvar Aalto: Architectural Monographs 4* (London, Academy Editions, 1978), p. 105.

28 Alvar Aalto, 'European reconstruction brings to the fore the most critical problems facing architecture in our time', *Abacus: Museum of Finnish Architecture Yearbook 3* (1983), p. 131.

29 For a fuller account of the building and comprehensive photographs and drawings, see my monograph, *Town Hall, Säynätsalo* (London, Phaidon Press, 1993).

30 Schildt, *Mature Years*, pp. 143–4.

31 Demetri Porphyrios, *Sources of Modern Eclecticism* (London, Academy Editions, 1982), p. 55.

32 Malcolm Quantrill, *Alvar Aalto: A Critical Study*,

(Helsinki, Otava, 1983), p. 134.

33 Text in the Alvar Aalto Archive.

34 Schildt, *Mature Years*, pp. 157-8.

35 Ibid., p. 158. Original in Aalto Archive.

36 Alvar Aalto, 'Architecture in Karelia', *Sketches*, p. 82.

37 In his RIBA Discourse in 1957, Aalto attributes the '1 millimetre' remark to one of his 'chief lieutenants' (*Sketches*, p. 145). He told Malcolm Quantrill that the 'planning module should always be as small as possible, preferably not much more than a centimetre' (Quantrill, op. cit., p. 243). Aalto's disinterest in the 'harmony of numbers' was much derided in the 1950s – a favourite saying in the Aulis Blomstedt circle was that he was 'churning butter from Corbu's cream' (Roger Connah, *Writing Architecture*; Cambridge, MIT Press, 1989; p. 151).

38 Text of lecture in the Alvar Aalto Archive.

39 Schildt, *Mature Years*, p. 159. The quotation is from a paper in the Alvar Aalto Archive.

40 Demetri Porphyrios, *Sources of Modern Eclecticism*, op. cit., p. 31.

41 Ibid., pp. 160–1.

42 Malcolm Quantrill, op. cit., pp. 134–5.

43 Ibid., p. 134.

44 Ranulph Glanville, 'Finnish Vernacular Farmhouses', *Architectural Association Quarterly*, vol. 9, no. 1 (1977), pp. 36–51. Glanville's essay concludes with an intriguing but highly speculative comparison of the additive character of much Finnish architecture and the 'agglutinative' structure of the Finnish language.

45 Text in the Alvar Aalto Archive.

46 Hannah Arendt, *The Human Condition* (Chicago, University of Chicago Press, 1958), pp. 52–3.

47 The phrase 'the little man' (sometimes translated as 'the small man', appears throughout Aalto's writings and lectures from the mid-1930s onwards. By it he referred to 'everyman' – himself included – all individuals in his eyes being dwarfed and threatened by the massive machinery of modern civilization.

48 Susanne K. Langer, *Feeling and Form* (London, Routledge and Kegan Paul) 1953, p. 99.

49 Yi-Fu Tuan, *Space and Place: The Perspective of Experience* (Minneapolis, University of Minnesota Press, 1977), pp. 183–4.

50 Schildt, *Mature Years*, p. 157.

51 Quoted by Christian Norberg-Schulz, 'Meaning in Architecture', *Architecture Meaning and Place* (Rizzoli, New York, 1987) p. 24.

52 In Alison Smithson (ed.), *Team 10 Primer* (London, Studio Vista, 1968), p. 96.

53 See Frederick Gutheim, *Alvar Aalto*

(New York, George Braziller, 1960), p. 29.

Individual, Institution, City

1 Alvar Aalto, 'Speech for the hundred-year jubilee of the Jyväskylä Lycée', *Sketches*, p. 163.

2 Quoted in *Nordic Classicism 1910–1930*, (Helsinki Museum of Finnish Architecture, 1982), p. 90.

3 Alvar Aalto, 'Culture and technology', *Sketches*, pp. 94–5. Originally published in *Suomi-Finland – USA*, 1947.

4 Alvar Aalto, 'Between humanism and technology', *Sketches*, p. 130. Aalto refers to Chaplin in the same passage. See also Schildt, *Decisive Years*, pp. 9–11.

5 Alvar Aalto, 'The architect's conception of Paradise', *Sketches*, pp. 157–9. Lecture given to a meeting of Swedish city planners in Malmö in 1957.

6 Alvar Aalto, 'The geography of the housing question', *Sketches*, pp. 44–6. Article originally published in *Arkitektur och sanhälle*, 1932.

7 Alvar Aalto, 'The architect's conception of paradise', op. cit., p. 159.

8 Alvar Aalto, 'Speech for the hundred-year jubilee of the Jyväskylä Lycée', op. cit., p. 162.

9 Kerstin Smeds, 'The image of Finland at the world exhibitions 1900-1992', in Peter B. MacKeith and Kerstin Smeds, *The Finland Pavilions: Finland at the Universal Expositions 1900–1992*, tr. John Arnold (Kustannus Oy City, 1993), p. 74.

10 Benedict Ziliacus, 'Finland', in Erik Zahle (ed.), *Scandinavian Domestic Design* (London, Methuen, 1963), p. 23.

11 Alvar Aalto, 'Lecture upon installation in Finnish Academy', *Sketches*, pp. 126–9. Lecture delivered on 3 October 1955.

12 Göran Schildt, 'Alvar Aalto and the classical tradition', the proceedings of The Second International Alvar Aalto Symposium, *Classical Tradition and the Modern Movement* (Helsinki, 1985), pp. 107–37.

13 Peter Kropotkin, *Mutual Aid: A Factor of Evolution*, (London, Freedom Press, 1987), p. 229 (originally published in 1902).

14 Alvar Aalto, 'European reconstruction brings to the fore the most critical problems facing architecture in our time', *Abacus: Museum of Finnish Architecture Yearbook 3* (1983), p. 127.

15 Alvar Aalto, 'National planning and cultural goals', *Sketches*, pp. 99–102.

16 Alvar Aalto, 'Finland builds: exhibition at the Ateneum, Helsinki', *Sketches*, pp. 113–4. Radio lecture given on 11 November 1953.

17 Alvar Aalto, 'Speech for the hundred-year Jubilee of the Jyväskylä Lycée', op. cit., p. 164.

18 Theodor Adorno, *Minima Moralia: Reflections from Damaged Life*, tr. E. F. N. Jephcott (London, Verso, 1984), p. 40. (Originally published in German in 1951).

19 Alvar Aalto, 'The RIBA Discourse: "The architectural struggle"', *Sketches*, p. 147.

20 George Baird, *Alvar Aalto*, (London, Thames and Hudson, 1970), p. 16.

21 Andres Duany, 'Principles in the architecture of Alvar Aalto', *Harvard Architecture Review 3: Precedent and Invention* (New York, Rizzoli, 1986), pp. 104–19.

22 Ibid., p. 116.

23 Ibid., p. 119.

24 In Fleig (ed.), *Alvar Aalto*, vol. 3, p. 68.

25 This does not appear in the transcript of the lecture, but is recalled by Patrick Hodgkinson in 'L'Annunziazzione Secondo Aalto' (*Spazio e Societa*, no. 35, September 1986, pp. 32–7), who regards it as a typical example of Aalto's attempts to disguise his real intentions with bogus functional rationalizations.

26 Alvar Aalto, 'The Decline of Public Buildings', *Sketches*, pp. 111–12. Originally published in *Arkkitehti* in 1953. Aalto is referring to branches of the Bank of Finland in provincial cities rather than the Bank itself, which occupied a monumental building in Helsinki completed in 1882.

27 Ibid.

28 Fleig (ed.), *Alvar Aalto*, vol. III, p. 71.

29 For a provocative series of essays on this theme see Michael Sorkin (ed.), *Variations on a Theme Park: The New American City and the End of Public Space* (New York, The Noonday Press, 1992).

30 Artek originally occupied the basement and the ground-floor shop to the left of the main entrance, with the Artek Gallery on the first floor; the gallery moved out in the 1960s and the shop moved to Esplanadi in 1990. The first floor has now been drastically modified.

31 Malcolm Quantrill (*Alvar Aalto: A Critical Study*; Helsinki, Otava, 1983), makes this point, which I have confirmed with Finnish friends.

32 Erkka Lehtola, 'Close encounters', *Books from Finland*, 3/1993, pp. 195–6.

33 Ibid.

34 In Fleig (ed.), *Alvar Aalto*, vol 1, p. 264.

35 Ibid., p. 265. See also Quantrill, op. cit., p. 162.

36 Demetri Porphyrios, *Sources of Modern Eclecticism*, (London, Academy Editions, 1982), p. 94.

37 Pointed out by Simo Paavilainen in 'Classicism of the 1920's and the classical tradition in Finland', *Nordic Classicism 1910–30* (Helsinki, Museum of Finnish Architecture, 1982), p. 90.

38 See Fleig (ed.), *Alvar Aalto*, vol. 1, pp. 268–73.

39 See Kirmo Mikkola, 'Eliel Saarinen and town

planning', in Marika Hausen, Kirmo Mikkola, Anna-Lisa Amberg and Tytti Valto, *Eliel Saarinen: Projects 1896-1923* (Cambridge, MIT Press, 1990), pp. 214–17, and p. 327.

40 See catalogue entry on Kallio by Simo Paavilainen in *Nordic Classicism*, op. cit., p. 99.

41 Schildt, *Mature Years*, p. 289.

42 Nils Erik Wickberg, 'Finnish Architecture in the Early 1900's and Alvar Aalto' from the proceedings of The First International Alvar Aalto Symposium (*Alvar Aalto vs. the Modern Movement*; Helsinki, 1981; pp. 45–65).

43 Fleig (ed.), *Alvar Aalto*, vol III, pp. 188–95.

44 See the bitter review of the scheme by the Director of the Museum of Finnish Architecture, Marja-Riitta Norri: 'Holl's Helsinki banana' (*The Architectural Review*, September 1993, p. 11); Holl's response in the October issue, pp. 13–14, and the letter by Peter Wilson criticizing the review in the November issue, p. 13.

45 Quoted in Schildt, *Mature Years*, p. 299.

The Town Centre and the Academic Campus

1 Alvar Aalto, 'National planning and cultural goals', *Sketches*, p. 100. (Originally published in *Suomalainen Suomi*, 1949).

2 Alvar Aalto, 'The geography of the housing question', *Sketches*, p. 45.

3 See Camillo Sitte, *Der Städtebau nach seinen Künsterlichsen Grundsätzen*, 1889, first translated into English by C. T. Stewart as *The Art of Building Cities* (New York, Reinhold, 1945).

4 See introduction, p. 13.

5 Alvar Aalto, 'Building heights as a social problem', *Sketches*, p. 92. (Originally published in *Arkkitehti* in 1946).

6 Alvar Aalto, 'National planning and cultural Goals', op. cit., p. 101.

7 See Fleig (ed.), *Alvar Aalto*, vol. 1, pp. 214–5.

8 See Jussi Rautsi, 'Alvar Aalto's urban plans', loc. cit., pp. 54–6.

9 Schildt, *Mature Years*, pp. 79–81.

10 See Aalto's description in Fleig (ed.), *Alvar Aalto*, vol. 1, p. 231.

11 Fleig (ed.), *Alvar Aalto*, vol. II, p. 119.

12 Malcolm Quantrill, *Alvar Aalto: a Critical Study* (Helsinki, Otava, 1983), p. 183.

13 See Porphyrios, *Sources of Modern Eclecticism*, (London, Academy Editions, 1982), p. 87.

14 See Göran Schildt, 'The Travels of Alvar Aalto' (*Lotus 68*, 1991), p. 40.

15 Andres Duany, 'Principles in the Architecture of Alvar Aalto', *Harvard Architecture Review 3: Precedent and Invention* (New York, Rizzoli, 1986), p.

119.

16 Alvar Aalto, 'The decline of public buildings', *Sketches*, pp. 111–2 (originally published in *Arkkitehti* in 1953).

17 This of course alludes to Le Corbusier's celebrated definition of architecture as translated by Frederick Etchells in *Towards a New Architecture* (London, Architectural Press, 1970).

18 Quoted in Göran Schildt, *Mature Years*, p. 128.

19 Ibid., p. 134.

20 The main 'student village' was planned by Kaija and Heikki Sirén, who were also responsible for the exquisite student chapel.

21 Jussi Rautsi, 'Alvar Aalto's urban plans', *RIBA Transactions*, 1986, (vol. 5, no. 1). p. 52.

22 See the description in Fleig (ed.), *Alvar Aalto*, vol. 1, p. 194.

23 See the description in ibid., p. 198.

24 Frederick Gutheim, *Alvar Aalto* (Braziller, New York, 1960), p. 26.

25 Demetri Porphyrios, *Sources of Modern Eclecticism*, op. cit., p. 8.

26 His own studio boasts an open air amphitheatre and projection wall in which Aalto visualized himself giving impromptu slide talks – events which, according to Mikko Merckling, a long-standing member of the studio, never in fact took place!

Places of Assembly

1 Alvar Aalto, 'Motifs from times past', ed. Göran Schildt, *Sketches*, tr. Stuart Wrede (Cambridge and London, MIT Press, 1985, pp. 1–2). Originally published in *Arkkitehti* in 1922.

2 Göran Schildt, *Early Years*, p. 184.

3 Quoted in Schildt, *Decisive Years*, p. 226.

4 See Asko Salokorpi, *Modern Architecture in Finland* (London, MIT Press, 1970), p. 28.

5 See J. S. Sirén, 'The Architectural Morals of our Church Building', re-published in the exhibition catalogue *J S Sirén: Architect: 1889–1961* (tr. The English Centre; Helsinki, Museum of Finnish Architecture, 1989), pp. 27–31.

6 See description in Fleig (ed.), *Alvar Aalto*, vol. 1, p. 218.

7 Reima Pietilä, 'A "gestalt" building', *Architectura and Urbanism*, special issue on Aalto, op. cit., p. 12.

8 For a discussion of the role of the line in Aalto's work, see Mark A. Hewitt, 'The imaginary mountain: the significance of contour in Alvar Aalto's sketches' (*Perspecta*, no 25).

9 This has previously gone unnoticed due to the lack of a published section of the Jyväskylä building, tending to reinforce the popular perception of the Imatra church as a unique *sui generis* perfor-

mance.

10 This dubious statistic counts each pane of the curving glazed screens on the north elevation as separate 'windows'!

11 Robert Venturi, *Complexity and Contradiction in Architecture* (New York, Museum of Modern Art, 1966), p. 82.

12 Reyner Banham, *Age of the Masters: a Personal View of Modern Architecture* (London, The Architectural Press, 1962; rev. ed., 1975), p. 136.

13 Quoted in Schildt, *Early Years*, pp. 188–9.

14 My view is shared by Quantrill, who in the conclusion of his monograph observes that: 'Aalto's mastery of interior quality . . . appeared to stop short of the creation of a truly satisfactory religious space.' (*Alvar Aalto: A Critical Study*; Helsinki, Otava, 1983; p. 244).

15 In this respect the plan and sectional form are reminiscent of the church at Olari by Käpy and Simo Paavilainen.

16 Schildt, *Early Years*, p. 257.

17 Fleig (ed.), *Alvar Aalto*, vol. 1, p. 188.

18 Göran Schildt, *Mature Years*, pp. 245–6.

19 Demetri Porphyrios, *Sources of Modern Eclecticism* (London, Academy Editions, 1982), pp. 2–3.

20 The phrase 'banks of cubist clouds' is taken from Quantrill, op. cit., p. 230.

21 Ibid, p227.

22 Ibid., p. 229.

Conclusion

1 Social housing, sadly, is a notable exception, having been dominated for many years by inflexible panel-construction systems.

2 The phrase first appeared, so far as I am aware, in P. Morton Shand's review of the 1930 Stockholm Exhibition (*The Architectural Review*, vol. 68, pp. 67–72), and reappeared in *The Review*'s advocacy of 'The New Empiricism' after the Second World War – see, for example, 'The New Empiricism: Sweden's Latest Style' (*The Architectural Review*, June 1947), pp. 199–204.

3 Manfred Tafuri and Francesco Dal Co, *Modern Architecture*, tr. Robert Erich Wolf (London, Academy Editions, 1980), p. 365.

4 Alvar Aalto, 'Culture and Technology', *Sketches*, pp. 94–6.

5 Schildt, *Early Years*, p. 216. This is written about the clothes line shown in Aalto's drawing of the Casa Väinö Aalto.

List of Works

1918
Remodelling of Aalto family house, Alajärvi
1918–9
Addition of belfry to church, Kauhajärvi
1921–2
Association of Patriots Building, Seinäjoki
1922
Industrial Exhibition, Tampere
1922–3
Two-family house, Jyväskylä
1923
Finnish Parliament House, Helsinki (competition project)
1923–4
Apartment building, Jyväskylä
1924
Workers' Club, Jyväskylä
Church restoration, Äänekoski
Church restoration, Anttola
1924–9
Defence Corps Building, Seinäjoki
1925
Church, Jämsä (competition project)
Church remodelling, Viitasaari
1926
Villa Flora, Alajärvi (architect Aino Aalto)
Casa Väinö Aalto, Alajärvi
1926–7
League of Nations, Geneva, Switzerland (competition project – sketches only)
1926–8
South-Western Agricultural Co-operative Building and Finnish Theatre, Turku
Apartment building, Turku
1926–9
Muurame Church, near Jyväskylä
1927
Kinkomaa Sanatorium, Kinkomaa (competition entry)
Office block, Vaasa, (competition project with Erik Bryggman)

Church, Töölö, Helsinki (competition project)
Church, Viinikka, Tampere (competition project)
Church, Taulumäki (competition project)
Belfry restoration, Pylkönmäki
Church, Pylkönmäki
Turun Sanomat Building, Turku
1927–9
Standard Apartment Block, Turku
Association of Patriots Building, Jyväskylä
1928
Summer houses, *Aitta*, magazine competition
Church restoration, Korpilahti
1929
Columbus Memorial Lighthouse, Dominican Republic (competition project)
Church restoration, Kemijärvi
700th Anniversary Exhibition, Turku (with Erik Bryggman)
1929–33
Paimio Sanatorium, Paimio
1930
Institute for Physical Education, Vierumäki (competition project)
Tehtanpuisto (Mikael Agricola)
Church, Helsinki (competition project)
Stadium and sports centre, Helsinki, (competition project)
University Hospital, Zagreb, Yugoslavia (competition project)
1930–1
Cellulose factory, Toppila, Oulu
1932
Prefabricated one-family house (competition project)
Prototype Week-end cabin design for Enso-Gutzeit Co (competition project)
1932–3
Villa Tammekan, Tarto, Estonia
Housing for the employees and doctors of Paimio Sanatorium, Paimio

1933
Redevelopment plan for Norrmalm, Stockholm, Sweden (competition project)
Helsinki stadium (competition project)
1933–5
Viipuri Library, Viipuri
1934
Railway station, Tampere (competition project)
Stenius housing development, Munkkiniemi, Helsinki
National Exhibition Hall, Helsinki (competition project)
1934–5
Aalto's own house and studio, Munkkiniemi
1936–7
Sunila Pulp Mill, Sunila
1937
Museum of Art, Tallin, Estonia (competition project)
Finnish Pavilion, *World's Fair*, Paris, France
Savoy Restaurant, Helsinki
Nordic United Bank, Karhula
1937–8
Director's house, Sunila
Two-storey housing, Sunila
Two-storey terrace housing, Wrst and second groups, Sunila
1938
Forestry Pavilion, Agricultural Exhibition, Lapua
Blomberg Film Studio, Westend, Helsinki (competition entry)
University of Helsinki Library extension (competition project)
Anjala paper factory, Inkeroinen
1938–9
Elementary school, Inkeroinen
Anjala apartment buildings, first group, Inkeroinen
Anjala apartment buildings, second group, Inkeroinen
Anjala housing for engineers, Inkeroinen

Finnish Pavilion, *World's Fair*, New York, USA
1938–40
Terrace housing, Kauttua
1938–41
Three-storey terrace housing, first and second groups, Sunila
Villa Mairea, Noormarkku
1939–45
Apartment buildings for Ahlström Company, Karhula
1940
HAKA housing development, Helsinki (competition project)
Traffic plan and design of Erottaja Square, Helsinki (competition project)
1941
Plan for an experimental town (produced with students from MIT)
1941–2
Regional plan for the Kokemaki Valley for Ahlström Company
1942–3
Women's dormitory, Kauttua
1942–4
Urban design project for Säynätsalo
1943
Town centre, Oulu (competition project)
Merikoski power station, Oulu (competition project)
1944
Villa Tvistbo (unbuilt project)
Town centre, Avesta, Sweden (competition project)
Strömberg housing development, Vaasa
Extension to factory, Kauttua
1944–5
Urban design for Rovaniemi (project)
Ahlström mechanical workshops, Karhula
1944–7
Strömberg meter factory and terrace housing, Vaasa
1945
Engineer's house and sauna, Kauttua
ARTEK Exhibition Pavilion, Sweden

1945–6
Sawmill extension, Varkaus
One-family housing development, Varkaus
1946
Heimdal housing development, Nynäshamn, Sweden (competition project with Albin Stark)
Master plan for Nynäshamn, Sweden (competition project)
One-family house, Pihlava
1947
Strömberg sauna and laundry, Vaasa
Johnson Research Institute, Avesta, Sweden
1947–8
Dormitory, Baker House, Massachusetts Institute of Technology, Cambridge, USA
1947–53
Regional plan for Imatra
1948
Forum Redivivum: Cultural and Administrative Centre (later referred to as National Pensions Institute) Helsinki, Finland (competition project)
1949
Ahlström factory warehouse, Karhula
General plan for Helsinki Technical University, Otaniemi (competition project)
Woodberry Poetry Room, Lamont Library, Harvard University, Cambridge, Massachusetts, USA
1949–50
Tampella housing, Tampere
1949–52
Säynätsalo, Town Hall, Säynätsalo
1949–54
Sports hall, Helsinki Technical University, Otaniemi
1950
Church, Lahti (competition project)
Funeral chapel, Malmi, Helsinki (competition project)
Kivelä Hospital, Helsinki (competition project)

1950–5
Regional plan for Finnish Lapland
1951
Erottaja Pavilion, Helsinki
Regional theatre, Kuopio (competition project)
Paper factory for Enso-Gutzeit, Kotka
One-family house, Oulu
Workers' housing, Inkeroinen
1951–2
Typpi Oy nitrogen factory and housing for Typpi Oy employees, Oulu
1951–3
Enso-Gutzeit paper mill, Summa
1951–4
Paper mill, Chandraghona, Pakistan
Cellulose factory, Sunila, Finland (second stage of construction)
Three-storey apartment house, third group, Sunila, Finland
1952
Cemetery and funeral chapel, Lyngby, Copenhagen, Denmark (competition project)
Association of Finnish Engineers Building, Helsinki
Enso-Gutzeit Country Club, Kallvik
1952–4
Housing for the personnel of the National Pensions Institute, Munkkiniemi
1952–5
Rautatalo office building, Helsinki
1952–6
National Pensions Institute, Helsinki
1952–7
Jyväskylä University, Jyväskylä
1953
Sports and congress hall, Vogelweidplatz, Vienna, Austria (competition project)
Imatra Centre Design Project, Imatra
Aalto's summer-house, Muuratsalo
1954
Studio R.S., Como, Italy
AERO housing, Helsinki (project)

1955
Urban design project for Summa
Bank building, Baghdad, Iraq (competition project)
Theatre and concert hall, Oulu, (project)
1955–6
Aalto Studio, Munkkiniemi
1955–7
Hansaviertel Apartment building, Berlin, Germany
City Hall, Gothenburg, Sweden (competition project)
1955–64
Main building, Helsinki Technical University, Otaniemi
1955–66
Department of Architecture, Helsinki Technical University, Otaniemi
1956
Drottning Torget, main railway station, Gothenburg, Sweden (competition project)
Director's house, Typpi Oy, Oulu
Master plan for the University of Oulu
Finnish Pavilion, *Biennale*, Venice, Italy
1956–8
Operating room, Paimio Sanatorium, Paimio
1957
Kampementsbacken housing development, Stockholm, Sweden, (competition project)
Town hall, Marl, Germany (competition project)
1957–9
Church of the Three Crosses, Vuoksenniska, Imatra
1957–61
Korkalovaara housing development, Rovaniemi
Sundh centre, Avesta, Sweden
1958
Town hall, Kiruna, Sweden (competition project)
Art Museum, Baghdad, Iraq (project)
Post Office Administration Building,

Baghdad, Iraq
Opera House, Essen, Germany (competition project)
House of Culture, Helsinki
1958–60
The Cross of the Plains Church, Seinäjoki
1958–62
High-rise apartments, Neue Vahr, Bremen, Germany
1959
Villa Carré, Bazoches-sur-Guyonne, France
Bjornholm housing development, Helsinki
Finnish War Memorial, Suomussalmi
1959–61
Project for Opera House, Essen
1959–62
Central Finland Museum, Jyväskylä
Enso-Gutzeit Headquarters, Helsinki
Parish centre, Wolfsburg, Germany
1959–64
Project for the city centre, Helsinki
1960–1
Shopping centre, Otaniemi
Lieksankoski power station, Lieksa
1960–3
Cultural centre, Wolfsburg, Germany
Thermo-technical laboratory, Helsinki Technical University, Otaniemi
1960–4
Main Building, Helsinki Technical University, Otaniemi
1961–2
Housing for nurses, Paimio Sanatorium, Paimio
Office and apartment block, Rovaniemi
1961–4
Opera House, Essen, Germany (second project)
1961–5
Town Hall, Seinäjoki
1962
Apartment blocks, Tapiola
Enskilda Bank building, Stockholm, Sweden (competition project)

Index

Page numbers in *italics* refer to pages on which captions to illustrations occur.